Lernkrimi Englisch

Crime Time

Michael Bacon
Tracy Bowens
Alison Romer
Caroline Simpson

circon

Baierbrunner Straße 27, 81379 München
Ausgabe 2023
3. Auflage

Redaktion: Sarah Portner
Fachkorrektur: Fiona Cain, Nathalie Russell
Produktion: Ute Hausleiter
Titelillustration: Karl Knospe
Lernkrimi-Logo: Carsten Abelbeck
Gestaltung: EKH Werbeagentur GbR
Umschlaggestaltung: red.sign GbR, Stuttgart

ISBN 978-3-8174-2901-1
381742901/3

Besuchen Sie uns auf Instagram und Facebook: circonverlag

www.circonverlag.de

Vorwort

Liebe Leserin, lieber Leser,

sicher zum Lernerfolg – mit Spaß und Spannung! Die Compact Lernkrimis mit ihrer Kombination aus Lektüre und didaktischem Übungsanteil eignen sich hervorragend, um breite Sprachkompetenzen in der Fremdsprache zu erwerben. Der Lerner wird dabei durch die spannende Handlung, das angemessene Sprachniveau und den stetig ansteigenden Schwierigkeitsgrad der Übungen gefördert und motiviert.
Entwickelt nach neuesten Erkenntnissen der Fremdsprachendidaktik, sind Compact Lernkrimis das ideale Medium für einen Lernerfolg im Selbststudium. Durch die kleinen Texteinheiten und den hohen Übungsanteil sind sie aber auch als Unterrichtslektüre bestens geeignet.

So lernen Sie mit Compact Lernkrimis:

- **Mit Begeisterung lernen:** Die packende Krimihandlung motiviert Sie beim Lesen des englischen Originaltextes.
- **Wissen intensivieren und erweitern:** Durch die Kombination aus didaktisch aufbereiteter Lektüre und textbezogenen Übungen testen und trainieren Sie Ihre Sprachkenntnisse effektiv. Vokabelangaben auf jeder Seite unterstützen Sie beim Lesen.
- **Systematisch lernen:** Knüpfen Sie an Ihr individuelles Sprachniveau an und setzen Sie eigene Lernziele.
- **Unabhängig sein:** Lernen Sie individuell – wo und wann immer Sie wollen.

Viel Spaß beim Erlernen der englischen Sprache
wünscht Ihnen

Prof. Dr. Christiane Neveling
Didaktik der romanischen Sprachen, Universität Leipzig

Inhalt

Death at Land's End

Caroline Simpson

Anne Sophie aus Heidelberg arbeitet als Au-pair in Cornwall. Bei einem Spaziergang am Hafen stößt sie mit einem Mann zusammen, der von einem der Segelboote wegrennt. Kurz darauf stirbt genau auf diesem Boot ein Segler. Schnell wird klar, dass sein Tod kein Unfall war und die Polizei beginnt zu ermitteln. Anne Sophie sagt als Zeugin aus und gerät dadurch selbst in tödliche Gefahr …

A1

1 The Jolly Roger

It's a lovely summer day. Anne Sophie is sitting on the **harbour** wall in Sennen Cove, Cornwall.(i) She is writing a postcard to her family in Heidelberg.

*Wednesday, 9th July, 2014. Dear Mum and Dad, I am writing to you in English **for practice** :-) My au pair job is still going well. Mr and Mrs Barber are very friendly. The children are **noisy** but sweet! This week we are on holiday in Cornwall. It's very beautiful here **at the seaside**...*

harbour	Hafen
for practice	zum Üben
noisy	laut
at the seaside	an der Küste
except (for)	bis auf, außer
sailor	Matrose
pipe	Tabakspfeife

It's so peaceful, she thinks. There is no one else at the harbour, **except for** an old man who is cleaning one of the yachts. He looks like an old **sailor** with his cap and **pipe**. She sees that the boats have names painted on the side, like *Sea Horse*, *Mary Jane* and ***The Jolly Roger***. How nice! she thinks and stands up to take a photo.

Just at that moment a man jumps from the deck of the

> **i** Cornwall ist der südwestlichste Landesteil Englands und ein beliebtes Urlaubsziel. Raue, steile Felsen, die sich mit langen Stränden und malerischen Buchten (Engl. **cove**) abwechseln, prägen die Küstenlandschaft.

Jolly Roger and **runs past** Anne Sophie. He is carrying a large bag which **bumps** her leg. It makes a sound like metal and it hurts.
"Ouch! Hey, watch where you're going!" Anne Sophie shouts.

The Jolly Roger	Totenkopfflagge, *wörtl.*: der fröhliche Roger
to run past	vorbeirennen
to bump	anrempeln
in his mid-40s	Mitte vierzig
↯ Aye, aye!	Jawohl! Zu Befehl!

But the man doesn't stop running.
Anne Sophie finishes her postcard and starts to leave. She walks past the old sailor, who is still working hard. A red sports car drives into the harbour car park. A man **in his mid-40s** gets out of the car. He is wearing expensive sailing clothes and sunglasses.
"Hey, George! Is my boat ready?" he shouts to the old sailor.
"**Aye, aye**, Mr Hartley. I checked it this morning."

Exercise 1: Opposites. Wie lautet das Gegenteil der folgenden Adjektive?

1. small ______*large*______
2. peaceful ____________
3. friendly ____________
4. cheap ____________

At 7 p.m. on the same day, Jake Smith is sailing out to sea. He likes fishing in the evening when the tourist boats are

mainland England	das englische Festland
in the distance	in der Ferne
binoculars *pl*	Fernglas
coastguard	Küstenwache
to capsize	kentern
lifeboat	Rettungsboot
to set	*hier*: untergehen

gone. He sails round Land's End, the most westerly point of mainland England, and away from the coast. After a while he sees something in the distance. He picks up his binoculars and sees a yacht that is lying on its side. Its big white sail is lying in the water. He sails closer.
"Hello! Are you alright? Is anyone there?" he shouts.
But there is no answer. Jake takes out his mobile phone. i
"Land's End Coastguard Station, McGregor here!"
"It's Jake Smith here. I have found a yacht in trouble. It has capsized."
"OK, Jake, tell me where you are and we will come quickly in the lifeboat."
Jake waits by the capsized yacht. He smokes a cigarette and watches the sun setting over the sea. Soon he hears the lifeboat coming. It's getting dark now. Liam McGregor, the coastguard rescue officer, takes out his torch. He searches the boat, but there is no one there.
"Help me lift the sail out of the water," he says to his partner, Sam Nolan.
The two men move over to the other side of the boat and lift the heavy sail. Under it they find a body in the water.
"Good God, I know him!" shouts Jake in shock.

> Im Englischen wird das Wort **handy** nur als Adjektiv verwendet (praktisch, handlich) und nicht als Bezeichnung für ein Mobiltelefon (*mobile phone*).

Exercise 2: True or false? **Welche Aussagen sind korrekt? Markieren Sie mit richtig ✓ oder falsch – !**

1. Jake likes fishing when it is quiet. ❒
2. He sees something far away. ❒
3. He calls the police. ❒
4. Liam McGregor works alone. ❒
5. Jake reads a book while he is waiting. ❒

It's breakfast time at the Sea View B&B[i] at Sennen Cove. Mrs Smith, the **landlady**, is carrying tea and toast into the dining room.

> Als **Bed and Breakfast** (kurz: *B&B*) bezeichnet man eine Unterkunft bei Privatleuten, in deren Preis immer ein warmes Frühstück enthalten ist.

"Did you hear about the sailing **accident**?" she asks the Barbers. "It was on the local radio news this morning. Last night a yacht capsized and a man died. My husband found his boat."

"How **terrible**!" says Mrs Barber. "Was it a tourist?"

"No, he was called Roger Hartley. He lived here as a boy. But he **moved** to London as a young man and **went into business**. They say he was very rich!"

rescue officer	Rettungshelfer(in)
torch	Taschenlampe
body	*hier*: Leiche
landlady	Wirtin
accident	Unglück
terrible	furchtbar
to move	*hier*: umziehen
to go into business	ein Geschäft gründen

"How did the accident happen?" asks Mr Barber.

yet	schon, bis jetzt
strange	*hier*: merkwürdig, seltsam
surprised	überrascht

"No one knows that **yet**. It's very **strange**," says Mrs Smith. "Roger was a good sailor. I can't understand it! It really is terrible!"

Exercise 3: Choose the correct alternative. Lesen Sie weiter und wählen Sie das richtige Wort!

"Roger Hartley?" Anne Sophie repeat / repeats. "Was his boat called *The Jolly Roger*?"

"Yes! How did you know that?" asks Mrs Smith **surprised**.

Anne Sophie tells / tell the Barbers what she saw at the harbour the day before.

"I think you should tells / tell that to the police!" says Mr Barber.

"Mrs Smith, where is / are the nearest police station?"

"In Penzance," the landlady replies.

"OK. Anne Sophie, got / get your bag. I'm driving you to Penzance!"

2 Fishing for Clues

Detective Inspector Jack O'Reilly is sitting at his desk at the Penzance Police Station.

clue	Hinweis, Spur
to nod	nicken
slim	schlank
hood	Kapuze
suspicious	verdächtig
forensic officer	Gerichtsmediziner
keel	Kiel

"OK, so you saw a man running from the yacht," the inspector says.
Anne Sophie nods.
"What did he look like?"
"He was quite tall and slim. He was wearing[i] jeans and a jacket with a hood. I didn't see his face. It happened so fast."
"Did you see anything else suspicious?"
"Yes. He had a big bag and it hit me when he ran past. There was something made from metal inside it."
At that moment Inspector O'Reilly's mobile phone rings.
"Excuse me," he says, and he goes out of the room to take the call.
"Jack, it's Brendan here," the police forensic officer says. "We have found something interesting. We think someone took a piece off the keel of the boat."
"Brendan, you know I'm not an expert sailor. Can you explain it to me simply?"

Um zu beschreiben was in dem Moment gerade war, als etwas anderes passierte, verwendet man das **Past Progressive.** Es wird mit *was/were* plus *-ing Form* gebildet.

Exercise 4: Correct the mistakes. Lesen Sie weiter und korrigieren Sie die sechs Fehler!

"Haha, Jack! Your the only man in Cornwall who doesn't like boats."
"Firstly, I'm from Dublin, as you know. And secondly, I get **seasick** if I just look at a boat. Just say me, Brendan."
"OK, the keel is the part that keeps a boat stable in the water. If you **damage** him, the boat is no longer stable. It can capsize easy."
How interesting, O'Reilly things. So maybe that german girl is a **witness** to a **crime**!

1. ______________ 2. ______________

3. ______________ 4. ______________

5. ______________ 6. ______________

Later that morning an elderly man and woman come into O'Reilly's office. The man looks angry and the woman is crying.

seasick	seekrank
to damage	beschädigen
witness	Zeugin
crime	Verbrechen
elderly	ältere(r/s)
angry	wütend

"Mr and Mrs Hartley, thank you for coming back. I know this is very hard for both of you. But I must ask you a few more questions about your son," the inspector says.
"We identified him 4 hours ago and the story is already in the newspapers!" Mr Hartley says angrily.

"Yes, I'm afraid **bad news**[i] **travels fast**," O'Reilly replies.

"Was it an accident?" Hartley's father asks.

"We are not sure. Did Roger have any problems?"

"No idea! He didn't talk to us much. He only came here to sail his boat," says Mr Hartley bitterly.

"Or did he have any **enemies**?" O'Reilly asks.

"Yes, lots. You can start with the neighbours. The Jones's boy **hated** Roger. He was **jealous** of him."

"Jones...?"

"Yes, Philip Jones. He was at school with Roger," says Mrs Hartley. "After school, they wanted to start a business together. But Philip isn't any good at business things. So Roger went to Surrey and started a company with Giles Hill **instead** – 'Hartley and Hill'. They produce electronic parts for the computer industry."

"What about Roger's personal life? Was he **married**?"

"He was. And **divorced** – and a terrible divorce it was, too. Sheila lives in Canada now with her new husband. I'm **glad** she's gone."

O'Reilly writes in his notebook: Philip Jones, the jealous school friend; Giles Hill, the business partner; Sheila, the

Das Wort **news** (Nachrichten, Neuigkeiten) verlangt im Englischen immer ein Verb im Singular, obwohl es wie ein Substantiv im Plural aussieht.

bad news travels fast	schlechte Nachrichten verbreiten sich schnell
enemy	Feind
to hate	hassen
jealous	neidisch
instead	stattdessen
married	verheiratet
divorced	geschieden
glad	froh

ex-wife. Very interesting, he thinks. But first I should go to the harbour and check out Anne Sophie's story.

Exercise 5: Match up the phrases. Welche der folgenden Satzteile gehören zusammen? Ordnen Sie zu!

1. [d] The elderly couple	a) were not happily married.
2. [ ] Philip Jones is not	b) make parts for computers.
3. [ ] 'Hartley and Hill'	c) a good businessman.
4. [ ] Roger and Sheila	d) identify their dead son.

In a small terraced house in Penzance, Philip Jones sits down on his sofa and puts his feet on the table. He opens a can of beer and picks up the local newspaper. When he reads the headline, 'Local man drowns in freak sailing accident', he has a big smile across his face.

to check sth. out	etw. untersuchen
terraced house	Reihenhaus
can	Dose
headline	Schlagzeile
to drown	ertrinken
freak	*hier*: außergewöhnlich
landlord	Wirt

O'Reilly parks in the harbour car park next to the Sailor's Safety pub in Sennen Cove. There is a lot of noise and shouting inside the pub. Suddenly the door opens and a young man falls out onto the street.
"And don't come back until you can pay for your beer!" the landlord shouts after him angrily.

The man **staggers** away towards the harbour and O'Reilly follows him. In the harbour, he sees an old man wearing a sailor's cap. He is cleaning one of the yachts. The young man speaks to him.

"Not a penny[i] more! Go home and get some sleep until you're **sober**!" the old sailor shouts, and the other man staggers away without saying a word.

> Der **penny** ist der hundertstel Bruchteil des britischen Pfunds. Die Mehrzahl ist **pence** (Abkürzung – "p").
> *The apple costs 90p.*

"Good afternoon, I'm Inspector O'Reilly from the Devon and Cornwall police. What's your name? Do you work here?"

"Yes, I clean the boats for the tourists. Everyone calls me Old George."

"Who was that young man who spoke to you?"

"That's just Clive, my **good-for-nothing** son. **Drunk** again!"

"I see. Were you here yesterday afternoon?" O'Reilly asks.

Old George nods.

"Did you see Roger Hartley?"

"Yes, I did," Old George replies. "He sailed out to sea at around 4 o'clock. Lovely boat, the *Jolly Roger*! Hartley's dead now, isn't he? I read it in the newspaper."

to stagger	wanken, torkeln
sober	nüchtern
good-for-nothing	Taugenichts
drunk	betrunken
I'm afraid	Es tut mir leid, aber ...; leider

"Yes, **I'm afraid** he is. Did you see anything suspicious earlier in the afternoon?"

"No, it was very quiet all afternoon. There was no one here," Old George replies.

imagination	Fantasie
liar	Lügnerin
to have a fight	streiten
anything else	sonst noch etwas

"We have a witness. She saw a man running from the *Jolly Roger* at around 3 o'clock," O'Reilly replies.

"Oh yes, I remember. There was a young girl, about 17 or 18. But I didn't see a man. Young girls have a lot of imagination, you know. You can't believe everything they say."

But O'Reilly isn't so sure. He doesn't think that Anne Sophie is a liar.

"Well, I saw something strange two days ago," Old George tells the inspector. "I was at the pub [i] over there, the Sailor's Safety. Hartley was outside in the beer garden with another man. They were having a fight."

"Do you know who the other man was?"

"Yes, it was Alan Walker, a Londoner. He keeps his boat here too, the *Mary Jane*."

Inspector O'Reilly's phone rings. "Sergeant Cole here, sir! I've got that telephone number you wanted for Giles Hill, Hartley's business partner."

"Thank you, Cole. I also want to find a Mr Alan Walker. He lives in London and he has a boat in Sennen Cove."

"I'll see what I can do," answers Sergeant Cole.

"What about Philip Jones?" asks O'Reilly.

"I'm on my way to talk to him now, sir!" Cole replies.

Der **Pub** ist im Vereinigten Königreich und Irland eine Kneipe und hat dort seinen festen Platz im sozialen Leben. Der Begriff leitet sich ab von "Public House", einem der Öffentlichkeit zugänglichen Haus.

"OK, that's all for now," O'Reilly says to Old George. "Here's my card. Phone me if you think of anything else."

Exercise 6: Pronouns. Ersetzen Sie die markierten Wörter durch die entsprechenden Pronomen!

1. O'Reilly doesn't think **Anne Sophie** is a liar.
   *O'Reilly doesn't think **she** is a liar.*
2. Did you see **Roger Hartley**?
   ____
3. **Hartley's parents** identify his body.
   ____
4. Walker keeps **his boat** at Sennen Cove.
   ____
5. Do you believe **Anne Sophie**?
   ____

O'Reilly gets in his car and dials Giles Hill's number.
"Hartley and Hill, Linda Jenkins speaking."
"Good afternoon, can I speak to Giles Hill, please?"
"I'm sorry, but Mr Hill is not in the office. He's on his way to Cornwall for a funeral. Mr Hartley is dead, you know!" replies the secretary excitedly.
"No problem. I'll meet Mr Hill there," says O'Reilly and he hangs up.

funeral	Beerdigung
excitedly	aufgeregt
to hang up	*hier*: auflegen

3 Red Herrings

In a dark corner of the Queen's Head pub in Newquay, Alan Walker sits alone at the bar. He is watching the local news on TV.

"This is Fred Cohen for the Nine O'Clock News. I'm standing outside the Penzance police station." At that moment a car arrives. The driver gets out and walks towards the **entrance** of the police station. The TV cameraman follows him and Cohen runs behind him with a microphone.

red herring	falsche Fährte
entrance	Eingang
rumour	Gerücht
path	Pfad, Weg
to appear	erscheinen
nosy	neugierig
nasty	gemein

"Inspector, there are **rumours** that Roger Hartley's death was not an accident. Do you have anything to say about that?"

"No comment at this time," O'Reilly says and walks away quickly.

I'm in big trouble now! thinks Walker. He drinks his double whisky and puts his head in his hands.

Newquay ist ein beliebter Ferienort an der Nordküste Cornwalls, etwa 40 Meilen von Sennen Cove entfernt. Die Stadt nennt sich selbst 'The Surfing Capital of Britain' und ist Austragungsort von Surfwettbewerben.

Exercise 7: Prepositions. Lesen Sie weiter und ergänzen Sie die fehlenden Präpositionen!

at | on | ~~onto~~ | for | to | to

"Come on, Anne! I want to see the dead man's boat!"

"Me too, me too!" Little Jamie and his sister Louise are holding **1.** *onto* Anne Sophie's hands as they run along the **path** **2.** ______ the harbour.

"The boat isn't here now," Anne Sophie explains **3.** ______ the children. "The police are looking **4.** ______ it. Let's go for a walk **5.** ______ the beach instead."

Suddenly Old George **appears** behind them.

"What are you doing here?" he asks angrily.

"The children just want to look **6.** ______ the boats."

"Go away!" he shouts. "You are much too **nosy**!"

"Why is that man so **nasty**, Anne?" Louise asks.

"I don't know. But let's leave here quickly!"

Meanwhile in Penzance, Sergeant Cole rings the doorbell to a small terraced house. A **middle-aged** man opens the door. He is wearing old jeans and a dirty T-shirt.

"Mr Jones? I'm Sergeant Cole from the Penzance police. Can I come in?"

Jones shows Cole into the living room. The room smells of cigarettes. There are pizza boxes and empty cans of beer on the table and on the floor.

meanwhile	währenddessen
middle-aged	mittleren Alters

to light	*hier*: anzünden
to let sb. down	jmd. im Stich lassen
unemployed	arbeitslos
↯ dump	Drecksloch
churchyard	Friedhof

"So what do you want?" Jones asks as he sits down and **lights** a cigarette.

"Did you know Roger Hartley?"

"Roger? Yes, he's dead, isn't he? I read it in the newspaper." Jones smiles.

"You don't seem very sad about that," says Cole.

"No, I'm not. Roger was my friend once. But he **let me down**. Look at Roger with his sports car and his big house. And look at me, **unemployed** and living in this **dump**!"

Exercise 8: Definitions. Vervollständigen Sie die Definitionen mit den angegebenen Wörtern!

dirty | nasty | nosy | angry | empty

1. A person who wants to know about other people's private lives is ________.
2. Someone who is aggressive or unfriendly is ________.
3. If you don't wash your clothes they are ________.
4. When you drink all the milk the bottle is ________.
5. If you shout because you are not happy about something, you are ________.

Friday morning is cold and rainy. Inspector O'Reilly is standing in the Sennen churchyard under a big umbrella. Next to him is Giles Hill. Old Mr and Mrs Hartley are talking to the vicar. No one else is in the churchyard.

local man	Einheimischer
decision	Entscheidung
to cancel a contract	einen Vertrag kündigen
supplier	Lieferant
bankrupt	bankrott

"Hartley was a local man. Why aren't there more people here at his funeral?" O'Reilly asks Hill.
"Roger was not very popular, Inspector. To him business was important – friendship was not."
"Was he difficult to work with?"
"He sometimes made very hard decisions. Last April he cancelled a contract with one of our suppliers. That man is now completely bankrupt!"
"Really! Who do you mean?"
"A man called Alan Walker," replies Hill.
Alan Walker? I know that name, thinks O'Reilly. Old George told me about him. He had a fight with Hartley outside the pub. I must talk to him as soon as possible. But first I must finish with Hill.
"Do you have any other ideas? What about his private life?" asks O'Reilly.
"I think Roger was having women problems. I heard him on the telephone. He sounded very angry."

Ein **vicar** ist ein Gemeindepfarrer der *Church of England* (anglikanische Kirche). Das anglikanische Kirchenoberhaupt ist der jeweils regierende britische Monarch, also Königin Elisabeth II.

Exercise 9: Asking questions. Lesen Sie weiter und setzen Sie die Fragewörter richtig ein!

who what where when

"**1.** ______ did this happen?" Inspector O'Reilly asks.
"**2.** ______ did he say?"
"It was a couple of weeks ago. He said, 'Leave me alone, you stupid woman. Don't phone here again!'"
"**Charming**! Do you think it was his ex-wife, Sheila?"
"No, she lives too far away. And I don't think Sheila and Roger were in contact anymore."
"OK, Mr Hill, I must ask you this question. **3.** ______ were you on Wednesday afternoon?"
"Sitting in a plane! I was on my way home from a business meeting in Chicago."
"I see. Do you have any idea **4.** ______ damaged Hartley's boat?"

"No, Inspector. I don't know anything about boats except that they make me seasick!" Hill says and he laughs.
"I understand," says O'Reilly with a smile. "I have the same problem. Thank you for your time, Mr Hill."
On the other side of the churchyard, O'Reilly sees Old George. He is watching the funeral from a distance and is smoking his pipe.
O'Reilly's mobile phone rings.

"Hello, it's Sergeant Cole here, sir! I've got an address for Alan Walker. His wife says he is on a golfing holiday in Newquay. I phoned him but he didn't answer. So I phoned the hotel. The receptionist said he checked out an hour ago. He's **probably** on his way home now."

Charming!	Wie charmant!
probably	wahrscheinlich
to keep an eye on sb.	jmd. im Auge behalten

"Good work, Cole! What about your talk with Philip Jones?"
"Yes, I met him yesterday. He really hated Hartley."
"Where was Jones on Wednesday afternoon?"
"He says he was at home alone. He didn't leave the house all day."
"So he's got a motive and no alibi," O'Reilly replies.
"That's right, sir."
"You **keep an eye on him**. I'm going to talk to Alan Walker."

4 Old Friends

"Please sit down, Inspector. My husband should be home soon. Can I get you a cup of tea?"
"Yes, please, Mrs Walker."
She goes into the kitchen and O'Reilly looks around the living room. He sees some sailing trophies on a **shelf**. Mrs Walker comes back with the tea.
"Your husband is a **keen** sailor, isn't he?"
"Oh yes! He loves boats. He's an expert! Alan has his own yacht. He keeps it at Sennen Cove, next to Roger's boat."

shelf	Regal
keen	leidenschaftlich, eifrig
business associate	Geschäftspartner
to impress sb.	jmd. beeindrucken

She shows O'Reilly a photo of a man on board a yacht. On the side of the yacht is the name *Mary Jane*.
"That's my name, Inspector. Alan named the boat after me."
"Does your husband come from Cornwall, Mrs Walker?"
"No, he's a Londoner. But Roger taught him how to sail. Roger liked to take his **business associates** on board his yacht. He wanted to **impress** them!" she says bitterly.
"Is it true that your husband lost a lot of money because of Roger?" O'Reilly asks.

"Yes, it's a disaster. When Roger cancelled our contract, we lost everything. Now we **even** have to sell this beautiful house!"
Well, that's a strong motive, thinks O'Reilly. And Alan is an expert on yachts. Did he sabotage Hartley's boat?

even	sogar
to go for a run	joggen gehen
figure	Gestalt
shadow	Schatten
package	Paket

Exercise 10: Opposites. Wie lautet das Gegenteil der folgenden Begriffe?

1. stand up ____________________
2. wife ____________________
3. won ____________________
4. hate ____________________
5. weak ____________________

"I'm **going** out **for a run**. The children are already in bed," Anne Sophie tells Mrs Barber that evening.
"Thanks, Anne! Don't be too late. Eric and I want to go to the pub later and we need you to babysit."
Anne Sophie runs along the beach. It's getting dark and the tourists and surfers have gone. At the ice cream kiosk she stops to have a rest. The kiosk has closed now. On the beach she sees two dark **figures** in the **shadows**, one tall and one short. The tall one gives a **package** to the other one. Then he turns and walks away. The short figure comes

scared	verängstigt
to hold one's breath	den Atem anhalten
to grab	greifen, fassen
several times	mehrmals
cruel	grausam
selfish	egoistisch
doorway	Türöffnung
at top speed	mit voller Geschwindigkeit

along the beach in Anne Sophie's direction.
She feels **scared**. She hides behind the ice cream kiosk and **holds her breath**. Suddenly a man's face looks round the corner of the kiosk.
"You again!" Old George shouts. "I warned you not to be so nosy," and he **grabs** her arm.

"Mrs Walker, did you know Roger Hartley personally?"
"Yes, Inspector, I met him **several times**. And his wife, Sheila."
"What happened between Hartley and Sheila?"
"Roger was a **cruel**, **selfish** man! Sheila left him and moved to Canada. I believe she is much happier[i] there."
"If you think of anything else, please call me. Here's my card and here's the number of the police station..."
Inspector O'Reilly hears a noise and looks up. A man is standing in the **doorway**.
"Alan Walker?" asks O'Reilly.
The man turns and runs out of the room. Quickly, O'Reilly follows him into the street. Walker gets into his car and drives off **at top speed**. O'Reilly runs to his car and drives after him. He turns a corner and sees that the road ahead is empty.

> Bei Adjektiven, die auf -y enden, wird in der Steigerung das -y durch ein i ersetzt. z.B.
> *happy, happier, happiest*

Oh no, I've lost him! Where has he gone? he thinks. But then he sees Walker's car parked on the other side of the road. Walker is sitting behind the **steering wheel** with his head in his hands.

Exercise 11: Contracted forms. Lesen Sie weiter und ergänzen Sie die Kurzformen!

"Penzance Police Station, Sergeant Cole speaking. How can I help you?"

"My **1.** name is ___*name's*___ Eric Barber. **2.** I am ______ phoning to report a missing person. Our au pair, Anne Sophie Niedermair, has **disappeared**. She went for a run and never came back."

"Anne Sophie? **3.** She is ______ a **potential** witness in the Hartley **case**, **4.** is not ______ she? **5.** We will ______ **treat** this as a top priority!"

Walker sits on the back seat of O'Reilly's car in **handcuffs**. "You are our top **suspect**, you know, Mr Walker. You were in Cornwall all week. You have a motive. And you know how to sabotage a yacht. All the **evidence** is **against** you."

steering wheel	Lenkrad
to disappear	verschwinden
potential	möglich
case	Fall
to treat	behandeln
handcuffs *pl*	Handschellen
suspect	Verdächtiger
evidence	Beweis(mittel)
against	gegen

"I know! That's why I tried to run away. I panicked! But Inspector, you must believe me. I didn't sabotage that boat. I was very angry with Hartley, but I'm not a **murderer**."

"Why were you really in Cornwall?"

murderer	Mörder
to change one's mind	sich anders entschließen
to beg sb. for sth.	jmd. anflehen um
She didn't want me to know.	Sie wollte nicht, dass ich es erfahre.
to hit sb.	jmd. schlagen
right away	sofort

"I wanted to sail my yacht one last time! I have to sell the *Mary Jane*, Inspector. I'm bankrupt."

"A witness saw you fighting with Hartley outside the Sailor's Safety on Monday evening."

"Yes, that's true. Hartley was an arrogant pig! My wife called him two weeks ago. She tried to make him **change his mind** about the contract. She **begged him for** help. **She didn't want me to know**, but Hartley told me. He laughed about it. He thought it was funny. So I **hit him**! But I didn't kill him!"

"You knew Hartley's boat well, didn't you? Hartley took you sailing. Isn't that true?"

"Yes, the three of us had some good times together on the *Jolly Roger*."

"Three? Who was the third person?" asks O'Reilly.

"Giles, of course. He and Roger often went sailing together and sometimes I went with them."

"Giles Hill? He told me he gets seasick just by looking at a boat!" O'Reilly says in surprise.

"He said that?" Walker asks and he laughs.

Just then O'Reilly's phone rings. "Hello? Yes, Cole, what is it? Anne Sophie has disappeared? OK, I'll come back to Cornwall right away!"

Exercise 12: True or false? Welche Aussagen sind korrekt? Markieren Sie mit richtig ✔ oder falsch – !

1. Walker went to Cornwall to play golf. ☐
2. Walker lost all his money. ☐
3. O'Reilly thinks Walker could be the murderer. ☐
4. Giles Hill gets seasick on boats. ☐

5 The Net Tightens

Anne Sophie is trapped inside the cabin of a small boat in Sennen Cove harbour. Her hands are tied behind her back and there is tape over her mouth. Old George and another man are sitting at a table on the other side of the cabin.

to tighten	sich zusammenziehen, enger werden
trapped	gefangen
tied	gefesselt
tape	Klebeband
mess	Durcheinander
to get rid of sb.	jmd. loswerden
deal	Handel

"What a mess!" says the younger man. "I only wanted to get rid of Roger, the pig! Do you know, he tried to block my deal with the Americans. I told him that that was the best way to make money. But he didn't listen."

"I know, Mr Hill. Hartley never listened to anybody."

"But what are we going to do[i] with this girl now? She isn't part of our plan," Hill says nervously.

"How about another sailing accident, sir?"

going to + Infinitiv bezieht sich auf die Zukunft. Es wird verwendet:

a) um persönliche Pläne und Absichten für die Zukunft auszudrücken:
*I'm **going to drive** to Paris next summer.*

b) für Ereignisse in der Zukunft, die man als logische Folge einer Handlung ansieht.
*Oh no, look! The cat **is going to catch** that bird!*

"Don't be stupid, George! The girl isn't a sailor. It must look like a swimming accident. We'll sail out towards the beach. Then we'll hit her on the head and throw her in the water. How's that for a plan."
"Aye, sir. That'll work."

Exercise 13: Choose the correct alternative. Lesen Sie weiter und wählen Sie das richtige Wort!

"Sergeant Cole here, sir. **1.** Where / Who are you now?"
"I'm turning onto the road to Sennen Cove. **2.** What are / What is the news on Anne Sophie?" O'Reilly asks.
"We had a call from a local woman. She was walking **3.** his / her dog near the beach. She saw two **4.** men / mens **dragging** a young woman in the direction of the harbour. She **5.** is thinking / thinks one of the men was Old George."
"Right. I'm on my way," O'Reilly replies.

He drives at top speed to the harbour, parks his car and runs towards the boat park. There is no one there except a young man, sitting alone on the harbour wall and drinking a can of beer.
"Hey, I know you," O'Reilly says. "You're Clive, Old George's son, aren't you?"
The young man **jumps up** and tries to run away. O'Reilly jumps up onto the harbour wall and grabs his arms.

to drag	schleppen
to jump up	aufspringen

"You're not going anywhere. You **are under arrest**."
"It wasn't my idea!" Clive shouts **drunkenly**.
"What do you mean? What was not your idea? Tell me everything you know," O'Reilly **orders**.
"It was Mr Hill's idea. He wanted it to look like a sailing accident. He asked my father to organize it. I had to do the **dirty work**, as usual. But I need the money, Inspector!"

to be under arrest	verhaftet sein
drunkenly	betrunken
to order	befehlen
dirty work	Drecksarbeit
wave	Welle

"Clive, are you talking about the *Jolly Roger*?" O'Reilly asks.
Clive nods his head.
"And where is your father now?"
"He just went out to sea in his motorboat."
"Where is he going? Is he alone?"
"No, there are two other people on board. They are going towards the beach," Clive replies.
O'Reilly takes out his mobile phone and rings the Coastguard Station.

Ten minutes later, Inspector O'Reilly is on board the lifeboat with the coastguards, Liam McGregor and Sam Nolan, sailing out to sea.
"The **waves** are quite high this evening. There is a storm coming," says Nolan.
"Are you alright, Inspector?" asks McGregor. "You look a bit green in the face."

"Don't worry about me. We must catch the other boat. Look over there! I think I can see them!" O'Reilly shouts.

Exercise 14: Verb forms. Setzen Sie die Verben in der richtigen Form ein!

be (2x) go (2x) have

1. Where ___ you ___?
2. Don't ___ stupid!
3. ___ you sure?
4. Old George ___ a son called Clive.
5. Anne Sophie often ___ to the harbour.

On the deck of the motorboat, Hill and Old George are preparing to throw Anne Sophie overboard.
"Untie her hands," Hill says. "And take the tape off."
"Help, help! Someone help me!" Anne Sophie shouts as soon as her mouth is free.
"There's no one here to help you, my dear," says Old George with a nasty smile.
"Shut up, George. Listen! Can you hear something?" Hill asks.
"Just the wind, sir. There's a storm coming."
"No, listen! There's something else," Hill shouts nervously.
They hear the sound of an engine in the distance.

to worry about	sich Sorgen machen um
to catch	*hier*: einholen
to prepare	vorbereiten
to untie	losbinden
engine	Motor

to splash	schwappen
in despair	verzweifelt
life buoy	Rettungsboje

"Thank God! It's the lifeboat. Over here! Over here!" shouts Anne Sophie and waves her arms.

"Damn! Forget the girl, George. Let's get out of here!"
Hill starts the engine and turns the boat away from the coast and out to sea.

"Can't you go any faster?" O'Reilly shouts at McGregor.
"Don't worry, sir. That little motorboat can't get far in bad weather like this."
"Faster, sir! They're getting closer," shouts Old George.
Suddenly a big wave splashes over the side of the boat and the engine stops.
"It's all over, George. We're finished!" Hill says in despair.
Seconds later the lifeboat arrives. Nolan ties the two boats together. McGregor helps O'Reilly to go on board the motorboat.
"You two are under arrest for sabotaging Roger Hartley's boat and for kidnapping Anne Sophie Niedermair!" the inspector shouts as soon as he is on deck.

Das englische Wort **wave** wird sowohl als Verb als auch als Substantiv verwendet, jedoch mit unterschiedlichen Bedeutungen. Das Verb **to wave** bedeutet „winken", während das Substantiv **wave** eine Welle bezeichnet.

McGregor helps him to handcuff the two men. "Now, where is she?"
"Look, there she is! In the water!" McGregor shouts. "The waves washed her overboard."
He grabs a life buoy and jumps into the water.

afloat	über Wasser
to cling onto	sich fest-klammern an
safety	Sicherheit

Anne Sophie is trying to stay **afloat** in the stormy sea. The waves are very high now, and her mouth and nose are full of salt water. McGregor swims towards her as fast as he can. Suddenly a big wave hits her and she goes under. But McGregor gets to her just in time. He grabs her arm before she sinks. She **clings onto** the life buoy and McGregor swims with her back to **safety**.

Exercise 15: Hidden words. Finden Sie zehn Begriffe rund um Boote und Wassersport!

M	A	L	W	E	M	W	O	T	S
O	V	E	R	B	O	A	R	D	A
G	K	I	S	R	T	V	D	E	I
D	E	S	U	A	O	E	A	C	B
P	E	W	R	T	R	I	C	K	O
I	L	I	F	E	B	U	O	Y	T
L	E	M	I	N	O	T	U	Z	N
L	Y	T	S	E	A	S	I	C	K
O	R	E	T	S	T	M	A	B	E
D	E	A	K	Y	A	C	H	T	E

Two days later the sun is shining and the sea is calm. Anne Sophie is sitting in a deckchair in the garden of the B&B.

deckchair	Liegestuhl
to look forward to sth.	sich auf etw. freuen

"Here's a cup of tea for you, Anne," says Mrs Barber. "Is everything OK?"

"Yes, thank you. I'm fine," Anne Sophie replies.

She takes out her mobile phone to write a text message.

> Dear Mum and Dad, I am feeling much better now. I am looking forward to seeing you next week in Heidelberg. You won't believe how many exciting stories I have to tell you!

Learning by Killing

Michael Bacon

Die Schüler einer Sprachschule an der Südküste Englands führen ein Kriminalstück auf. Doch aus dem Spiel wird blutiger Ernst, als die Aufführung tatsächlich mit einer Leiche endet. Wie konnte das vor aller Augen geschehen? Schüler und Lehrer sind schockiert und Inspector Watsons Spürsinn ist gefragt.

A2

1 Check-In

Tracy Dean, the secretary, smiles at the young man.
"Now, what's your name?"
He must be French, she thinks. He's wearing a raincoat in the middle of July – and he's looking at the women in the corner of the room. The young man laughs loudly and grins at Tracy.
"My name? Pierre! Pierre Leclerc, of course!"
His teeth are perfectly white, and his long, black hair **matches** his deep, brown eyes. The two women in the corner **giggle** and **stare** at Pierre Leclerc. He **shrugs** his shoulders, and they giggle again.
"Well, Pierre, your class is B1. Your teacher is Jim Ryan. Would you like a cup of coffee? Join the others over there. They're in your class, too. Next please!"

to match (with)	(zusammen) passen; verglei-chen (mit)
to giggle	kichern
to stare	starren
to shrug	die Achseln zucken
plump	pummelig, mollig
to shuffle	*hier*: schlurfen
glasses *pl*	Brille; Gläser
by the way	übrigens

A short, rather **plump** man **shuffles** forward. He's wearing **glasses**.
"My name is Mr Schultze. I am a German. Do you want my pass-port?"
"No," says Tracy, "that isn't neces-sary, Mr Schultze. You're on my list – and you're in Jim Ryan's class as well. Follow Pierre and have a cup of coffee. **By the way**, we always use first names (i) here

at Church Hill. My name is Tracy – and yours?"

Mr Schultze **hesitates** and then almost **whispers**.

"It's Karl. Karl with a K!"

"Pleased to meet you, Karl. How was your journey?"

to hesitate	zögern
to whisper	flüstern
to offend	kränken, beleidigen
to tick off	abhaken

Karl Schultze takes a step backwards. He is a little uncertain about the question. The flight from Hanover to London was punctual, efficient and cheap. The Underground from Heathrow to Waterloo Station was also cheap, but with two heavy suitcases it was, quite honestly, unpleasant. The train to Eastcastle was late and slow, with too many people. The taxi from the station was fast, much too fast, and also very expensive. Can he say all this in one sentence, or does he need his dictionary? He doesn't want to **offend** Tracy, who is very attractive – and very friendly. Karl remembers a phrase from his English class in Gifhorn!

"Let's cut it short!" he laughs. "My journey was excellent."

Tracy **ticks off** Karl's name and points to the corner with the coffee. Karl, pleased with himself, walks towards the girls. He puts down his two suitcases, takes a cup of coffee and then studies his dictionary.

Tracy Dean continues to note all the new arrivals and send them to the tables with coffee and tea. In all, there are twenty students who want to stay for three weeks at The Church Hill School for English. Three weeks in Eastcastle, a little village on the South Coast. It is not very far from Brighton, about fifteen minutes by train, and the beaches and the cliffs are superb.

> In England und den USA ist die Anrede mit dem Vornamen sehr viel häufiger als im Deutschen. Anders als das Duzen im Deutschen ist dies nicht unbedingt Ausdruck einer engeren persönlichen Beziehung.

Exercise 1: Match up the opposites. Welche Gegenteile gehören zusammen? Ordnen Sie zu!

1. laugh	☐ terrible
2. plump	☐ light
3. whisper	☐ cry
4. cheap	☐ slow
5. late	☐ shout
6. short	☐ expensive
7. superb	☐ slim
8. heavy	☐ tall
9. fast	☐ early

The school is a large Victorian building with a long garden at the back and a **drive** at the front. There's one car parked near the steps that lead to the front door. But what a car! A Rolls Royce from the late fifties! It **sparkles** in the afternoon sunshine. This **is the pride and joy of** Colonel Lessons, the owner of Church Hill School for English. He's a retired army officer, and he **runs** his school with military precision. However, he doesn't **appear** in the building too often. Most of the time, he's at the 19th hole of Eastcastle's Golf Club. This **ex-**

drive(way)	Auffahrt zu einem Haus
to sparkle	funkeln
to be sb.'s pride and joy	jds. ganzer Stolz sein
to run	*hier*: leiten
to appear	auftauchen, erscheinen

pression is often confusing for foreign students. Golf? Aren't there only 18 holes? That's quite right, but people often call the club house the 19th hole or the "watering hole". This is a perfect place where you can relax and have a drink – or two, or three and often even more.

expression	(Gesichts-)Ausdruck
confusing	verwirrend
accounts *pl*	Geschäftsbücher
mock	*hier*: gespielt; falsch
mobile	Handy
speck	Körnchen; Pünktchen
to switch on	*hier*: (Motor) anlassen
marvellous	wunderbar, fantastisch
ϟ money for old rope	leicht verdientes Geld
fee	*hier*: Schulgeld; Gebühr

Occasionally the Colonel comes to the school to check the accounts and the reservations for the next course. When he leaves, he raises his hand in mock salute and always shouts: "Any problems, call me on the mobile. I'll be at Number 19." Then he marches down the steps and gets into his car. He wipes a few specks of dust off the passenger seat and, like a small boy opening a Christmas present, he switches on the engine. He listens carefully. No, he can't hear a thing, so all is in order.

A "Roller", (i) he says to himself, is a car that must be seen and not heard. What a marvellous life! All the summer courses are full. This language school business is money for old rope! The students pay the exorbitant fees before they start; the teachers get their low salary four weeks after their teaching finishes. And the difference between what comes in and what goes out lands in my bank account. In about five years, I'll be a millionaire! I can move to the South of France and forget this stupid little town for ever! And then he drives off to the golf club and his first gin and tonic of the day.

Was Colonel Lessons hier liebevoll als „Roller" bezeichnet, ist natürlich – ganz standesgemäß – sein Rolls Royce.

Tracy is a very attractive woman in her mid-thirties. She's taller than Colonel Lessons and has long, blond hair and a healthy, sun-tanned complexion. This comes from her interest in sailing. When she's not at Church Hill, you can almost always find her at the harbour, working on her small yacht.

Like all sailors, male or female, she spends more time painting and cleaning her boat than actually sailing. She was born in Eastcastle and loves the relaxed atmosphere of a small, coastal town. The fishing boats, the promenade with its terraced houses and shops, the three pubs for the tourists, the seagulls screech-ing over the small pier, the Punch and Judy show next to the entrance.

complexion	Teint
male	männlich
coastal	Küsten...
Punch and Judy show	Kasperletheater
fairly	ziemlich
staff	Kollegium; Personal
ϟ conman	Schwindler
case	Fall

Yes, she says to herself, when she's cleaning a railing or washing down the deck, this is heaven on earth! And the job is marvellous, I can't complain at all. Well, except for the boss.

Tracy doesn't really like the Colonel. She's fairly sure that he only runs the school to make a profit. He's a businessman! But there are always fresh faces. Every summer new students, as well as new teachers. Colonel Lessons has only one permanent member of staff – and this is his daughter, Rose. All the other teachers are looking for summer work; they are often people who want to earn a little extra money teaching their mother tongue – sometimes teachers who are between jobs. Occasionally a conman who has no idea how to teach the language but needs the money. For example Henry, last year. A sad case, in fact a complete and total failure. But – so it goes. Not everyone can be like Jim Ryan, the new Irish recruit for this summer. His contract is for two courses, six weeks in all. The second course is just beginning. This Sunday, as she begins to paint the mast, Tracy thinks about the changes in her life during the last three weeks. In fact, she's in love with Jim Ryan. OK, it is true that he is a little younger than she is – 29, in fact – but he's so romantic. This may be her last chance.

contract	Vertrag
↯ pep talk	aufmunternde Worte

Exercise 2: Odd one out. Welches Wort ist das „schwarze Schaf"? Unterstreichen Sie das nicht in die Reihe passende Wort!

1. attractive ugly beautiful handsome
2. yacht boat car ship
3. building house school garden
4. leave depart arrive stay
5. clever stupid silly ridiculous
6. sailor secretary soldier officer
7. small tiny miniature huge
8. pier seagull harbour coastal town
9. students teacher sailor pupils

Rose, Colonel Lessons's daughter, is giving a pep talk to the staff.

"Now, we're all here. The students are here as well. Teaching begins on Monday and, as you know, the motto of Church Hill is

'Learning by Doing'. Each of you has five students, and we expect a presentation, in the widest sense of the word, after the three weeks of teaching. You all have a theme. Yours, Terry, is 'English Food', are you happy with that?"

Terry **nods** and makes a few **notes**.

"I'll **manage**," he says. "We can put a menu together that covers everything. With prices and **recipes**. No problem!"

Rose continues. "Janet, your group should concentrate on music. Anything connected with music. And Patricia – or do you prefer Pat?"

Patricia Jones shrugs her shoulders. Rose smiles.

"OK – Pat! Your theme is 'The Village Fair'. You know, the standard stuff about **jumble sales**, **sack races**, and so on."

Patricia Jones feels uncomfortable. She comes from Sunderland in the North-East of England. "The Village Fair" or "The Village Fête" seems to be a very middle-class topic. Typical for the South Coast!

"Rose, that's not easy. I'll manage somehow – but what about Jim?"

Rose turns to Jim Ryan, pauses and takes a deep breath.

"Jim, you know Church Hill's motto. 'Learning by Doing'. We want to change it a little for your theme. You should produce a short drama with the title 'Learning by Killing'. So, it's **obviously** a **rather violent** play. But **remember** – it is a play! We don't want the local police **involved**!"

to nod	nicken
note	Notiz, Zettel
to manage to do sth.	es schaffen, etw. zu tun
recipe	Kochrezept
jumble sale	Flohmarkt, Basar
sack race	Sackhüpfen
obviously	offensichtlich
rather	eher, ziemlich
violent	gewalttätig, brutal
to remember sth.	sich erinnern an
involved	verwickelt, involviert

Exercise 3: Find the verbs. Lesen Sie weiter und unterstreichen Sie alle Verben im folgenden Textabschnitt!

The four teachers smile and laugh a little. Jim Ryan looks around.
"Rose, all of you. I come from Ireland. That means I know all about violence, **murder**, and so on. Not personally, of course. But I think, with a little bit of **imagination**, I can produce a short play. Dramatic but short! It **depends on** the students I have, naturally."

The others clap their hands. Rose's mobile rings.
"Ah, there's the boss-man. My father's ringing to find out whether everything's going **smoothly**. OK. **Let's call it a day**. See you all tomorrow. Remember! Monday, 9 a.m. sharp!"
The teachers for the Summer School of 2017 collect their notes, smiling, laughing and ready to start teaching.

Later, at the harbour, Tracy finishes painting the mast. She looks up at the cliffs. On the highest cliff, she sees the castle. It must be at least 800 years old. The stone is grey but, in the sunlight, now seems very white. The seagulls are still screeching.
And this is England, she thinks. The England I love. And Jim Ryan? He's not English – he's Irish. But that doesn't matter.

murder	Mord
imagination	Fantasie; Vorstellung
to depend on	abhängen von
smoothly	problemlos, reibungslos
Let's call it a day.	Machen wir Schluss (für heute).

sea shanty	Seemannslied
⚡ to tickle sb.'s fancy	jdn. reizen
to set	*hier*: untergehen
Channel	Ärmelkanal
tranquillity	Stille

Tracy goes back to her car, singing a well-known **sea shanty** quietly to herself.

"Where have you been all the day, Billy Boy, Billy Boy, where have you been all the day, my Billy Boy? Oh, I've been walking all the day with my darling Nancy Grey, and my Nancy **tickled my fancy**, oh my darling Nancy Grey."

Billy Boy and Nancy Grey, she thinks. Or Jimmy Ryan and Tracy Dean?

The sun begins to **set** on Eastcastle. The English **Channel** shimmers in the background. One of the large Dover car ferries, a speck on the horizon, is moving slowly towards France. Four or five yachts are returning to the harbour after a day's sailing. The weather forecast is positive. Can anything, anything at all, disturb this **tranquillity**?

2 Departure Lounge

"Good morning, ladies and gentlemen!"
Jim Ryan sees five students sitting in the room. Two men and three women. They're all a little nervous in their first lesson.
Pierre Leclerc is talking to Elke, a young lady from Zurich. Elke has long blond hair, very large blue eyes and a figure that Pierre is familiar with from magazines. Pierre is certain that Elke is a model who needs to learn English. He smiles at her and shakes his head of dark hair.

figure	*hier*: Gestalt; Figur
familiar (with)	vertraut (mit), sich auskennen (mit)
biro	Kugelschreiber
briefcase	Aktentasche
proudly	stolz
to adjust sth.	etw. zurechtrücken

Karl Schultze is sitting at his desk. In front of him, he has a folder, two pencils and a biro. The biro is blue – not black and not red. His dictionary is in his briefcase, which stands proudly next to the desk. Karl adjusts[i] his glasses and looks at Mr Ryan, ready and waiting.

> Ein kleiner Tipp:
> Nutzen Sie bereits bekannte Wörter, um unbekannte Vokabeln herzuleiten. Manchmal helfen dabei auch Fremdwörter im Deutschen weiter: **to adjust** „zurechtrücken, gerade rücken" ist verwandt mit dem deutschen „justieren".

Next to him is Franca from Spain. A very beautiful woman – with red hair! A redhead! From Spain? Yes, indeed. She can't speak English very well, but she can produce a beautiful "th" – the others always

splutter, particularly Karl. The fifth student is Mahdi. He comes from Oman. He's not interested in the girls, the women, the ladies! He wants to learn English. He wants to be **successful** and develop his country. English! THE language! The "lingua franca" of globalisation. Or is it globalization? He **makes a mental note** to ask the teacher later.

Jim Ryan stands in front of the class. He pauses, and then he says:

to splutter	hervorstoßen, stammeln
successful	erfolgreich
to make a mental note of sth.	sich etw. merken
to bow	(sich) verbeugen
modestly	bescheiden
blank	*hier*: verständnislos, leer

"My name is Jim. Jim Ryan. And what's your name?"

He goes round the class. They all introduce themselves. Pierre gives his name and laughs. Karl gives his name and stares. Elke and Franca say their names very clearly. Mahdi is the only person who introduces himself formally.

"Teacher, I am Mahdi – from Oman. My country needs people who speak good English. I am here to learn English. I like fish and chips. Thank you very much."

Mahdi **bows modestly** and sits down.

Jim Ryan opens his notebook. "So, we have a Pierre, a Karl, an Elke, a Franca and a Mahdi. That's good, very good. Does anyone know why?"

His students look at him with **blank** faces.

"OK, I'll tell you why. We're going to learn English in the next three weeks. 'Learning by Doing' is the motto of Church Hill School. And we, you five students and myself, are going to produce a play. Not a comedy, not a tragedy – just a simple murder story. 'Learning by Doing' may be the motto of Church Hill, but the title of our little play is 'Learning by Killing'!"

Exercise 4: Unscramble the definitions. Enträtseln Sie die folgenden Definitionen!

1. A newspaper with lots of pictures: agzanemi

   ____

2. A small table where you can work: edks ____________
3. Something you can write with: oibr ____________
4. A bag for carrying papers and books: sefibcrae

   ____

5. Something you organize your papers in: rlfdoe

   ____

6. Pieces of fried potato: ichsp ____________
7. A person with red hair: ahddeer ____________
8. A group of pupils or students who are taught and study together: saslc ____________

Jim Ryan begins to hand out some sheets of paper.
"Now, I know that all of you have about two or three years of English behind you. That means that we have to keep the dialogue in this play fairly simple. Its success depends on... Yes, Mahdi?", Jim Ryan looks at the young man. "You've got a question. That's good. Any questions – just ask!"

success	Erfolg
slightly	etwas, ein bisschen
embarrassed	verlegen

Mahdi is slightly embarrassed. He's not sure what the word "dialogue" really means. He

knows the verb "to die", and he also knows that "a log" is a piece of wood. You can put logs on a fire. But "dialogue"? Karl picks up his biro and opens his notebook. Pierre laughs again and looks once more at Elke. He knows all about dialogues, especially dialogues with beautiful Swiss women.
Jim Ryan explains enthusiastically:

Exercise 5: Verb forms. Lesen Sie weiter und setzen Sie die richtige Verbform ein!

"A dialogue, Mahdi, **1.** be ______________ when two people talk to each other. At the moment, I **2.** talk ______________ to you, and I **3.** try ______________ to tell you what this word **4.** mean ______________. Now you can tell me that you understand the meaning of the word. OK?"
Mahdi **5.** nod ______________ his head but **6.** say ______________ nothing.

Jim Ryan asks once more: "Do you understand the meaning of 'dialogue' now?"
Mahdi waves his hands and grins. "Dialogue," he says. "OK, two people talking to each other – like in the movies." He **emphasizes** the word "movies".
Karl Schultze carefully writes the word "movies" next to the word "dialogue" and then **adds** a question mark. He must check

to emphasize	betonen, hervorheben
to add	hinzufügen

this when he goes back to his bed and breakfast[i] **accommodation**.

"Exactly," says Jim Ryan. "But this is not a movie, Mahdi. This is a play. For us the dialogue is in the play. Now, look at your sheets of paper. There are five characters in this short play. I think we can use your real names. The play has got two scenes. The first scene takes place in a small studio, well, a **bedsit** really, and there are two actors, let's say Karl and Franca. Karl is an artist, and Franca is his model. In the beginning, a business relationship, but now they are lovers."

Mahdi and Karl **exchange** glances. This word sounds **suspicious**.

"Karl, however, has a **patroness**. That will be you, Elke. You are much older than Karl, and you are a very **jealous** woman."

At this point, Elke closes her dictionary, very loudly.

"Jim, Mr Ryan, this is not true. I am not jealous. Nobody in Switzerland is jealous of other people. Other people are jealous of the Swiss. We have got the mountains, the lakes – and the Swiss Franc!"

"Yes, Elke, you're quite right, of course. But don't forget that the Swiss Franc is a kind of money. In Britain, we think the Swiss Franc is cold and antiseptic. We think that the Swiss are people who show no emotions. Let's see – do you know what the difference between heaven and hell is?"

The students are quiet again and listen **attentively**.

> Typisch britisch! Reisende finden in Großbritannien ein flächendeckendes Netz an privaten Gästezimmern oder Frühstückspensionen. *B&Bs* schonen nicht nur den Geldbeutel und sind individueller als Hotels, sondern sie punkten oft auch mit Familienanschluss.

accommodation	Unterkunft
bedsit	möbliertes Zimmer, Einzimmerwohnung
to exchange	wechseln, austauschen
suspicious	misstrauisch; verdächtig
patroness	Mäzenin
jealous	eifersüchtig
attentively	aufmerksam

serious	ernst
impressed	beeindruckt
guardian	Wächter(in)

"In hell," Jim explains, "the English are the cooks, the Germans are the police, the French are the mechanics, the Swiss are the lovers, and the Spanish are the bankers."

Jim Ryan pauses dramatically. Nobody laughs except Mahdi. Elke looks very unhappy. Pierre tries to give moral support with his dark brown eyes. He smoothes back his long black hair and looks very **serious**. The other two, Karl and Franca, aren't sure if this is a joke.

"In heaven, on the other hand," Jim Ryan continues, "the English are the police, the Germans are the mechanics, the French are the cooks, the Swiss are the bankers, and the Spanish are the lovers. You see, that's the difference between heaven and hell."

Mahdi raises his hand. "Teacher, Mr Jim Ryan, what about the Omanis?"

Then Franca raises her hand. "Jim, where are the Irish in this little story?" She smiles sweetly.

Jim Ryan is **impressed**. They understand the story. They understand the humour.

"Well, if you must know... hmmm... the Omanis are the **guardians** of heaven and, well, the Irish must be the guardians of hell."

Everybody laughs. They are beginning to relax. Jim Ryan hands out some more sheets.

"Now, the second scene is in a pub – you all know what a pub is, of course."

Karl raises his hand, removes his glasses and says very seriously: "A pub, Mr Ryan, is a building where people go to drink and meet their friends. Pubs serve alcoholic and other drinks, and often also food."

"Excellent, Karl," says Jim Ryan, "that's an excellent definition. How do you know that?"

Karl Schultze **blushes** and then puts his glasses back on. He picks up the dictionary.

"It is here, Mr Ryan, in this dictionary." He pronounces the word "dictionary" very slowly, very carefully with an air of triumph.

Jim Ryan raises both thumbs in **appreciation**. "Yes, the dictionary. Have you all got a dictionary?"

Three students look in their briefcases. One student grins and does nothing. This, of course, is Pierre Leclerc. He's a Frenchman. Like all Frenchmen, he thinks that the English language is really French. All you need to do is to speak French with an English accent. Voilà – or, in English 'There you are!' Easy, isn't it?

"Brilliant," says Jim Ryan. "Pierre, I see that you haven't got a dictionary. Buy one, as soon as possible! You'll need it! And Karl, remember that we use first names here. My name is Jim, short for James. Now, let's talk about the second scene of our play."

Karl is slightly **upset** and a little embarrassed. First you get **praise**; then you get criticism. These English, they're so unfair! Pierre is angry. His dark brown eyes **send daggers** in the **direction** of Jim Ryan. Elke **smirks**, and Franca claps her hands. Jim, she thinks. Jim Ryan – yes, you are a very **witty**, clever and **handsome** man.

Jim carries on. "Elke and Pierre are sitting in the pub. Elke is **passionately** in love with Karl, the artist – she's older than he is – and she knows that Karl is having an affair with his model

to blush	rot werden, erröten
appreciation	Anerkennung
upset	aufgeregt, verärgert
praise	Lob
↯ to send daggers	tödliche Blicke zuwerfen
direction	Richtung
to smirk	süffisant lächeln
witty	geistreich, witzig
handsome	gutaussehend
passionately	leidenschaftlich

Franca. Elke feels **betrayed**. After all, she pays the bills for this artistic genius and wants something more than just paintings in return. She decides that Karl must die."

"This is a very drastic decision," Jim explains. "She will lose the young man she is in love with, and the world will lose a potentially great artist. But there we are – jealousy is an uncontrollable passion. She **hires** Pierre, a professional killer, who shoots Karl."

Karl nods his head slowly. He likes the idea. And the more he thinks about it, the more he likes it. He has an affair with two women in this play. Both are very attractive. He cleans his glasses and focuses on the redhead from Spain. He is beginning to enjoy this three-week **stay** in Eastcastle, with **opportunities** that he never thought about before in Gifhorn.

"Jim," Mahdi says **shyly**, but with more **confidence** than before, "Jim, what is my role in the play? I cannot possibly be the barman. I'm a Muslim."

betrayed	betrogen; verraten
to hire	einstellen, anheuern
stay	Aufenthalt
opportunity	Gelegenheit, Möglichkeit
shyly	schüchtern
confidence	(Selbst-)Vertrauen, Zuversicht
innocent	unschuldig; ahnungslos
witness	Zeuge, Zeugin
corpse	Leiche
to remind sb. (of sth.)	jdn. (an etw.) erinnern

"All very simple, Mahdi. You are an **innocent witness**, and you discover the **corpse**."

Mahdi likes the sound of the word "corpse". It **reminds** him of "cops". This is a very good role in the play. He lowers his head, closes his eyes and puts his hands together. He is very proud and remembers a phrase from the Christian Bible and says: "Thy will be done, on earth as in heaven."

The others laugh, and Jim is happy that the ice is broken. Even Elke is giggling. Pierre points two fingers and a thumb at Jim Ryan and says, “Bang, bang”. Franca looks at Karl, who is making more notes.

to break the ice	das Eis brechen
to point (to)	zeigen (auf)

Yes, she thinks, he’s rather short and rather plump, and I hope I don’t have to kiss him – but, after all, it is only a play.

Exercise 6: Word order. Wie lauten die Wörter in der richtigen Reihenfolge?

1. you put can on fire logs a

____

2. picks Karl biro his up

____

3. with French speaks accent Pierre a

____

4. pub in meet people friends their a

____

5. Karl die that must decides she

____

6. witness an are innocent you

____

7. broken happy is ice Jim is that the

____

It's Sunday, and there are five days left until the play is performed. Jim and Tracy are down at the harbour, enjoying the sunset. Their affair is now five weeks old. Tracy is throwing a few pebbles into the water, wondering how she can turn the conversation to the future – that is, if there is a future for her with Jim Ryan.

to be performed	aufgeführt werden
pebble	Kieselstein
bright	intelligent
tax-free	steuerfrei
allowance	*hier*: Beihilfe, Zulage
ties *pl*	Bindungen
to hand in one's notice	kündigen

"Jim," she smiles. "I want to talk about us. You must know that I'm very much in love with you. What I need to know is where I stand and where you stand in this relationship."

Jim looks out to the sea and shrugs his shoulders. "What can I say? You're a wonderful woman, Tracy. You're very attractive, you're great fun, and you're bright. But – I'm the wrong person for you. My contract finishes next week, the day after the final presentations. And then I'll move on. In fact, I've already got another teaching post. The chance of a lifetime. A five-year contract in the Middle East – tax-free, overseas allowance plus marriage and family allowance plus..."

Tracy laughs happily and says: "Why, Jim, that sounds marvellous. OK, I love Eastcastle, but I've got no real ties here. Well, except for the yacht, but I can easily sell that. And I only rent the flat.(i) Where is the contract exactly?"

"If you must know, it's Saudi Arabia, teaching Business English to Saudis in one of the big oil companies. But Tracy, I don't think you quite understand what I'm trying to say."

In her mind, Tracy is already planning how she can hand in

Flat ist das britische Wort für „Wohnung", während Amerikaner hierzu **apartment** sagen.

her notice to the school and her landlord. That won't be a problem. In fact, she could leave within a couple of weeks, and she knows that her neighbour is looking for a yacht just like hers. She laughs happily and pulls at Jim's arm.

"Oh, Jim. Don't make things so complicated. I can join you after you move in. Saudi Arabia sounds wonderful. OK, it may be a little hot, but I'm sure I can find some sort of secretarial work. Why are you telling me this only now? It's too good to be true!"

For a few seconds a cloud covers the setting sun, and the horizon begins to glow pink and red. Jim turns and stands in front of Tracy. His silhouette casts a long black shadow that envelops Tracy totally.

"There's something you should know, Tracy. I'm a married man. I've got two children. The plan is that they join me in Riad in September. Church Hill is just a temporary post. I'm sorry. I'm afraid you and I have no future, none at all."

As the sun reappears, Tracy stands up. Her face says everything. She is shocked. So shocked that she begins to shiver, although a warm breeze is blowing off the Channel.

"But the last five weeks – last Thursday – last Monday. Does all that mean nothing? You said that..."

"I know, I know. This is all my fault. I'm an impulsive bastard. I always involve innocent people. I'm sorry. This, here, is the end for us."

Tracy scrambles off the beach towards her car. She is heartbroken. What a fool she is. She loves someone who is already married with two children. The impostor!

landlord	Vermieter; Gastwirt
to glow	leuchten
to cast	*hier*: werfen
shadow	Schatten
to envelop	einhüllen
to shiver	zittern
to scramble	stürzen, hasten
impostor	Betrüger(in)

She turns round and screams at Jim: "Is this really true!? You flirt with me, you invite me out for drinks and dinner, you make love to me, you even tell me you love me. And all the time you're a married man. How can you do this to me?"

shame	Scham, Schande
actor/ actress *m/f*	Schauspieler(in)
kind	Art, Sorte
⚡ to roar off	davondonnern

Jim looks into the distance. Perhaps he feels some shame, because he answers in a very deep voice. But then Jim is a very good actor.

"I'm sorry, Tracy. I'm afraid, this is the end of our affair."

Tracy tries to control herself. "You know what? You're not an impulsive bastard, Jim. You are a total bastard. A bastard of the worst kind. Don't ever speak to me again!"

Tracy runs off to the car, gets in and roars off. Jim kicks a few pebbles, puts his hands in his pockets and walks to the nearest pub.

Exercise 7: True or false? Welche der folgenden Aussagen sind wahr? Markieren Sie mit richtig ✔ oder falsch – !

1. Jim and Tracy meet at the harbour early in the morning. ❑
2. Jim thinks Tracy is very stupid. ❑
3. Jim has got a contract in Singapore for five years. ❑
4. Tracy can hand in her notice to her landlord quite quickly. ❑
5. Tracy does not want to move to Saudi Arabia. ❑
6. Jim Ryan has got three children. ❑
7. It is quite warm at the harbour. ❑

3 Departure

On Thursday of their third week, Class B1 is word perfect in the two scenes of the play. They know the dialogue **by heart**. They're all enjoying themselves and are now very relaxed in each other's company. Elke really wants to play the part of the older patroness and is experimenting with make-up and a couple of **wigs** from the local Amateur Dramatic Society. Pierre is very enthusiastic about his part. As the murderer, he must appear totally cool. He must be a professional and mustn't show any emotions. This could be difficult for a Frenchman – but, after all, it is only a play. Karl is happy. He can finally show everyone that under his North German exterior he actually[i] is a romantic artist, a man with passion. Franca is now quite happy to be Karl's model. She doesn't have to take off her clothes, and she doesn't have to kiss Karl. Mahdi goes back to his bed and breakfast every day and thanks Allah that he is simply an innocent witness. And he's learning English very fast, which pleases him.

by heart	auswendig
wig	Perücke
dress rehearsal	Generalprobe
props *pl*	Requisiten

Actually wird häufig falsch verwendet. Auch wenn es an das deutsche „aktuell" erinnert, bedeutet es doch „tatsächlich", „eigentlich". „Aktuell", „derzeitig" kann z. B. mit dem Adverb **currently** übersetzt werden: *The teacher is* ***currently*** *unavailable.*

After the **dress rehearsal**, the players collect all their papers and **props** and leave for the pub.

Jim Ryan stays in the school. He has something important to do. He knocks at the door of Colonel Lessons's office, **whistling** an old Irish folk song and **feels** totally **at ease**. The "Tracy thing" is over. The B1 class are absolutely marvellous, and he knows that the performance on Friday will be a great success. The contract for Saudi Arabia is signed and ready to be posted. Of course he's not married! Two children? What a crazy idea!

"Come in!" shouts Colonel Lessons.

Jim Ryan opens the door.

"Ah, Jim. Sit yourself down. Everything OK? Any problems? Would you like a whiskey – it's Irish, you know."

The Colonel reaches up to a shelf and takes down a **volume** of the Oxford English Dictionary. He puts it upright on the table, opens one side and takes out a small **hip flask**. He smiles. He's dreaming about the South of France, and he **suspects** that Jim Ryan wants his salary before the contract finishes. No way! Ryan is a very good teacher, but he has to wait four weeks!

to whistle	pfeifen
to feel at ease	sich wohl fühlen
volume	*hier*: Band, Buch
hip flask	Flachmann
to suspect	verdächtigen
dedicated	engagiert
to get sth. off one's chest	sich etw. von der Seele reden

Jim folds his hands very modestly. "No thanks, Colonel," he says, "I still have to do some work on the presentation. Last minute changes."

The Colonel grins. This man is **dedicated**! He pours himself a large glass of whiskey. Perhaps Majorca would be better than Cannes? He looks at Jim and waits.

"Fire away, young man! **Get it off your chest**!"

"Well, Colonel. My contract finishes on Saturday, as you well know."

Colonel Lessons nods his head encouragingly.
"The thing is," Jim says, "I need some money, quite a large amount of money, before I take up my next job. And I think you can give it to me."

Exercise 8: Prepositions. Setzen Sie die richtigen Präpositionen ein!

1. They know the dialogue ____________ heart.
2. Pierre is very enthusiastic ____________ his part.
3. They leave ____________ the pub.
4. Jim feels totally ____________ ease.
5. He takes ____________ a small hip flask.
6. Get it ____________ your chest!
7. She takes ____________ her clothes.

A long silence follows. Colonel Lessons takes a gulp of whiskey and almost chokes. The impertinence! The fellow really does want payment in advance! These Irish are so cocky!
"I'm not sure what you're getting at, Ryan," the Colonel says. Jim settles back in the chair and takes out a notebook.
"Colonel, just listen to the notes I have here," he goes on. "You charge £800 per student for a course of three weeks. You

encouragingly	ermutigend
gulp	(großer) Schluck
to choke	ersticken; würgen
impertinence	Frechheit, Dreistigkeit
fellow	Kerl, Bursche
ϟ cocky	großspurig, frech
to settle back	sich zurücklehnen

pay the teacher £600 pounds for three weeks. You get a 20% **cut** from the bed and breakfast accommodation. You pick up 10% from the two pubs where the students drink. You give the students mock certificates for completing the course. You aren't even registered with any of the agencies that control courses for teaching English as a foreign language. In fact, Church Hill School for English is a gold mine and, at the moment, all the gold goes to you."

cut	*hier*: Anteil, Provision
white as a sheet	kreidebleich
fireproof	brandsicher, feuerfest
under false pretences	unter Vorspiegelung falscher Tatsachen
blackmail	Erpressung
to report	melden, berichten; anzeigen
mist	Nebel

The Colonel is as **white as a sheet**. He takes another gulp of whiskey. Jim Ryan stands up and looks around.

"This building isn't **fireproof**. There are no escape routes from upstairs. You even illegally employ Polish migrants to do the repairs. All in all, you are making a great deal of money **under false pretences**."

The Colonel finishes his whiskey and pours another. His voice is now very loud. "This is **blackmail**, Ryan! Everything you say may be true. But – and it's a big but – it may NOT be true. Now, you're a man of business. What do you really want?"

Jim Ryan's answer is calm and cool: "Colonel, I can **report** all of this tomorrow to the Ministry of Education or the Department of Health and Safety. Then you're ruined. Am I right – or, am I right?"

There is a long pause as the Colonel thinks. He sees Majorca sinking, the South of France disappearing in a **mist**.

"How much?" he asks

Jim Ryan grins, sits down and crosses his legs. He puts the notebook into his pocket.

"30 **grand**, Colonel. That's a **bargain**. I leave for Saudi Arabia on Sunday. Give me the money at the station, and then everything's OK."
The Colonel hesitates. He tries to work out the price of **property** between Cannes and Calais.
"20," he says, in a very military tone.

ϟ grand	tausend Pfund
bargain	günstiges Angebot, Schnäppchen
property	*hier*: Immobilien
envelope	Briefumschlag
vigorously	energisch, kräftig
to dial	wählen

Ryan smiles. "OK, let's make it 25. Sunday, at the station, used notes in a brown **envelope**."
Jim Ryan stands up and holds out his hand. Colonel Lessons shakes it **vigorously**.
"You're a bastard, Ryan. Now get out!"
As soon as Jim leaves the office, Lessons **dials** Tracy's number.
"Tracy! We need some cash, fairly quickly. I'll give you the details tomorrow, but we're talking about 25,000. That's possible, isn't it?"
"Of course, Colonel. What's wrong?"

Exercise 9: Synonyms. Welche Wörter haben eine ähnliche Bedeutung? Ordnen Sie zu!

1. cocky	☐ energetically
2. cut	☐ relaxed
3. hip flask	☐ impertinent
4. under false pretences	☐ thousand
5. calm	☐ commission
6. grand	☐ bottle
7. vigorously	☐ illegally

Colonel Lessons tries to pour another whisky, but the hip flask is now empty.
"Nothing, Tracy. Nothing at all. We'll sort it out tomorrow. Just take the money out of the bank and keep it in your flat till Sunday."
Friday is the day of the presentations. The four groups are all ready and waiting. Janet's group starts at 10 in the morning. They sing traditional songs like "Greensleeves", but also have a Karaoke session. Pat's group organizes various activities in the back garden: a traditional English Fête – the sack race is a great success. The third group, with Terry in charge, produces a midday meal. The students can choose from bangers and mash, toad-in-the-hole or shepherd's pie. They can also drink "Real Ale," traditional English beer. This item on the menu, however, is not very popular, particularly with the Japanese students.
At 3 p.m., it's the turn of Jim Ryan's group. Everybody goes into the main hall, a large room with a stage at the back. Here they all sit down in a sort of circle. The students are laughing and talking, some in their own language, but most of them in English. They're very pleased with their progress and are looking forward to the final presentation. Jim, Elke, Franca, Karl, Mahdi and Pierre walk to the front and disappear behind a large curtain. Karl steps out and talks to the audience.
"Ladies and gentlemen, it is our pleasure to present a short play. Look, please, at your programme. You all know the motto of

to sort sth. out	etw. regeln
in charge (of)	verantwortlich, zuständig (für); leiten
bangers and mash	Würstchen mit Kartoffelbrei
toad-in-the-hole	in Teig gebackene Würstchen
shepherd's pie	Auflauf aus Hackfleisch und Kartoffelbrei
hall	*hier*: Saal
to look forward to	sich freuen auf
to disappear	verschwinden
curtain	Vorhang
audience	Publikum

Church Hill School, namely 'Learning by Doing', but the title of our play is 'Learning by Killing'. This is an example of English irony."

to chuckle	kichern, in sich hineinlachen
to clap	klatschen
to sweat	schwitzen
betrayal	Verrat
awkwardly	ungeschickt
to recognize	erkennen
canvas	Leinwand
convincing	überzeugend
setting	Schauplatz

The students chuckle and begin to clap. Karl is sweating but very happy that they like his joke. He continues.

"The plot is simple. Love, betrayal, jealousy and murder. I hope that you enjoy our little play. The text, by the way, is included in your programme."

Karl bows rather awkwardly, holding his glasses, and then disappears backstage. The curtain is drawn back. The students smile and begin to clap again. Jim Ryan and his team have created an authentic flat with props. Most students recognize the sort of bedsit that they live in. They see a bed, a table, two chairs, a wash basin but also canvasses and half-finished paintings.

In the short first scene, Karl and Franca are very convincing. All the students understand that passion plays an important role in this little play.

They now know that something "dramatic" will happen in the second scene. After the curtain is opened again, there is even more applause.

This time the setting is a pub. It looks just like the "The Cherry Tree," [i] the pub where most of the students spend their evenings. It's only two hundred

> Die fantasievollen Namen der Pubs in Großbritannien gehen zurück auf Zeiten, in denen weite Teile der Bevölkerung noch nicht lesen und schreiben konnten. Die meisten Pubnamen erinnern an historische Ereignisse. Tier- oder Pflanzennamen gehen meist auf lokale Wappen zurück. Der mit Abstand häufigste Pubname ist **The Red Lion.**

metres from the school. Of course, they don't know that Colonel Lessons has "an arrangement" with the landlord. Ten per cent! There are several comfortable chairs and a table as the bar, with pieces painted to look like dark, Victorian wood. Lots of glasses hanging upside down and bottles behind, also upside down. Music is playing quietly in the background. Elke and Pierre are sitting at a table, whispering. The students study the text in the programme.

↯ tiff	Geplänkel, kleiner Streit
solution	Lösung
to apologize	(sich) entschuldigen
temptation	Versuchung
wrinkle	(Gesichts-)Falte
to offer	(an)bieten

E: So, Pierre, you know what to do. Have you got the gun?

P: Do you want to see it? I can show it to you.

E: Not here, you fool. People may be looking at us. You know the plan. I have an argument with Karl. A lovers' **tiff**, as they say. I tell him that I know he is having an affair – an affair with that silly young woman, Franca.
I leave and go to the car park. He follows me. I know he will. He wants my money and my contacts. I drive away, and then you shoot. It's all a great tragedy, and the world will lose a great artist. But there is no other **solution**. Think of... Aaah, here he comes!

Pierre moves to another table when Karl enters the pub. Karl **apologizes** for being late and sits in a chair. Then he tells Elke all about Franca, how pretty she is, much prettier than his previous model.

The audience smile and chuckle. Dramatic irony. They already know much more about what is happening than Karl does.

Then Karl says that he wants to give his new painting the title "Temptation". There is a long pause. Then Elke takes out a mirror and looks at her wrinkles.

E: Oh, sweet bird of youth! And I am so old and wrinkled and tired. I have nothing to offer anymore.

K: Now, Elke. You know that that's simply not true. You're the most beautiful woman in the world. You are my muse, you are my inspiration, my sun and my moon – and you are also the love of my life!

The audience cannot help laughing. After all, Elke, despite her make-up, is a very attractive woman, and Karl – well, Karl is rather short and plump. And he wears glasses. Elke continues.

E: Thank you, Karl. But that's not enough. I may be the love of your life but you don't really love ME! You only love my money! You're only interested in me because I pay your bills! Listen, I know what's going on. I know you are having an affair with this woman, this girl. So we must end our affairs, both of them. The sexual affair... and the business affair!

Exercise 10: Simple present or present continuous?
Lesen Sie weiter und setzen Sie die Verben in der richtigen Form ein!

K: Don't say that, Elke! I love you more than words can say. I **1.** think ________________ of you every minute of the day.

E: We are finished. Goodbye!

Elke **2.** leave ________________. Karl, **stunned**, sits for a moment longer and then **3.** run ________________ out. Pierre **4.** hurry ________________ to the door and **5.** follow ________________ him. A shot is heard in the background. Suddenly Mahdi appears.

M: Help! Call the police. Call an ambulance. A man **6.** lie ________________ in the car park! I think he **7.** die ________________.

Mahdi exits and returns a few moments later. He raises his hands and looks at the audience.

M: The man is dead. This is a terrible tragedy. His last words were "Elke, Franca, temptation". May he **rest in peace**.

The curtain is drawn, and the students of Church Hill School begin to applaud. Colonel Lessons appears from the front of the hall, marches to the stage and then turns to the audience. They clap their hands, louder and louder. What a superb end to three weeks in Eastcastle. All the presentations. Food, songs, village life!

The players step round the curtain, holding hands. Elke bows first, and the others follow. They are all smiling, pleased that the production is so successful. Karl polishes his glasses, raises his arms in triumph and then waves his hands to **silence** the audience. He's absolutely **thrilled**.

"Ladies and gentlemen," he says. "Thank you for your appreciation. You obviously liked our little play. Now we must give thanks to our teacher, director and producer – Jim Ryan!! Jim, please come out!"

Karl turns to the curtain, but nothing happens.

The students continue to clap – and clap – and clap. Nobody appears. Karl whispers to Mahdi, who then disappears behind the curtain. The clap becomes a slow handclap. Everybody is waiting for Jim Ryan.

> Anders als im Deutschen werden Relativsätze nur dann mit einem Komma vom Bezugswort abgetrennt, wenn sie eine zusätzliche Information enthalten und das Bezugswort nicht definieren.
> *Karl whispers to **Mahdi, who then** disappears.*
> Aber: *Tracy loves **someone who** is already married.*

Suddenly Mahdi runs through the curtain, pulling it down and **knocking over** several of the props. He's **frantic**. He turns to the players and then to the audience. He raises his hands and begins to cry.

The students begin to sit down. Is this part of the play? they **wonder**.

Mahdi turns to Pierre and whispers something. Pierre marches forward. He looks at the audience **grimly**.

"Something is very wrong here. Sacre-bleu! Jim Ryan is dead. Please leave the room. This is not a play. Jim Ryan, our teacher, is dead!"

The curtain closes again. Some of the younger students begin to **scream**.

stunned	benommen; fassungslos
to rest in peace	in Frieden ruhen
to silence	zum Schweigen bringen
thrilled	begeistert, hingerissen
to knock over	umwerfen, umstoßen
frantic	völlig verzweifelt
to wonder	sich fragen
grimly	grimmig, streng
to scream	schreien, kreischen

Exercise 11: Translation. Übersetzen Sie folgende Sätze ins Deutsche!

1. They are ready to present their tasks.

___

2. The students are laughing and talking.

___

3. They are looking forward to the presentation.

___

4. Mahdi disappears behind the curtain.

___

5. I drive away and then you shoot.

___

6. Karl polishes his glasses.

___

7. Some students begin to cry.

___

4 Left Luggage

Inspector Watson from the local police is tired. It's Saturday morning, and the temperature is already around 30 degrees. But he must continue with the interviews. Most of the students want to leave on Sunday. The five members of Jim Ryan's class are extremely upset and can give no useful information. The revolver from the play is on the desk in front of him. It's plastic, of course, and cannot be used to kill anyone.

Pierre still has the **receipt** from the local toyshop – £5.50. Watson also has the first report from **forensics**. This says that the murderer must have shot Ryan from a corner behind the stage, probably the left-hand corner, because that's where the door to the back garden is. The murderer must be familiar with guns. After all, the distance from the door to Ryan's body is about 10 metres.

receipt	Quittung
forensics	Kriminal-technik

The next student, a young man from Terry's class, knocks and enters the room.

"Ah, let's see." Watson looks at his list. "You must be Mr Olsen, from Denmark, I think."

"That's right, Inspector. How can I help?"

"Well, according to my plan here, your seat was in the second row, the last one on the right-hand side, so perhaps you could actually see this door which leads into the garden?"

Jens Olsen smiles and says:

Exercise 12: Simple past. **Lesen Sie weiter und setzen Sie die Verben in der passenden Verbform ein!**

"I understand, Inspector. Now let me think back." He concentrates. "The play **1.** be ______________ great fun. The actors **2.** be ______________ superb. Very good English. We **3.** understand ______________ everything. After Elke **4.** leave ______________ the pub, the audience were all very quiet. We **5.** know ______________ that something was going to happen, a fight or a murder. When the gun **went off**, there was some laughter – we all knew it was a toy gun. And I can tell you this. After the shot, I **6.** hear ______________ three sounds very clearly. One was a cry of pain. Well, we **7.** think ______________ that was part of the play."

"Go on," says Inspector Watson softly.

"The second was a **thud** – is that what you say in English?" Watson looks up from his notebook and nods.

"It was like a body that falls to the ground," the young man continues. "Or the floor. The main hall has wooden floorboards. And then, in the total silence before the applause, I heard that someone **slammed** a door. It must be this door on your plan. So the killer left the main hall by this door – is that what you think?"

to go off	*hier*: losgehen
thud	dumpfes Geräusch
to slam	zuschlagen, zuknallen

"Thank you, Mr Olsen. Very helpful. When do you return to Denmark?" Watsons asks.
"Monday, Inspector. From Heathrow to Kastrup, that's the airport in Copenhagen."

strange	merkwürdig, seltsam
unsolved	ungelöst
to mop	wischen
investigation	Ermittlung, Untersuchung

When Jens Olsen has left the room, Watson leans back in his chair. So! His hypothesis is correct. The killer shot from behind and exited into the garden. But who is the killer? And where is the weapon? And what is the motive? Questions, questions – and no answers!
The interviews continue. After the students, the teachers – and then, finally, the staff. Rose can give no helpful information. She was there at the performance but saw and heard nothing **strange**. Tracy was at home. She always has Friday afternoons free. The last person to come in is Mrs Bradley, the cleaner. Inspector Watson begins to feel that this case may remain **unsolved**. It could be "the perfect murder".
"Sit down, Mrs Bradley. Now, I wonder if you can tell me why someone wanted to kill Jim Ryan?"
"Well, Inspector, I'm not really sure. I mean, perhaps it's nothing important – but on Thursday evening, when I started to **mop** the floor..."
While Inspector Watson is doing his interviews, Colonel Lessons is at Number 19. He's happy that he doesn't need to be at Church Hill until the late afternoon. Tracy is organizing everything, and Rose is there, too. He orders another gin and tonic and smiles at the barmaid.
Well, he thinks, that's all over. Jim Ryan's dead. No **investigations** from the Ministry of Education. OK, those students from the B1 class are rather upset, and one or two others may miss their flights back home. Perhaps I'll lower their fees – say £50 –

and then everything will be forgotten. An unfortunate incident. Very unfortunate for Jim Ryan!

Exercise 13: Questions about the text. Beantworten Sie folgende Fragen auf Englisch!

1. Why can Ryan's class give no useful information?

____

2. How much did the toy gun cost?

____

3. Where was Olsen's seat?

____

4. How many sounds did Olsen hear?

____

5. Where was Tracy on Friday?

____

6. What is the cleaner's name?

____

7. Where does Olsen live?

____

The Colonel, a military man through and through, turns to the collection of antique guns behind the bar.

"Judy, tell me. That collection behind you. Do all those guns still work?"

The barmaid shrugs her shoulders and pours another pint of beer.

"Colonel, to be honest, I've no idea," she says. "They belong to the Secretary of the Golf Club. He's a collector, you know. But why don't you ask Tracy Dean. She was the barmaid here before me. She'll know. Another gin and tonic, Colonel?"

incident	Zwischenfall, Ereignis
to sip	nippen
confident	*hier*: zuversichtlich
to solve	lösen
to loosen one's collar	den Kragen lockern
to afford	sich leisten

"Yes, of course! I'm feeling lucky today!"
While the Colonel is **sipping** his gin and tonic, the phone rings. Judy picks it up. After a few seconds, she turns to Lessons.
"It's the police, Colonel. An Inspector Watson. He wants to see you down at the school – immediately!"
"Damn!" says Lessons. "OK, Judy, tell him I'm on my way."
The Colonel gulps the rest of his drink and heads out to the Rolls Royce.

Inspector Watson is now very **confident** that he can **solve** the murder. He **loosens his collar**. When Colonel Lessons comes in, he writes the time in his notebook: 15:34.
"Colonel, how good of you to come so quickly. No problems, I hope."
The Colonel is extremely angry.
"Now, listen Watson," he says grimly. "This is a murder case, obviously. And I want you to find the murderer. I can't **afford** to have this sort of scandal hanging over Church Hill!"
Watson looks out to the garden and then stares at Colonel Lessons.
"But you can afford to take out £25,000 from your bank – one day before Jim Ryan is murdered. I wonder if there's a connection?"
Lessons is stunned. "Now, look here, Inspector! I don't think you realize how much my school pays in local taxes. Without this

school, Eastcastle is nothing. And how do you know about the £25,000, anyway?"

"Have you got a cleaning lady, Colonel?"

Lessons sits down. What on earth is this little inspector trying to say?

"Of course we've got staff," shouts the Colonel. "Ask my daughter, Rose. She's in charge of all that."

Watson deals his trump card.

fire precautions	Brandschutz-maßnahmen
insurance	Versicherung
ϟ moonlighting	Schwarzarbeit
to sigh	seufzen
ceiling	(Zimmer-)Decke

"Yes, I know. And I also know that your cleaner's name is Mrs Bradley. She comes in every weekday around six. Now, where were you, Colonel, between six and seven on Thursday? Not at the Golf Club, so they tell me."

Lessons begins to splutter. He knows exactly where he was – in his office with that bastard Jim Ryan.

"Er – wait a second, Inspector. Let's see – Thursday. Back from the clubhouse around four to check up on accounts. Last-minute preparations for Friday, you know, **fire precautions**, and so on. Ah, yes! A short talk with Jim Ryan about his references. He wants – sorry, he wanted to take up a post in Saudi Arabia. Well, there were no problems. He was an excellent member of staff here during his six-week stay. Then down to the Pig and Whistle for dinner. Yes, that's it. Thursday. Oh, and a phone call to Tracy to withdraw the £25,000. And, dear Inspector Watson, I need that money to pay for certain repairs to the roof, and so on. Cash payments, you know. Cash, Inspector – no tax, no **insurance**. I think you call it '**moonlighting**'."

Inspector Watson **sighs** and looks at the **ceiling**.

"A good story, Colonel," he says. "It sounds very convincing. But Mrs Bradley tells me a very different story. She's cleaning the floor outside your office and hears a loud argument between you and Ryan. Now, she isn't an eavesdropper, but she hears a reference to the Ministry of Education and the word 'blackmail' – and the sum of £25,000. After a few minutes Ryan comes out, whistling cheerfully. Then, around seven, you come out. You are so angry that you don't even say goodbye. By the way, I also know that you have several prizes for shooting with a pistol. I'm afraid, Colonel, that I must ask you to come down to the police station."

eavesdropper	Lauscher(in)
cheerfully	fröhlich, heiter
constable	Wachtmeister, Polizist
reason	Grund
handcuffs *pl*	Handschellen
relieved	erleichtert
detective work	Ermittlungsarbeit
promotion	Beförderung
to gather	*hier*: (ein)sammeln
mansion	Villa, Herrenhaus
mellowed brickwork	alter Ziegelsteinbau

Watson stands up and calls in the constable waiting outside. The Colonel laughs, slightly hysterically. For some reason, he sees the sun setting on Majorca and the South of France, yet again. Even on Calais.

"You've got this all wrong, Inspector. I'm totally innocent..." the Colonel splutters.

But he has no time to explain. The constable puts on the handcuffs and leads him out to the police car. The Colonel sees his gleaming Roller in the drive. This time it will be a police cell – not Number 19.

Watson is relieved. He congratulates himself. Excellent detective work, he thinks. I may get promotion for solving this case so quickly. He gathers his notes, walks to his car and then decides to have a good pint of bitter in his local pub. Church Hill School, the old Victorian mansion, is now empty. The mellowed brickwork reflects the sun as Watson slams the front door shut.

to admire	bewundern
to hum	summen

About two miles out from the harbour, Tracy, on her yacht, is gliding through the waves of the English Channel. She looks towards the town and **admires** the old castle standing at the top of the cliffs. She doesn't feel sorry for the Colonel. He's an arrogant bastard anyway. Only Tracy knows who really killed Jim Ryan. She gently **hums** the sea shanty about Billy Boy and Nancy Grey. She thinks about the £25,000 in a brown envelope and her flight to New York on Monday. Then she suddenly turns and throws the revolver into the water.

Exercise 14: Questions. **Formulieren Sie folgende Sätze als Fragen!**

1. Watson is doing his interviews.

   ____

2. They order another gin.

   ____

3. He turns to the gun collection.

   ____

4. His school pays local taxes.

   ____

5. She's cleaning the floor.

   ____

6. The sun is setting on Eastcastle.

   ____

The Butterworth Mystery

Alison Romer

In einem Dorf in Lancashire werden Gemälde eines berühmten Künstlers gestohlen. Dabei verletzen die Diebe eine Museumswärterin schwer und entkommen unerkannt. Sergeant Rose tappt zunächst im Dunkeln, aber dann weisen die Bilder selbst auf das Motiv hin. Kann er das Rätsel rechtzeitig lösen, um die Gemälde sicherzustellen?

A2

1 Scary Stories

Michael Rose had been working for the Lancashire Police for seven years. He loved his job. Because he lived and worked in a small village, he knew many people by name. Even though he was only thirty-three, he was an **old-fashioned** type of policeman: friendly, caring and ready to help. He liked the people of Pendle Lee, and the people of Pendle Lee liked Sergeant Rose.

Crime was not a big problem. At the police station, days went by quite slowly. Many other officers liked to be in a bigger town or a city. But Michael loved being part of a small **community**. The village itself was also a lovely place to live. The church, which was in the centre, had been built in 1376. Many of the houses had been standing for a very long time. Even the pub, which was called "The White **Witch**", was hundreds of years old. At the **edge** of the village a river **flowed** through the fields and woods. On summer evenings, it was as beautiful as a painting.

However, there was not very much for young people to do. Bored teenagers were often getting into trouble. In fact, most of the problems Michael had to **deal with** were caused by teenagers. Loud music, graffiti and bad behaviour were the main

old-fashioned	altmodisch
crime	Verbrechen
community	Gemeinschaft
witch	Hexe
edge	Rand, Ecke
to flow	fließen
to deal with	sich beschäftigen mit, zu tun haben mit

things. Usually he just talked to the young people and their parents. He hardly ever had to take one of them to the station. In seven years, he had only arrested five people. Yet in those seven years, he had found eleven lost dogs and returned them to their homes. Some policemen would have found that kind of life boring. But Michael was happy.

to arrest	verhaften
kind	Art, Sorte
to set	*hier*: untergehen
shift	Schicht(dienst)
bureaucracy	Bürokratie
to purr	schnurren

Exercise 1: Translation. Wie heißt das Wort auf Deutsch? Übersetzen Sie!

1. fields ______________________
2. village ______________________
3. caring ______________________
4. ancient ______________________
5. cottage ______________________
6. happen ______________________
7. gate ______________________
8. painting ______________________

It was the middle of summer. The sun had just set, and it was very late. Michael was at the police station. He was on the night shift. For a few hours, he had been doing some paperwork. Even in a small village station, there was a lot of bureaucracy. He had also had some coffee and had read the newspaper. The police station cat, Harriet, was sitting on his knee. She was purring.

"Sorry, Harriet," Michael said. "You're going to have to move. I want another coffee."

He tried to push the fat tabby cat off his lap, but she didn't want to go.

Suddenly the phone rang.

That's strange, Michael thought. Nobody ever called late at night unless something was really wrong.

He picked up the phone.

"Pendle Lee Police Station," he said.

tabby	getigerte Katze
strange	seltsam
to recognize	erkennen
elderly	älter
cemetery	Friedhof
to sigh	seufzen
to gather	*hier*: (sich) versammeln
to upset sb.	jmd. ärgern
graveyard	Friedhof
grave	Grab
right away	sofort
glow	Leuchten

"Oh, Michael," said a voice he recognized.

It was Mrs White, an elderly lady who lived on the edge of the village.

"I'm sorry it's so late," she said. "But there's something happening in the cemetery."

Michael sighed. Every now and again, a group of teenagers would gather at the Pendle Lee Cemetery. Wearing black clothes, they would light candles and play loud music.

"Is it those kids again?" Michael asked.

"Maybe," Mrs White replied. "I can't sleep. And it upsets me that they go to the graveyard. My parents' and grandparents' graves are there."

"Of course," said Michael. "I'll go right away. Then maybe you can get some sleep."

Around ten minutes later, Michael parked the police car at the cemetery gates. He could hear music. The yellow glow of candles told him where the kids were. He got out of the car and

switched on his torch. Next to the gates was a very old house. In the past, the cemetery caretaker had lived in it. But the place had been standing empty for twenty years. Some of the windows were broken. Climbing plants had grown over the building. They had even gone through some of the windows.
Two hundred years ago, it had been really pretty. But now it looked like something from a scary movie. Nobody went inside. Birds had made their homes in the empty rooms.

to switch on	anschalten
torch	Taschenlampe
caretaker	Hausmeister

Exercise 2: Choose the correct alternative.
Kreuzen Sie die richtige Variante an!

1. The graveyard at night...
   a) ❐ looked how something from a scary movie.
   b) ❐ looked like something from a scary movie.
   c) ❐ looked as something from a scary movie.
2. Police work involves...
   a) ❐ much bureaucracies.
   b) ❐ more bureaucracy.
   c) ❐ a lot of bureaucracy.
3. He knew many people by name.
   a) ❐ He called people names.
   b) ❐ He knew lots of people quite well.
   c) ❐ Many people knew his name.

Using his torch to light the way, Michael went towards the teenagers. Candles were glowing on the graves. There was loud music, and some of the teenagers were standing in a circle singing.
When Michael appeared out of the darkness, he frightened some of them. A girl screamed.
"Sorry," he said to her. "It's only me. Are you trying to make a ghost appear?"
"It's none of your business," said a tall boy.
He stepped forward into the torchlight. Michael knew who he was. His name was Alex. He was seventeen years old, and his parents owned the bakery.
"It IS my business," Michael replied. "This is a cemetery. Having a party here isn't respectful."
The girl who had nearly screamed came across to Michael.
"We can do what we want," she said. She was trying to sound brave after her fright earlier.
Michael recognized her now. Katie Lewis. She was only fourteen, and she should have been at home in bed.
"What are you doing?" Michael asked. "Are you trying to make contact with witches? I don't think you'll have any luck tonight."

to glow	leuchten
to appear	auftauchen, erscheinen
to frighten sb.	jmd. erschrecken
to scream	schreien, kreischen
ghost	Gespenst
It's none of your business!	Das geht dich nichts an!
brave	mutig
fright	Schreck
Lancashire	engl. Grafschaft, benannt nach der Stadt Lancaster

Pendle Lee was in a part of Lancashire that was famous for its witches. In the early seventeenth century, some women and men from the area had been arrested. It was said that one talked to a black dog that was really the devil. The villagers believed that witches had made some people sick and even killed them. It was

believed that cows stopped giving milk because of **magic spells**. The unlucky women and men were kept in **prison** at Lancaster Castle. The witches had been **hung** in 1612. Many people went to watch. Now, the witches were seen as ordinary people who were **scapegoats** of the community. But the stories had continued until the present day.

to believe	glauben
magic spell	Zauberspruch
prison	Gefängnis
to hang sb.	jmd. erhängen
scapegoat	Sündenbock
to exist	bestehen, existieren

Exercise 3: Simple past. Lesen Sie weiter und setzen Sie die Verben ins Simple Past!

The Lancashire Witches **1.** bring ________________ many tourists to the area. People could buy toy witches. Lancaster Castle even **2.** have ________________ a special tour of the old prison rooms. And every year on Halloween, people from all over **3.** walk ________________ up Pendle Hill in the dark. Pendle Lee had its own stories, too. Some were about the cemetery. The first graves **4.** be ________________ over seven hundred years old. Long before the big Pendle Lee church was built, an even older church **existed** where the cemetery **5.** be ________________. The stories **6.** tell ________________ of witches meeting at the place where the old church once **7.** stand ________________.

It was said that they danced around large fires and tried to see the devil. The ghost of a witch called Agnes Cott was said to **haunt** the graveyard. Some people said that the caretaker's house was haunted, too. Strange noises were heard late at night. Strange lights were seen, too, even when the teenagers were in their beds.

Michael switched on his torch again.
"Time to go," he said to the kids, "before the ghost of Agnes Cott really does appear. Then you'll all run screaming back home anyway."
"You can't stop us," said Alex. "We'll come back again. The more this community hates us the happier we are."
"I'm sorry you feel that way," said Michael.
He did understand. There was nothing for teenagers to do in Pendle Lee. He thought that young people's discos at the **church hall** were a good idea. The villagers were worried about noise and alcohol. However, having teenagers on the streets at night was a bigger problem.

to haunt	spuken (in)
church hall	Gemeindesaal
headstone	Grabstein
to smash	zerschlagen, zerschmettern

After the kids left the graveyard, Michael looked around. There wasn't any graffiti on the graves tonight. In the past, there had been a problem with graffiti. Even some of the **headstones** had been **smashed**. That was a few years ago.
Alex and the other young people were angry and bored, but Michael didn't think they would do anything that bad. He decided to keep an eye on them anyway.

A few days later, Michael was on a normal afternoon shift. He liked to work during the day because there was more to do. He could walk around the village and talk to people. He could **stop by** the different shops and **chat** with the owners. At the station, other officers would come in from time to time. Even Harriet the cat liked the daytime best. On sunny days, she could lie on the step outside the station. Anybody coming in or going out would have to step over her.

to stop by	vorbeischauen
to chat	plaudern
allotment	Schrebergarten
rather	*hier*: eher
to admire	bewundern
mobile	Handy
emergency	Notfall
to burgle sth.	einbrechen in
siren	Sirene
art restoration	Gemälderestaurierung
to offer	(an)bieten
to think long and hard	es sich reiflich überlegen

Mr Murphy, an elderly man, had called in at the station to give Michael some beans. Mr Murphy had grown them himself in his **allotment**. He was always stopping by with fresh vegetables. Like many older people, he used his allotment for pleasure **rather** than needing the food. He grew more than he could eat. Michael was just **admiring** the fresh green beans when his **mobile** rang.
"I'll just get that," Michael said to Mr Murphy.
He put the beans down. The call was from his boss, who had an office in the city.
"We've just heard from the Oswald Gallery," the Chief Inspector said. "They called the national **emergency** number. Can you go there, Michael? They've been **burgled**."
Michael switched on the **sirens** as he drove quickly through the village in his car. As he drove, he thought about the gallery. He hadn't been there for over three years, but he used to go a lot. That was because his ex-girlfriend, Sarah, loved art. Sarah had left to go to America about three years ago. She worked in **art restoration** and had been **offered** a job in Boston. After **thinking long and hard**, she decided to take it. But Michael couldn't get a

job with the police in the United States. He didn't want to stop being a policeman either. So he stayed in Pendle Lee, and Sarah moved to Boston.

Exercise 4: Match-up. Welche Wörter passen zusammen? Ordnen Sie zu!

1. ☐	elderly	a) shift
2. ☐	thank	b) spell
3. ☐	stay	c) restoration
4. ☐	art	d) caretaker
5. ☐	magic	e) man
6. ☐	cemetery	f) calm
7. ☐	night	g) goodness

The Oswald Gallery was just outside the village. It was in a beautiful eighteenth-century house. A man called John Oswald had built the house, and the gallery was named after him. It took Michael around ten minutes to get there. When he arrived, he walked to the door. Two elderly women quickly came to meet him. They looked upset. Both of them started speaking at once.

"Oh Sergeant,[i] thank goodness you're here!" one of the women exclaimed. "I'm Joan Potts. I work here."

"We don't know how it happened," the other lady was saying

Nur als direkte Anrede oder als Teil eines Namens werden Titel und Berufsbezeichnungen wie **Sergeant** im Englischen großgeschrieben. In allen anderen Fällen schreibt man sie klein.

at the same time, "but it's my **fault**!"

"No, Lottie, of course it's not your fault," said Joan.

"Yes it is!" Lottie exclaimed. "I'm so angry with myself!"

Michael raised his hands.

"Let's stay calm," he said. "We'll go inside, and you can tell me all about it. Then we'll start searching for the **thief**."

upset	erschrocken, aufgebracht
at once	*hier*: gleichzeitig
Thank goodness!	Gott sei Dank!
to exclaim	ausrufen
fault	Fehler
thief	Dieb

2 Past Life

Once inside, Michael took out his notebook.
"Now tell me what happened," he said.
"No one had come to visit for over two hours," said Joan Potts. "It was a slow day."
Lottie Bingley sat down behind the reception desk.
"I'm afraid I left the reception," she said. "Every year we have a competition for artists. People from all over Lancashire send in their paintings. This morning we had some new paintings come in, and I was very excited. I wanted to see them, even though it's not my job to unpack them. I went upstairs to look. While I was gone, someone came in and stole one of our paintings. So it's all my fault."

reception	Empfang
competition	Wettbewerb
to unpack	auspacken
to steal	stehlen
security camera	Überwachungskamera

Michael looked all around the room.
"Don't you have security cameras?" he asked.
"No," Joan replied. "It would cost a lot of money. But we never imagined that someone would steal from the Oswald Gallery!"
"And neither of you saw anybody?" Michael asked.
"No." Both women replied at the same time.
"We didn't see or hear anything," said Lottie.
"Let's have a look at where the painting was hung," Michael said.
The women led him into one of the gallery's little rooms. Modern galleries had lots of space and white paint, but the Oswald Gal-

lery was different. The building had many small rooms and **halls**. The walls were covered in beautiful old wood. The windows were very small. As visitors walked around, they could imagine living three hundred years ago. Paintings were hung on all the walls, but in one place there was an empty spot.
"It was here," said Joan. "It was called 'Summer'."
Michael took out his phone.
"I'm going to call the **crime scene** police," he told Joan and Lottie. "Someone will come round and check for **finger-prints**. I'll also need a photo-graph of the painting, please. It'll help in the **investigation**."

hall	Flur
crime scene	Tatort
fingerprint	Fingerabdruck
investigation	Ermittlung

"I'll go and find one," said Lottie. "The artist was Butterworth, of course."

The Oswald Gallery was small and not very important. But it had the largest collection of Butterworth paintings in the country. Tristan Butterworth was a famous painter from the 1940s and 50s. He had lived near Pendle Lee for many years. When he died in the 1980s, many of his best paintings were given to the gallery. People came from all over the United Kingdom to see them.
Lottie came back into the reception and handed a large photograph to Michael.
"Here it is," she said. "This is 'Summer'. It's a wonderful picture, isn't it?"
Michael looked at it. It showed a beautiful summer scene. In the background, the sun shone on a river. Green fields and trees were all around. In the front of the painting, there was a large tree, and under it sat a young woman. She was wearing an old-fashioned yellow dress and a big hat.

"This was painted in 1951," Lottie said. "Looking at it makes me feel so calm. It almost feels like you're really there."
"It's lovely," said Michael. "I'll need to keep this photograph for our investigation. Is that okay?"
"Of course," said Lottie. "We'll do whatever we can to help."

Exercise 5: Question words. **Setzen Sie die richtigen Fragepronomen ein!**

which | who | where | why | what | when

1. ________ was the painting hung?
2. ________ kind of competition was it?
3. ________ does the gallery open?
4. ________ of the paintings was stolen?
5. ________ were Joan and Lottie so upset?
6. ________ works at the gallery?

Back inside his car, Michael phoned his boss, Chief Inspector Blake. He gave Blake all the information he had so far. The inspector was very busy. Michael could tell he wasn't very interested in a painting stolen from a village gallery. The city had more crime than the police could deal with.
"They should have had security cameras," Blake said angrily.
He told Michael to contact the Art Loss Register. It kept an international database of art that had

database	Datenbank

to alert sb.	jmd. alarmieren, warnen
burglary	Einbruch (-diebstahl)
mood	Stimmung, Laune
terror alert	Terroralarm
wavy	gewellt
to wonder	sich fragen
imagination	Vorstellung

been stolen or lost. If a rich person or a museum wanted to buy a piece of art, they could find out if it was stolen through the Register. If it was, the buyer could **alert** the police. The thief who was trying to sell the art could then be caught.

It was hard to find stolen art. Sometimes the buyer knew it was stolen, but didn't care. Sometimes a group of thieves would plan a big **burglary**, and then wait for many years before selling the art in places like Africa or South America.

"Can you deal with this?" Blake asked Michael. "I don't have another officer who can come down there right now. It's too bad we have to send you a crime scene officer just to take some fingerprints."

"I still think it's a good idea," Michael said.

The inspector was often in a bad **mood**, and Michael was glad he didn't have to work in the city with him.

"You know we're on **terror alert**, don't you?" Blake went on. "We may have to send officers to Manchester or London at any moment. You too, Sergeant."

"I know," Michael replied. "Leave everything to me, Inspector. I'll send you my reports."

After the phone call was finished, Michael opened the car window. He took a deep breath of fresh air. Then he looked at the photograph of 'Summer' again. The young woman in the picture was very pretty. She had long, **wavy** blonde hair. She looked out across the fields. Michael **wondered** if the woman had been real or if she had come from the painter's **imagination**.

Michael was soon back at the station. He immediately contacted the Art Loss Register. He informed them about the stolen painting and gave all the details. Then he went out and **interviewed** the villagers. He was hoping someone had seen something strange, like someone hurrying away from the village. **Meanwhile**, the crime scene officer was **exploring** the gallery. If fingerprints were found, they would be put into the police fingerprint database. If the thief had done anything wrong before, his (or her) prints would be in the database. They would **match with** the prints from the crime scene. Then the police would have a name.

to interview	befragen, verhören
meanwhile	währenddessen
to explore	erkunden
to match with	*hier*: passen zu
Crimestoppers number	Telefonnummer für sachdienliche Hinweise
stranger	Fremder
unconscious	bewusstlos
straight	direkt, geradewegs

Over the next two days, Michael was busy. He put up signs about the burglary. The signs asked people with any information to call the police or the national **Crimestoppers number**. He also went from house to house, asking the villagers if they had seen a **stranger** in the village. A few couples and families had had picnics or had stopped at the White Witch pub. But nobody had been behaving strangely. He made copies of the 'Summer' photograph. Then he took them to all the art shops and auction houses in the area. He sent the photo to colleagues in Preston, Manchester, and even London.

At the station, he put the photo on the wall. Instead of trying to find a stolen painting, he began to feel that he was trying to find the beautiful woman. It seemed very important to take her back to the gallery where she lived.

Exercise 6: Prepositions. Lesen Sie weiter und setzen Sie die passenden Präpositionen ein!

in | about | for | with | at | to | after

1. _____ a few days, the other police officers started to joke **2.** _____ Michael's painting. He looked **3.** _____ it a hundred times a day. Sometimes, when he was talking **4.** _____ someone, his eyes would go to the photograph. "Have you fallen **5.** _____ love?" some of the officers asked.

Michael no longer chatted **6.** _____ the villagers. He didn't seem to have time any more. Even Harriet the cat seemed in a bad mood because of 'Summer'. Michael only wanted to hunt **7.** _____ the painting, and was no longer interested in playing with her.

Whenever he had a moment, he was on the phone or visiting auction houses, asking about the painting. Even when he was not at work, he'd visit places that sold old paintings.

On Tuesday afternoon, the phone rang. It was exactly five days since 'Summer' had been stolen. Every time the phone rang, Michael hoped it was about the painting. It was Joan Potts from the gallery.

"Something terrible has happened!" she exclaimed. "Lottie has been taken to hospital. Another painting was stolen and this time, the thief pushed Lottie down the stairs. She's **unconscious**."

After going **straight** to the gallery and looking at the crime scene, Michael went to the hospital with Joan. They were both very worried about Lottie. Because she was old, her chances of getting better quickly were not good. She'd hit her head quite **badly** and broken one of her legs. Joan couldn't help crying as they stood in the waiting room at the hospital. The doctor **in charge** promised to call Michael as soon as there was a change. Michael needed to ask her about what happened. Perhaps Lottie saw the thief coming up the stairs. But while she was unconscious and in danger, all he could do was wait and hope.

badly	*hier*: heftig, schwer
in charge	verantwortlich, zuständig
landscape	Landschaft
still-life	Stillleben
clue	Hinweis, Spur

Meanwhile, he needed to contact the Art Loss Register about the second stolen painting. It was another Butterworth, called 'Evening in June'. This time it was of a terrace outside a lovely old house. There was a table with teacups and a teapot, and a large strawberry cake. On one of the chairs sat a woman. Michael recognized her as the woman from 'Summer'. This time she was dressed in a pretty purple dress. She was reading a book. In the background were green hills, and the sun was just going down. The sunset seemed to make the picture glow.

Michael thought it was strange that both paintings were of the same woman. There were many Butterworth pictures that showed **landscapes** or **still-life** scenes. Only a few had the young woman in them. Perhaps that was a **clue**.

"Who was she?" Michael asked when he called Joan that night.

"Don't you know?" asked Joan. "It's Sylvia. Sylvia and Tristan Butterworth got married in 1950. She was very beautiful and was his model for some of his paintings."

"Maybe if we find out more about Sylvia Butterworth, it might give us a clue," Michael said. "Perhaps the thief wants to collect paintings of her."

"Good idea," said Joan. "Maybe he's **obsessed with** her. We have an **archive** at the gallery. It has a lot of information about Sylvia in it. You can look at it if you like."

Exercise 7: Opposites. Finden Sie das passende Gegenteil!

1. ☐ few	a) strange
2. ☐ push	b) quiet
3. ☐ wrong	c) pull
4. ☐ friendly	d) ugly
5. ☐ normal	e) many
6. ☐ slow	f) right
7. ☐ daytime	g) fast
8. ☐ beautiful	h) unfriendly
9. ☐ loud	i) night-time

The next day, after his afternoon shift, Michael went back to the Oswald Gallery. It had been closed, and there were plans to buy security cameras. The risk of someone getting **hurt** again was too big. Joan took Michael upstairs to a small office. It was filled with **filing cabinets**.
"This is the Butterworth archive," Joan said. "The filing cabinets are full of photographs and letters. They belonged to both Tristan

obsessed (with)	besessen (von)
archive	Archiv
to hurt	verletzen; schmerzen
filing cabinet	Aktenschrank

and Sylvia. There are also lots of papers about Butterworth's paintings and **exhibitions**. You can look through them, if you like."

Joan made him a cup of coffee. Then she gave him the keys to the gallery and the code number of the alarm system. She went back to the hospital, where she spent her evenings sitting with Lottie. Michael was alone. He didn't know where to start looking. All he knew was that someone had a **reason** for stealing Butterworth's paintings of Sylvia. Perhaps the past would give him a clue.

exhibition	Ausstellung
reason	Grund
file	Akte
confident	selbstsicher
down	*hier*: offen, lose
gorgeous	herrlich, wunderschön
honeymoon	Flitterwochen

First he pulled open some **files** of photographs. There were lots of black-and-white ones, and there were many of Sylvia by herself. Michael knew they were not important for the investigation, but he couldn't help looking. Some were of Sylvia when she was very young. Most showed her in her twenties and thirties.

Michael felt that he had never seen anyone more beautiful. Sylvia had big, dark eyes and a glowing smile. She was quite tall and looked strong and **confident**. When she was younger, she had worn her long hair **down**. When she was older, she wore it up, in the style of the 1950s. Her clothes were always pretty and looked good on her. In some of the photos, she was with a man. Michael recognized him as Tristan Butterworth. The names, places and dates were written on the backs of many photos.

There were many pictures, for example, of Tristan and Sylvia in a **gorgeous** landscape. In the background were lakes and mountains. On the backs of the pictures were the words '**Honeymoon**, Cumbria, 1950'. The couple looked very happy. Some of the photographs showed other people, too.

soldier	Soldat
serious	ernst

There were many that had been taken on the terrace of a house. Michael thought it was the same terrace as in 'Evening in June'. In the photos, lots of people were standing around. They had glasses of wine and cigarettes. In other photos, the same people were sitting under a tree, having a picnic. Behind them the Pendle Lee river flowed. Everyone was smiling at the camera. There were a few pictures of Butterworth with another man. The pictures said 'Nigel and Tristan', with different places and dates. There were also pictures of 'Nigel and Sylvia'.

Next he looked at some old letters. There were lots from Sylvia to Tristan. Michael began to read. He read for a long time. When he looked at his watch, he had been reading for over an hour. He had been in a different world. It seemed as though Sylvia was writing to him. He put down the letters and picked up some different ones. All of them were to Sylvia from a man named Nigel Huxley. Some were dated from 1941 to 1944 and had been sent from France.

Exercise 8: Adjectives or adverbs? Lesen Sie weiter und wählen Sie das passende Adjektiv oder Adverb!

Michael looked through them **1.** quick / quickly. Huxley had written about being a **soldier** in World War II. He wrote about being frightened when bombs fell **2.** close / closely by. He also told her about other soldiers, who had died. Some of the letters were very **3.** serious / seriously.

But others were **4.** full / fully of fun. In these light letters, he wrote about parties and friends. Huxley had written 'To my darling Sylvia' at the top of the letters. It was **5.** clear / clearly that he had been in love with her. Michael took out his notebook and wrote down Nigel's name. Perhaps he was still **6.** alive / alively. Maybe he had more information about Sylvia and the paintings.

Michael had been in the archive for hours. At last he decided to go home. He wanted to come back as soon as possible, because there were many more letters and papers to look at. But before he left, Michael opened the filing cabinet with the photos. There was one he wanted to see again. The photo showed Sylvia sitting on a beach. She was wearing a big sun hat and a white dress. Her hair was down. In her hands was a small book. She had stopped reading and was looking into the camera. But instead of smiling, Sylvia looked serious. Michael felt that she was looking right at him. Before he could stop himself, he had picked up the photo. Then he put it into his pocket. He had never stolen anything in his life. Now he was a thief, just like the person who had taken the paintings.

Michael had spent many hours in the archive, and it was now night-time. On his way home, he drove past the cemetery. He was worried that the teenagers were there again. Suddenly, he saw something. It looked like the glow from a candle or a torch. It seemed to be moving among the graves.
"Those kids!" Michael said out loud.

He looked at his watch: 12:16 a.m. Michael stopped the car at the gates and got out his torch. Then he went into the cemetery. The light seemed to have disappeared. He listened, but he couldn't hear anything. The moon was shining brightly, and the air smelled like cut grass and old flowers. He walked on. The graves looked quite scary in the dark. Although he didn't believe in ghosts, Michael didn't feel very brave. It was like a graveyard scene from a scary movie.

among	zwischen
to disappear	verschwinden
to hide	(sich) verstecken
to be about to do sth.	im Begriff sein, etw. zu tun

Suddenly he got angry. The teenagers were probably hiding from him. Maybe Alex and his friends were all sitting behind the headstones, waiting for him to go away. They probably thought this was funny. Michael decided to switch off his torch[i] and wait for the kids to come out.

The moonlight helped him to see quite well. But suddenly a cloud moved across the sky, and the moonlight disappeared. It was very dark. Michael turned around in a circle. Nothing. No light. And he still couldn't hear anything, either.

He was about to switch his torch back on when he saw a small light. It was near the old caretaker's house. There was someone there. Michael put on his torch again. He shone it across the graves towards the empty old house.

Bei vielen **Phrasal Verbs** kann das Objekt sowohl vor als auch nach der Präposition stehen:
He switched his torch off.
Ein Objektpronomen steht aber immer vor der Präposition:
He switched it off.

"Hello!" he called out.

Immediately the candlelight disappeared. Michael started to walk to the house.

"It's Sergeant Rose here," he shouted. "What are you doing?"

Exercise 9: Odd one out. Welches Wort passt nicht in die Reihe? Finden Sie das „schwarze Schaf"!

1. paint cook photograph draw
2. moonlight torchlight sunlight starlight
3. ghost witch vampire murderer
4. steal rob burgle sell
5. box circle triangle square
6. graveyard museum headstone cemetery
7. torch candle soldier lamp
8. clue confident obsessed frightened

When he reached the house, he shone his torch all around. There was nobody there. However, a strange symbol had appeared on the front door. It showed three stars inside a circle, painted in yellow paint. He tried the door, but it wouldn't open. He went up to some of the windows and shone his torch inside. The rooms were empty apart from some broken tables and chairs. There were spider's webs everywhere. "Whoever you are," Michael said to the empty air, "you should go home."

apart from	außer
spider's web	Spinnennetz

Suddenly he heard a ghostly laugh. He couldn't tell if it was a man's or a woman's voice. Before he could turn around, there was a sharp pain in his head, and he was falling towards the ground.

3 Young Woman with Flowers

When Michael finally opened his eyes, his clothes were wet from lying in the grass for a long time. He put his hand to his head. When he looked at his hand, there was something dark on his fingers. Blood. He felt sick, and his head hurt. His torch was lying on the ground, but it wasn't working any more. Michael looked around. He didn't know what to do. The best thing would be to call his boss, then go to the hospital and get a doctor to look at him. He stood up. All he wanted to do was get into bed. Slowly, he went back to his car and drove home.

witness	Zeuge

Early the next morning, Michael went to the station. He wrote a report about what happened in the graveyard. His head still hurt badly, but he didn't want to spend the day waiting to see a doctor. Instead he called the hospital about Lottie. She was still unconscious, and the doctors were doing all sorts of tests. After the hospital call, he phoned the homes of Alex and some of the other teenagers from the cemetery. He asked their parents to bring them down to the station as soon as possible. If[i] Alex had hit Michael, he was in serious trouble. Then he arranged for another officer to talk to the teenagers. Although Michael wanted to talk to Alex and the others himself, he was a witness

> Verwechseln Sie nicht **if** und **when**:
> *If Alex hit Michael, he would be in trouble.* (**if** = wenn, falls)
> ***When** Alex hit Michael, he was in trouble.* (**when** = wenn, als)

sculptor	Bildhauer
nearby	in der Nähe
to pay sb. a visit	jmd. einen Besuch abstatten
mansion	Villa, Herrenhaus

to a crime. He couldn't be the questioning officer, too. Then Michael searched the Internet for Nigel Huxley. Huxley might have information about the paintings or Sylvia. He found out that Huxley had also been an artist. He was a **sculptor**, but he was not as famous as Butterworth. His last sculpture was made in 1967. Now Huxley lived in a village only 20 kilometres from Pendle Lee. He was 85 years old, and it seemed that he was very rich.

Michael thought about everything he now knew about Huxley. He lived **nearby** and knew about art. And although he was old, you didn't have to be fit to push an old lady downstairs. He had been in love with Sylvia. Perhaps he had driven to the gallery. He could have stolen 'Summer' while Lottie was looking at the new paintings upstairs. The second time, Lottie may have seen him stealing 'Evening in June'. He might have pushed her down the stairs, then put the painting in the car and driven home.

Michael decided to **pay** Huxley **a visit**.

But first, he put out some cat food for Harriet. The big tabby was still in a bad mood. Michael just wanted to talk about, think about and dream about those paintings! He had no time for cats or the other villagers. When Mr Murphy came in that morning with a bag of aubergines, Michael had simply thanked him and looked back at the computer.

At lunch time, Michael drove to the nearby village. It took him a long time to find Huxley's house. The house was very large. In fact, it was a **mansion**, but it was hidden behind lots of trees on the edge of the village. Michael parked the police car in front of the house. It was a lovely old place. There were lots of steps leading to a big door. Michael went up and rang the bell. After a few moments, an elderly woman opened the door.

Exercise 10: Translation quiz. Übersetzen Sie und enträtseln Sie das Lösungswort!

1. Villa _ _ _ □ _ _ _
2. Taschenlampe □ _ _ _ _
3. Bildhauer _ _ _ _ _ _ □ _
4. Handy _ _ _ _ □ _
5. Friedhof _ _ _ □ _ _ _ _
6. selbstsicher _ _ □ _ _ _ _ _ _

Lösung: □□□□□□

"Mrs Huxley?" Michael asked.
"No, I'm the **housekeeper**," the woman said.
She looked at his police uniform and car. For some reason, she didn't seem too happy.
"Do you want to see Mr Huxley?"
"Yes, please, if he's at home," Michael replied.
"You'd better come in," said the housekeeper.
Michael followed her into the house.

housekeeper	Haushälterin
to point to	zeigen auf

"Wait here." The housekeeper **pointed to** a chair by the door. She wasn't friendly at all. Michael wondered if she ever smiled. He sat down. The big hall was painted a light green. The floor was made of gorgeous dark wood. In the corner stood a large

sculpture. Michael couldn't really tell what it was. It could have been a woman with long wavy hair. Or a tree. Whatever it was, it looked very modern.
Suddenly the housekeeper appeared again.
"You can see Mr Huxley now," she said. "He's in the living room."

Nigel Huxley sat in a big chair. He didn't look 85 at all. He seemed a lot younger. But perhaps that was because of his **bright** blue eyes. He looked intelligent and full of energy.
"I'm sorry about my housekeeper," Huxley said. "She's not very nice to visitors, even policemen."
Michael looked around the living room. The sun was shining through the large windows. There were two huge sofas and a few chairs. In the middle of the room was a round table. Lots of books were everywhere: on the table, on bookshelves and on the floor. There was also a beautiful old **fireplace**. Above the fireplace, on the wall, there was a painting. Michael immediately recognized Sylvia.

bright	*hier*: hell, strahlend
fireplace	(offener) Kamin

"That's a Butterworth picture!" he exclaimed.
"Yes," Huxley said. "It's called 'Young Woman with Flowers'. Tristan Butterworth gave it to me."
The painting showed Sylvia holding lots of flowers. They were pink, orange and red. The background was a dark green, and Sylvia was wearing a green dress.
Michael couldn't take his eyes off the picture. Even when the housekeeper came in with tea and biscuits, he couldn't stop looking at Sylvia.
"How can I help you?" Huxley asked, taking a cup of tea and a chocolate biscuit.

Michael finally took his eyes off the painting and looked at the old man.

"I'm sorry, Mr Huxley, I should have introduced myself. I'm Sergeant Rose from the police station at Pendle Lee. You heard about the **robbery** at the gallery?" asked Michael.

"Of course," Huxley replied. "I collect Butterworth paintings. I'm often at the Oswald Gallery."

robbery	Raubüberfall
to question sb.	jdn. befragen
detective work	Ermittlungsarbeit

"You know that Lottie Bingley is unconscious in hospital?" Michael asked, watching Huxley closely.

"Yes. It's very sad and upsetting," Huxley said.

Michael looked at the picture of Sylvia above the fireplace.

"Somebody wanted those pictures very badly," he said. "Badly enough to almost kill an elderly woman. Both paintings were of Sylvia. We should look for someone who is obsessed with her."

Huxley's eyes shone, and he gave a small smile.

"So you've come to **question** me," he said. "Good **detective work**, Sergeant Rose. It's true, I was in love with Sylvia. She and I grew up together. Our families were friends. We lived in the same village and went to the same church. Even when I was a teenager, I loved her. I met Tristan Butterworth at art school. Sylvia would model for us both. Then the Second World War started. I became a soldier, but Tristan couldn't join the army. He had polio when he was a baby, and there was something wrong with his leg. While I was in France, Tristan and Sylvia fell in love. I wanted them to be happy, so we stayed friends."

Ein falscher Freund!
to become heißt „werden".

"What happened to Tristan and Sylvia?" Michael asked. He'd almost forgotten about the stolen art.

Exercise 11: Choose the correct alternative. Lesen Sie weiter und unterstreichen Sie die richtige Variante!

"The Butterworths moved to America in the 1960s," Huxley **1.** goes / went on. "We **2.** have written / wrote letters at Christmas, but after a few years our letters stopped. I **3.** hear / heard they **4.** lived / were living in New York. Tristan had an exhibition at the Museum of Modern Art. Then I read in the paper that he had died in 1986. I never saw Sylvia again. I tried **5.** to find / finding her, but with no luck. Now my paintings **6.** of / from Sylvia **7.** bring / brought back wonderful memories of summer."

"Would you break the law to get more of those memories?" Michael asked.

"I'm sorry to disappoint you," said Huxley, "but I didn't steal those paintings."

"So you won't mind if I have a look around your house?" Michael asked.

memory	Erinnerung
to break the law	das Gesetz brechen
to disappoint sb.	jmd. enttäuschen
to mind sth.	etw. dagegen haben
search warrant	Durchsuchungsbefehl

"Yes, I do mind, Sergeant Rose," the old man replied, standing up. "My house is private. If you don't have a search warrant, please leave."

Huxley was starting to get angry. But Michael knew he was right. Without a search warrant, the police couldn't search someone's home. Michael had to leave. He thanked Huxley for his time.

On his way out to the car again, he thought about the old man. Firstly, he seemed obsessed with Sylvia and collected paintings of her. Secondly, he was **familiar with** the Oswald Gallery and lived close by. Thirdly, he didn't want the police looking around his house.

Michael decided to call Chief Inspector Blake to find out if he could get a search warrant for the mansion.

familiar (with)	vertraut (mit), sich auskennen (mit)
wallet	Geldbeutel
security	Sicherheit

Later that night, Michael decided to go to the gallery. He wanted to look in the archives again, and still had the key. He wasn't really thinking about the investigation. He was wondering if Sylvia was still alive in New York or somewhere else. She would be an old woman by now. In his imagination, however, she was a beautiful young woman. He wanted her to stay that way. He still kept the photo of Sylvia in his **wallet**. Every now and then, he took it out and looked at it.

Before he left for the gallery, he called Joan Potts. He wanted to let her know that he would visit the archive.

Now that the gallery was closed, she believed the paintings would be safe. However, she was still happy to know that a policeman was around. She also told him that they had bought a new **security** system. There were cameras for every room. In two days' time[i] it would be installed. Then they could open the gallery again. Meanwhile, Lottie was out of danger. She could open her eyes and talk a little bit. She had no

Statt in **two days' time** kann man auch einfach **in two days** sagen. Beides bedeutet „in zwei Tagen". Die Wendung *in ... days' time* hebt aber die Zeitspanne, die vergeht, etwas mehr hervor.

memories at all of the robbery. She was **confused** about being in the hospital. Still, Michael was **relieved** that she was getting better.

confused	verwirrt
relieved	erleichtert

Exercise 12: True or false? **Kreuzen Sie die richtigen Aussagen an!**

1. Nigel Huxley is 75 years old. ❐
2. Huxley had been in love with Sylvia. ❐
3. Michael thinks that Huxley might have pushed Lottie down the stairs. ❐
4. Huxley allows Michael to search his house. ❐
5. After the Second World War, Huxley lost contact to Sylvia and Tristan Butterworth. ❐
6. Michael kept a photo of Sylvia in his wallet. ❐

4 Voices in the Dark

By the time Michael got to the Oswald Gallery, the sun had nearly disappeared. He parked his car right in front of the door and was shocked about what he saw. There was graffiti all over the front of the building. It was the same yellow paint that he'd seen at the caretaker's house, and the same symbols. Then he saw the broken window. The hole was big enough for someone to climb through, but bits of glass were still sharp.

The robber had probably been hurt. Michael looked through the broken window. A big rock from the garden was lying inside, on the wooden floor. Bits of broken glass were everywhere. On one piece of glass, he saw something red. It looked like blood. The thief had been cut. This meant that the police could get an important DNA clue. Michael immediately took out his mobile phone. He called the city station. Another officer would come to Pendle Lee as soon as possible. The crime scene officer would come, too.

Michael didn't want to stand outside waiting. He decided to go in. Perhaps the thief was still in the gallery. Trying to stay calm, he opened the front door. Then he stopped and listened. He couldn't hear anything. He took another step. The wooden floor made a loud noise. Then, slowly and quietly, he went to the room with the broken window. There were paintings on the wall. Some of them were landscapes from the Butterworth collection. There were also sculptures. But Michael was more interested in the blood. It was a very dark red because it was almost dry. It made a small **trail** across the floor and into the hall. Michael followed it. The trail went up the stairs, along the hall, and into another room. It stopped in front of a wall. There was an empty space where a painting once hung.

Suddenly, there was a shout from downstairs. The two other policemen had arrived. Michael went downstairs and **greeted** them. He told them about the trail of blood and the stolen painting.

"Can you go through the building?" he asked the **constable**, whose name was John Ritchie. "I'm going to look in the garden."

"I'll get fingerprints and blood," said the crime scene officer. "But I don't think we'll get a **match**. There were no matches on our fingerprint database last time."

Just as Michael was about to go outside, the constable called him back.

trail	Spur
to greet sb.	jmd. grüßen
constable	Wachtmeister, Polizist
match	*hier*: Treffer

"You're the one who was hit in the graveyard, aren't you?" he asked. "I talked to those teenagers. Every single one has an alibi. Even Alex, who is an angry young man. One day he'll end up arrested for something, believe me!"

Michael thanked him, then took his torch and went outside.

There was no moonlight, so it was very dark. He walked all around the building, looking and listening. On one side of the garden was the car park. Two police cars were parked there. On the other side of the garden there were woods. They made a good hiding place. Michael went into the trees. It was very dark, almost black. The trees looked very tall in the white light from the torch. Michael thought about his visits to the cemetery. Now he was walking through woods at night. His torch had become his best friend. It was a good thing he did not believe in ghosts or witches. If they were real, he would have seen one by now. In fact, he felt like the ghost of Pendle Lee himself. That's what happened when you spent too much time in graveyards and dark places.

Exercise 13: Personal pronouns. Ersetzen Sie die hervorgehobenen Personen durch die richtigen Pronomen!

1. **Lottie** *She* was pushed down the stairs.
2. **Two policemen** ______ were helping with the investigation.
3. **You and I** ______ don't know who the thief is.
4. **Michael** ______ followed the trail of blood upstairs.
5. Michael told **Lottie and Joan** ______ to get cameras.
6. Can you tell **my friend and I** ______ where the gallery is?
7. We will visit **Lottie** ______ in the hospital.
8. Tell **Michael** ______ about the stolen painting!
9. "I'm here to help **the woman** ______," Michael told her.
10. "Don't ______ have security cameras?" he asked **Lottie and Joan**.

Suddenly, he heard a noise. He immediately[i] stopped walking and listened. He wondered if it was a small animal making noises in the dark. But then he heard a voice. Another voice answered. Two people were hiding in the woods. Michael took out his phone and called PC Ritchie. He spoke very quietly and quickly. The constable agreed to join him.

Abweichend zum Deutschen stehen **Adverbien in der Satzmitte** im Englischen nicht hinter dem konjugierten Verb, sondern davor.
*Sergeant Rose **often** goes to the cemetery.*
Er geht **oft** zum Friedhof.
*He **immediately** stopped walking when he heard a noise.*
Er blieb **sofort** stehen, als er ein Geräusch hörte.

In less than a minute, the constable was there, walking softly through the trees. Then they both switched off their torches. After a few moments, their eyes could see better in the darkness. They quietly walked towards the sound of voices. Two people were hiding in some bushes underneath a tree. They were dressed all in black, and had long black hair. This just made their white faces stand out even more in the dark. Michael recognized two young men from the cemetery. He gave a shout. The boys looked around and saw the officers, then jumped up and started to run. Michael and PC Ritchie raced after them through the trees. The teenagers were fast, but frightened. They kept looking behind them. Suddenly, one of them hit a tree and fell to the ground.

PC (Police Constable)	Wachtmeister
to manage to do sth.	es schaffen, etw. zu tun

"It's a good idea to look where you're going," said Michael as he pulled the boy to his feet.

Meanwhile, PC Ritchie had managed to stop the other one. The constable took the boy's rucksack and opened it. He shone his torch inside.

"What do we have here, boys?" PC Ritchie asked, shining his light on cans of yellow spray paint.

spray paint	Sprühfarbe
involved in	beteiligt an
insulting	beleidigend

At the police station, Michael and PC Ritchie questioned the teenagers. They said they'd painted the symbols on the walls, but had had nothing to do with the smashed window or the burglary. Just after doing the graffiti, they'd heard someone walking through the car park. They'd gone into the woods and then heard the sound of breaking glass. One of the boys' fathers was in the room with them, which was normal when a 15-year-old was involved in a crime.
"Why didn't you call the police?" he asked his son.
"I hate the pigs," said the boy, using the insulting word for policemen. "Can we go now?"

Exercise 14: Plurals. Geben Sie die Pluralform an!

1. thief ______________________
2. woman ______________________
3. gallery ______________________
4. information ______________________
5. memory ______________________
6. noise ______________________
7. system ______________________
8. witch ______________________

The police would wait until daylight to search the woods for the stolen painting. Michael didn't want to let the boys go until then, but he had to. There was no reason for arresting them. They were checked for cuts, because of the broken glass in the gallery window. But neither of the boys had been cut anywhere on their bodies.

They were in lots of trouble about the graffiti, but Michael didn't think anything serious would happen to them. He let them go home with their parents.

Back at his desk, he made some notes for his report. Then he made a list of things to do in the morning. At the top was the search warrant for Nigel Huxley's home. He wanted to visit the old sculptor as soon as possible. He wanted to have some of Huxley's blood for testing, too. The investigators could match it against the blood from the gallery. Next, he wanted to take Joan Potts to the gallery to ask her about the stolen painting. He was sure it was another one of Sylvia. Then, he wanted to go to the hospital to see if Lottie had any memories of the robbery. Suddenly, the phone rang. Michael picked it up.

"Hello?" he said.

"Michael, it's Mrs White," said the woman on the phone. "Sorry I'm calling so late. It's those kids in the cemetery."

"Not again." Michael sighed.

He was disappointed. There were bigger things than bad behaviour going on in Pendle Lee.

"I'll go immediately," he said. It wasn't illegal to be at a cemetery at night, but it wasn't respectful.

"Perhaps we can ask the ghost of Agnes Cott to give them a fright," Mrs White said. "Then they'll stay at home every night!"

Michael gave a short laugh.

"I'll ask her to pay them a visit," he said.

Once more, Michael drove to the cemetery. Once more, he parked at the gates and got out his torch. There were candles glowing among the graves. He could see young people sitting around. Loud music was playing. He recognized the tall **figure** of Alex. When he got close to the group, Alex saw him and stood up. The young man looked angry. Michael felt angry, too, but he didn't want to get involved in a fight with teenagers.

"Go away!" Alex **yelled**.

Michael was just about to reply when he heard a loud scream. It sounded like it was coming from the caretaker's cottage. Immediately Michael started to run to the old house. Alex ran, too.

"It's Katie!" Alex exclaimed. "She went into the house for a **dare**."

"Can't you kids stay out of trouble?" Michael shouted as he ran.

When he got to the house, he tried to open the door. It was still locked.

"She went through a window," said Alex.

Together they ran to the side of the building. Just then, Katie screamed again. Michael found the window. It was old-fashioned, and the old wood had made it easy to open from the outside. He shone his torch inside and called Katie's name. He saw her **rush** into the room, looking very frightened. When she saw Michael and Alex, she started to cry and immediately tried to climb through the window. Michael helped her.

Once outside, Katie fell on the ground. She lay on the grass.

"It's the witch!" she said. She couldn't stop crying.

"What did she look like?" Alex asked.

figure	*hier*: Gestalt; Figur
to yell	(laut) schreien
dare	Mutprobe
to rush	eilen, sich beeilen

Michael looked at the young man angrily. "There are no witches," he said. "Or ghosts."

Then he saw a strange glow coming from inside the house. It was very bright orange.
Katie and Alex saw it, too.
"I dropped my candle," said Katie.
The old house was on fire.
Michael immediately pulled his mobile phone from his pocket. He called the emergency number. But just as he was about to speak, he saw a figure inside the house.

to be on fire	brennen, in Flammen stehen
burning	brennend
to choke	ersticken, würgen

"There's someone in there!" he exclaimed.
"The witch!" Katie cried. "I told you. She's real!"
Michael threw the mobile to Alex, who immediately told the emergency services where they were. Then Michael climbed through the broken window into the burning house.
"Police!" he called out, but the figure had disappeared.
He ran through the room and into the hall. Spider's webs were on his face and in his hair. The fire seemed to come from the front room. He could feel how hot it was. He was choking on heavy smoke. He looked around, confused. Then he saw her: a woman was going up the stairs. He had no time. The fire was going to burn the old building down. He ran up the stairs. He could see quite well because of the orange glow from the fire. When he got to the top, he saw her standing very still, looking at him. For a moment, he thought that Katie was right. The woman was a witch.
Agnes Cott, he thought. She had long grey hair and dirty old clothes. She looked very old. Michael told her his name.
"I'm here to help you," he said.
She turned and ran down the corridor.
Michael followed her. He could see smoke from the fire coming up the stairs. He went into one of the bedrooms. Although it was

darker in the room, he could see the old woman. She was trying to pick up some large, flat objects. When Michael got closer, he saw that the objects were paintings. On every one, he recognized Sylvia.

old people's home	Seniorenheim
to remember sth.	sich erinnern an
disease	Krankheit
care	Pflege, Betreuung

The old woman looked at Michael and started to cry.
"Please help me!" she said.

Two months later, after his evening shift, Michael left the station. He walked up the road. When he got to the **old people's home**, he stopped. Nigel Huxley was waiting for him. It was the same every Wednesday and Sunday. The two men went inside together.
Sometimes Sylvia couldn't **remember**[i] their names. She couldn't remember pushing Lottie down the stairs, or laughing and knocking Michael out in the graveyard.
For weeks she'd been living in the old caretaker's cottage. She stole things to eat, as well as the paintings.
She couldn't be put in prison for her crimes because she had Alzheimer's **disease**. Instead, at the old people's home she had food, clothing and good **care**. She mainly remembered things that happened sixty years ago.
Michael knew she had been beautiful then, although he couldn't tell from looking at the old woman now. He and Nigel would listen to her stories about wonderful summer evenings, and her eyes would glow with happiness.

Achten Sie immer auf den Unterschied zwischen **remind** und **remember**!

to remember sth.	sich erinnern an
to remind sb. of sth.	jmd. an etw. erinnern

"Her eyes are the one thing that hasn't changed," Michael said to Nigel, looking at the photo of Sylvia in his wallet. "They're still beautiful."

Exercise 15: Questions about the text. **Beantworten Sie die Fragen zum Text in ganzen Sätzen!**

1. Who stole the Butterworth paintings and why?

 ____

 ____

2. Who was Agnes Cott?

 ____

3. What are the teenagers doing at the cemetery at night?

 ____

 ____

4. Why do the villagers think that the old caretaker's house is haunted?

 ____

5. Why is the gallery called the Oswald Gallery?

 ____

Long Time No Kill

Caroline Simpson

Das Mädcheninternat Shepton Mallet im beschaulichen Somerset feiert sein 100-jähriges Bestehen. Nach dem Fest verschwindet plötzlich eine ehemalige Schülerin und in ihrem zurückgelassenen Auto findet die Polizei Blutspuren. Wollte etwa jemand aus dem Internat sie loswerden, oder ist der Anwältin einer ihrer Fälle zum Verhängnis geworden? Inspector Hudson und sein Team von Scotland Yard ermitteln.

A2

1 The Open Day

It's a sunny Saturday morning in late July. In the beautiful little village of Shepton Mallet,[i] Henry, the school **caretaker** is working hard. Everything must look perfect before the guests arrive. He is hanging up a banner above the entrance. It says:

Shepton Mallet ***Boarding School****, 1915 – 2015. 100 Years of* ***Educating*** *Girls!*

"Very good, Henry," says a well-dressed, **middle-aged** woman, smiling. "Our **Open Day** will be a great **success**."

caretaker	Hausmeister
boarding school	Internat
to educate	(aus)bilden
middle-aged	mittleren Alters
open day	Tag der offenen Tür
success	Erfolg
stall	Verkaufsstand
handicrafts *pl*	Handarbeiten
head girl	Schulsprecherin
polite	höflich

She turns to a group of teenage girls. They all wear identical dark blue skirts, white shirts and blue and white ties.

"Now, Amy and Alice, you two set up the cake **stall** on the left of the garden, and Belinda, you can put up the **handicrafts** stall." She then turns to a tall girl with a ponytail.

"Joanna, your job as **head girl** is to welcome the guests. Be **polite** and charming."

"I'll do my best," Joanna says with a smile.

The woman smiles back at her.

Shepton Mallet ist eine kleine Stadt im Südwesten Englands. Sie gehört zur Grafschaft Somerset, die bekannt ist für ihre schöne Landschaft und ihre Apfelplantagen.

Three hours later, the garden is full of guests. Women and girls of all ages are standing in little groups, many with their families. On one side of the garden a family is eating muffins and chatting.

"When I was a girl, the teachers were very strict," a white-haired lady tells her granddaughter. "If I was lazy in class, the teacher hit me on the back of the hand."

"Oh Granny, I don't believe you," laughs the little girl.

"It's true! Once I had to write 'I must not run in the corridor' one hundred times! Of course things are very different now."

to chat	sich unterhalten, plaudern
strict	streng
lazy	faul
curly	lockig
wedding	Hochzeit
That's a shame!	Wie schade!
to change the subject	das Thema wechseln
bossy	bestimmend, herrisch
prime minister	Premierministerin

"Hello and welcome. Would you like a glass of champagne?" asks Joanna, the head girl, with a charming smile.

"See what I mean?" says the grandmother. "Very different!"

On the other side of the garden, two old school friends say hello. One of the women has curly red hair and is wearing a colourful skirt. The other has short blonde hair and looks very businesslike in a pencil skirt and blazer.

"Penny! How lovely to see you," says the red-haired woman. "You remember my husband, Brian, don't you?"

"Yes, Jennifer, of course. Hello Brian! Do you know, I haven't seen you both since your wedding," Penny replies.

Margaret Thatcher war von 1979 bis 1990 Premierministerin des Vereinigten Königreichs. Sie war die erste und bislang einzige Frau in diesem Amt und berühmt für ihre oft unerbittliche Haltung, was ihr den Spitznamen „The Iron Lady" (die eiserne Dame) einbrachte.

"That's a long time ago," Jennifer laughs. "What about you? Where's your husband? Didn't he come with you today?"
"No, Neil is busy this weekend," answers Penny.
"That's a shame," says Jennifer. "You two are such a lovely couple. Penny, are you alright? You look rather tired."
"I'm fine. I've just got some stress at work at the moment," says Penny.
She quickly changes the subject.

Exercise 1: Adjectives. Lesen Sie weiter und unterstreichen Sie alle 9 Adjektive!

"Look at those uniforms, those lovely blue skirts," Penny says. "Do you remember our uniform when we were young?"
"My God, yes! Those ugly grey skirts and yellow blouses. We all looked terrible!" laughs Jennifer.
Just then Joanna walks past and offers them some champagne.
"Wow, things have changed here," says Jennifer when Joanna has gone. "Do you remember the head girl when we started?"
"You mean Margaret Taylor. I could never forget her. She was so bossy and arrogant – more like a prime minister[i] than a head girl."
"Yes, that's why we called her 'Thatcher' behind her back!" replies Jennifer, and both women start to laugh.

lawn	Rasen
gate	Tor
to stub out	ausdrücken
probably	wahrscheinlich
choir	Chor
assembly hall	Aula
peeping Tom	Spanner
binoculars *pl*	Fernglas
wood	kleiner Wald
to join in	mitmachen

On the other side of the lawn, near the school gates, two women are standing watching the guests and smoking.
"Come on, Fiona. Let's go in," one of them says and stubs out her cigarette with the sole of her leather boot. "Don't you want to see how the others have changed?"
"Not really," says Fiona, lighting up another cigarette. "They're probably all rich, fat and boring."
Claire laughs. "You're terrible, Fi! They're not all bad."
A bell rings and the music teacher, Miss Wallis, appears.
"Ladies and gentlemen, we would like to invite you all to come inside. The school choir is about to sing in the assembly hall."
"Go on, Claire. I'll see you later at the Queen's Arms, okay?" Fiona turns to leave. "Claire, look over there. A peeping Tom!"
She points at a man on the other side of the gate. He is watching the school through binoculars.
The man sees her and moves away quickly towards the little wood behind the school. The two friends say goodbye and Claire walks up the path towards the huge stone building.

In the assembly hall, the choir sings the school song. Many of the women join in, some with tears in their eyes. This is too sentimental for Claire, so she goes out into the entrance hall. Here the walls are full of class photos from 1915 till the present year.
"Hello there!" says a voice beside her.
Claire looks up and sees a blonde woman in a business suit.
"Penny?" says Claire.

The woman nods. "Look, Claire. Here's our old class of 1985." They both look **closely** at the photo of a group of 11-year-old girls smiling at the cameraman.

"And here's Miss Foster," says Claire and points at the teacher standing beside the girls. "She looks so young!"

"Years younger than we are now," says Penny.

closely	genau
halfway human	halbwegs menschlich
to exclaim	ausrufen (Schock od. Überraschung)
row	Reihe

"I liked Miss Foster. What a shame she left the school."

"Yes," Claire replies, "she and Miss Musty were the only teachers who were **halfway human**."

Exercise 2: Prepositions. Ergänzen Sie die Präpositionen!

above   at   behind   on   through

1. The teacher points ______ the blackboard.
2. She is looking out ______ the window.
3. The women are standing ______ the left side of the lawn.
4. The child is hiding ______ the curtain.
5. There is a banner hanging ______ the entrance.

"Oh Claire, look here!" Penny **exclaims**. "It's Becky."

She points at a little girl in the second **row**. This girl isn't smiling. She is looking at the camera with a sad expression on her face.

"Do you ever think about what happened back then?"
"No, I try not to think about it. It was so sad," Claire replies.
"You know, I still don't really understand what happened that night," says Penny.
"There's nothing to understand. It was just a terrible accident."
"We were so young. Do you think they told us the whole truth? I sometimes think that they didn't."

truth	Wahrheit
suspicious of	misstrauisch gegenüber
crime	Verbrechen
lawyer	Anwältin
smart	*hier*: schick

"What do you mean?" asks Claire in surprise.
"Oh, it's just a feeling, probably nothing. My job makes me suspicious of everyone. I have too much to do with crime."
"Are you a policewoman?"
"No, I'm a lawyer," Penny replies.
So that explains the smart clothes, Claire thinks as she looks down at her own jeans and boots.

Exercise 3: True or false? Welche Aussagen sind korrekt? Markieren Sie mit richtig ✔ oder falsch – !

1. Penny and Claire were in the same class at school. ❏

2. Miss Foster was not a nice teacher. ❏

3. Becky was an unhappy child. ❏

4. Penny is now a policewoman. ❏

"Hello there! How lovely to see you after all these years."
The women turn round.
"Miss Musty! How are you?" asks Claire.

promotion	Beförderung
to retire	in Rente gehen
headmistress	Schulleiterin
Retirement Home	Altersheim

"Congratulations on your promotion," Penny says politely. "I'm fine," says Miss Musty. "And thank you, Penny. I've been headmistress for 15 years now and I love it. And here's someone that you both know. You remember Margaret, don't you?"
A woman in an expensive-looking designer dress steps out from behind Miss Musty and says 'Hello'.
Claire and Penny smile at each other, both thinking "Thatcher!"

Exercise 4: Choose the correct alternative. Lesen Sie weiter und unterstreichen Sie die richtige Variante!

"Come on, ladies, let's **1.** getting / get a cup of tea," Miss Musty says, and she **2.** leads / is leading Claire, Penny and Margaret into the next room.
Here the school secretary **3.** is standing / stands at a long table set with cups and saucers. When they come in, she **4.** is pouring / pours them tea from a large teapot.

"Mrs Motherwell, how are you? I didn't know you still work here," says Margaret.
"I'm very well, thank you, my dear. Yes, I'm still here, until I retire in a couple of years. Would you like sugar in your tea?"
"What happened to Miss Sharp after she retired?" asks Penny.
"She still lives in Shepton Mallet," replies Miss Musty. "At the Sunshine Retirement Home on the other side of the village."

"My goodness, I can't imagine Miss Sharp in an old people's home. I bet they're all afraid of her!" says Claire, half joking.
Miss Musty laughs. "Yes, she was a very strict headmistress."
"So what are you all doing now?" asks Margaret.

My goodness!	Meine Güte!
to imagine	sich vorstellen
to bet	wetten
Foreign Office *UK*	Außenministerium
to stay in touch	in Kontakt bleiben
business card	Visitenkarte
to sigh	seufzen
pale	blass

But before anyone can reply, she tells them what she is doing. "I'm at the Foreign Office. Terribly busy, of course. And I have to travel all the time. It was difficult while the children were young. But luckily they are both very clever. Adrian is studying at Oxford now and Prunella is a medical student at St. Thomas' Hospital."
Penny and Claire give each other a quick look, both thinking the same thing.
"This is such fun – meeting up again after so long," says Margaret. "We must stay in touch. Here, take these," she says, handing Penny and Claire two shiny business cards.
"Wait a second," says Penny, searching through her handbag. Eventually[i] she finds her business cards at the bottom of her bag under her mobile phone and gives them to the others. At that moment they hear the start of Beethoven's Fifth Symphony coming from Penny's handbag. She takes her phone out of her bag, looks at the display and sighs.
"Excuse me," she says nervously and goes outside.

False friends alarm!
eventually heißt „endlich, schließlich" und nicht „eventuell", was man mit **maybe** oder **perhaps** übersetzt.

Minutes later she returns. She looks pale.
"Are you alright, Penny?" asks Miss Musty. "You look worried."

"It's just a problem at work," Penny replies. She turns her phone off. "That's better. Now I won't be disturbed again." She smiles at the others. "Sorry, what were you saying, Margaret?"

to disturb	stören

Exercise 5: Pronouns. Ersetzen Sie die markierten Wörter durch die entsprechenden Pronomen!

1. Margaret gives **Penny and Claire** her business card.

   ____

2. Penny searches for **her mobile phone** in her bag.

   ____

3. Claire can't imagine **Miss Sharp** in an old people's home.

   ____

4. **Margaret's children** are both very clever.

   ____

It's early evening now and the guests are starting to leave.
"Are you driving back to Birmingham tonight?" asks Claire.
"No," Penny answers. "I'm staying overnight at the White Hart. You know, the hotel next to the pub."
"Me too. Let's walk back together. Are you ready to leave?"
"Let me just say goodbye to Jennifer," says Penny.
"I'll wait for you outside," says Claire and walks into the garden. It's quiet there now. She smokes a cigarette while she waits. Suddenly she hears a noise on the other side of the school gate.

It's the man with the binoculars again! He's *still* watching the school! What on earth does he want? thinks Claire.

What on earth...!	Was zum Teufel...?!
startled	erschrocken
to tap	klopfen, tippen
churchyard	Friedhof
in silence	schweigend
ϟ teacher's pet	Lehrers Liebling, Streberin
to oversleep	verschlafen

"Hey, you! What are you doing?" The man looks startled. He runs to a dark-coloured coupé parked by the gate and drives off. A minute later Penny taps her on the shoulder and now Claire is startled.

"Are you alright, Claire? I heard you shout."

Claire tells Penny about the peeping Tom.

"Well, there's no one there now, so let's go," says Penny, and they walk through the village towards the hotel.

It's getting dark as they pass a little church. They both turn to look at the churchyard and then walk on in silence until they arrive at the Queen's Arms pub next to the hotel.

"I'm meeting Fiona here," says Claire. "Do you want to join us?"

"No, I don't think so," answers Penny.

"Wait a minute. I'll just send Fiona a text message to tell her I'm here."

While Claire writes her message, Penny turns her phone back on. It beeps loudly several times. "Oh no, not more messages."

A woman with long black hair and wearing a leather jacket and jeans comes out of the pub and walks towards them.

"Hi Fiona! Look, I've brought Penny with me," says Claire.

"Hello Penny," says Fiona coldly.

"Hello Fiona," Penny replies without smiling. "Look, Claire, I'm tired, so I'm going to my room now. Let's meet for breakfast tomorrow around 8:30, okay?"

The other two watch as she walks quickly towards the hotel.

It's a warm evening, so Fiona and Claire sit in the beer garden. "Guess who was at the Open Day – Thatcher! And she's got this perfect life...it makes you sick!" Claire says.

"What about Miss Penelope, **teacher's pet**?" asks Fiona. "Is she still perfect, too?"

"Penny's a lawyer now. If you ask me, she's a workaholic. Her phone never stops ringing. And she is always thinking about crime. Do you know, she even told me she thinks there was something suspicious about that accident in 1985."

Fiona listens with interest. "Penny always was the cleverest girl in the class," she says.

Exercise 6: Unscramble the words. Lesen Sie weiter und bringen Sie die Buchstaben in die richtige Reihenfolge!

It's Sunday **1.** norgmin ________________ and Claire is sitting in the breakfast room at the White Hart Hotel. She looks at her **2.** chawt ________________: 9 a.m. That's funny, she **3.** kinsth ________________. Penny is always on time. **4.** sherapp ________________ she has **overslept**. She waits another 10 minutes and then goes to the **5.** porceeint ________________.

"Could you please call Mrs Sutton and tell her I'm waiting for her."

"Mrs Sutton has already checked out," answers the receptionist.

"Are you sure? We wanted to meet for breakfast."

"Yes, madam. She left early this morning, before I was on duty."
"How strange! So you didn't see her?"
"No. She just left the money and keys on the desk. And a note saying she had to get back to work."

Poor Penny, her job must be very stressful. As Claire turns to walk back to the breakfast room to finish her coffee, she bumps into a chambermaid. She has come from cleaning the bedrooms.
"Look, Michele," she says to the receptionist, "I found this in room 14." And she puts a mobile phone on the desk.

on duty	im Dienst
strange	merkwürdig, seltsam
to bump into	zusammenstoßen mit
chambermaid	Zimmermädchen
to dial	wählen

Exercise 7: Question and answer. Beantworten Sie die Fragen zur Geschichte!

1. Who is Miss Musty?

____

2. Where does Claire meet Fiona after the Open Day?

____

3. Why doesn't Fiona like Penny?

____

4. Where does the chambermaid find Penny's phone?

____

"Room 14 you say, Sharon? That was Mrs Sutton's room. Miss Hockey?" she calls after Claire. "It seems Mrs Sutton left her mobile phone here. Do you know how we can contact her?"

"Possibly. One moment," Claire says.

She gets out the business card that Penny gave her the day before. The number of 'Corbett & Co Lawyers Ltd' is written on it, but also what looks like a private number. Claire **dials** this number and hears it ring several times. Then she hears Penny's voice: "Neil and I are not at home, so please leave a message."

"Penny, it's Claire here. It's a shame you had to leave so early. It was nice seeing you again. Listen, you left your phone at the White Hart. Call me back. Bye!"

2 The Red Toyota

It's 10 p.m. on Monday evening. Sergeant Wilson and PC O'Malley are driving through Brixton[i] in their squad car.

"Mondays are boring, aren't they, sir?" comments O'Malley. "It's so quiet. Everyone's home watching the football match on TV."

"Yeah, but it's better than working at the weekend," says Wilson.

They come to a green light and start to cross.

"Watch out, sir!" shouts O'Malley as a car suddenly comes speeding from the right and nearly hits them.

Wilson immediately switches on the blue light and starts to follow the car. O'Malley picks up the walkie-talkie to contact the police station.

"PC O'Malley here. We're following a red Toyota down Stockwell Road. It crossed at a red light and nearly hit us. Now it's speeding up. The driver is trying to get away."

Wilson puts his foot down on the accelerator. Soon the police car is right behind the Toyota and starts to overtake. The driver of the Toyota panics, loses control and crashes into a large metal fence by the side of the road.

PC (police constable)	Polizeibeamter
squad car	Streifenwagen
to speed	rasen
accelerator	Gaspedal
to overtake	überholen
fence	Zaun
case	Fall
to arrest	festnehmen
to joyride	eine Spritztour machen
scrapyard	Schrottplatz
to trace	aufspüren

"We've got them!" says O'Malley into his walkie talkie.
Wilson stops the squad car. The two policemen get out and walk over to the wreck.
"Get out and put your hands up!" shouts Wilson.
The car doors open slowly. The driver and passengers get out.
"Well, look at that! It's just a group of kids," says PC O'Malley.

Exercise 8: Verb forms. Lesen Sie weiter und setzen Sie die korrekte Verbform ein!

It **1.** be ____________ early Tuesday morning at Scotland Yard. Inspector Hudson **2.** knock ____________ on Sir Reginald's door and goes inside.
"Morning James, I've got a new **case** for you. Last night two of our officers in Brixton **arrested** a group of teenagers. They **3.** be ____________ **joyriding** in a stolen car. The teenagers are from Basingstoke.[i] They say they **4.** find ____________ the car at a **scrapyard** there and **5.** think ____________ it would be fun to drive it up to London."

"But joyriding isn't a job for Scotland Yard," Hudson replies. "It's not that simple. Our men in Brixton have **traced** the car's owner – a Mrs Penelope Sutton," Sir Reginald explains.

Brixton ist ein Stadtbezirk von London. Er liegt südlich der Stadtmitte und ist ein sozialer Brennpunkt.
Basingstoke liegt auf halber Strecke zwischen Brixton und Somerset.

"Have they spoken to Mrs Sutton yet?"
"No. They found her business card in the car and tried to call her. No one answered at her private number so they rang her work number – a law firm in Birmingham. The secretary told them Mrs Sutton was in Somerset at the weekend. She was staying at the White Hart Hotel in Shepton Mallet. They expected her at work yesterday, but she didn't come."
"So Mrs Sutton is missing," says Hudson.
"Yes," Sir Reginald replies. "Sergeant Wilson and PC O'Malley searched the car, looking for drugs."
"Did they find any?" asks Hudson.
"No," replies Sir Reginald. "But when they opened the car boot, they found a lot of blood. I'm afraid Mrs Sutton may be the victim of a violent crime."

law firm	Anwaltskanzlei
to expect	erwarten
car boot	Kofferraum
victim	Opfer
violent crime	Gewaltverbrechen
database	Datenbank
recent	aktuell
next-of-kin	nächster Angehörige
straight away	sofort
denim jacket	Jeansjacke

"Listen, everyone," says Hudson. "A woman called Mrs Penelope Sutton is missing and she may be in danger. Harvey, put Mrs Sutton's name in the national database of missing persons. And find out what you can about her background. I need a recent photo of her and the name of her next-of-kin."
"Yes, sir!" says Constable Harvey.
She is young and very enthusiastic about her job. She starts working straight away.
Hudson turns to a man with round glasses and a denim jacket.
"Bradley, I want you to go to the scrapyard in Basingstoke."
"A scrapyard in Basingstoke?" DI Joe Bradley asks. He doesn't sound very enthusiastic.

"Yes, that's where the teenagers found Mrs Sutton's car. The forensic team is already searching for clues there. Your job is to question the owner of the scrapyard. Find out if he saw who left the car there. And ask people around the area of the scrapyard if they saw anything suspicious."

forensic	gerichtsmedizinisch
clue	Hinweis
suspicious	verdächtig
shoulder-length	schulterlang
jealous	neidisch

"Yes, sir," says Bradley quietly.

"We already know that Mrs Sutton lives in Birmingham. She works for a law firm in Pritchett Street," says Hudson.

Next he turns to a young woman with shoulder-length brown hair.

"Jarvis, I want you to go to Birmingham. Talk to Mrs Sutton's boss and colleagues. Maybe they have an idea where she might be."

"It sounds like an interesting case, sir," says DI Wendy Jarvis.

Bradley gives her a jealous look.

Exercise 9: Match-up. Welche der folgenden Begriffe gehören zusammen? Ordnen Sie zu!

1. ☐ next-of-	**a)** firm
2. ☐ car	**b)** crime
3. ☐ law	**c)** kin
4. ☐ violent	**d)** boot

"Excuse me, sir. I've found Mrs Sutton's home address and her husband's mobile phone number," says Constable Harvey.

"Thank you, Harvey. Jarvis, go to this address. Talk to Mr Sutton and say you want to search his house. If he won't help you, get a **search warrant**. Look for any clues – anything that explains why Mrs Sutton has **disappeared**. And ask the Birmingham police force to send you an assistant to help."

search warrant	Durchsuchungs-befehl
to disappear	verschwinden
to frown	die Stirn runzeln
to examine	untersuchen
to compare	vergleichen
to be in charge	die Verantwor-tung tragen
Constabulary	Polizeirevier

"No problem, sir," says DI Jarvis with a smile.

Bradley **frowns**. He didn't give *me* an assistant, he thinks.

"Dr Barrington is already **ex-amining** Mrs Sutton's car," Hudson continues. "Jarvis, while you're at the Suttons' house, try to find something that the forensic team can use to **compare** the DNA with the blood in the car, like a tooth-brush or a hairbrush."

Jarvis smiles and nods.

Hudson turns to the others. "I'm driving to Somerset – to the hotel where Mrs Sutton spent the weekend – to talk to the people who saw her last. While I'm gone, I'd like you, Harvey, to be **in charge** of things in the office. You can ask Sir Reginald to give you an assistant if you need any help. Do you think you can manage?"

"Oh yes, sir! Thank you, sir!" says Harvey, giving him a big smile. "I'll certainly do my best."

Even *she* gets an assistant! Bradley thinks angrily.

"And Harvey, can you also let the Somerset **Constabulary** know that I'm coming," Hudson tells her. "I may need their help with the case. Remember, team, we must all work quickly. A woman's life is in danger."

It's 12:30 midday. Hudson is sitting in a motorway cafe on the M3.

"Sir, I've spoken to the police in Somerset," says Harvey on the phone. "Inspector Matthews at the station in Warminster is your contact. He sounds quite **excited** about working with you." She gives Hudson the number and rings off.

Hudson reads through his notes on the Sutton case. This will be an interesting job, he thinks. But it means I'll be away from home for a while. I should tell Miss Paddington. He picks up his mobile and dials his home number in London.

"Hello, it's James here."

"James, I **was just about to** call you. I'm cooking **shepherd's pie** this evening. What time will you be home for dinner?"

excited	aufgeregt, begeistert
to be just about to	gerade dabei sein, etw. zu tun
shepherd's pie	Auflauf mit Lammfleisch und Kartoffelbrei
housekeeper	Haushälterin
emergency	Notfall
investigation	Ermittlung

"Miss Paddington, I'm afraid I'm not coming home this evening. I've got a new case. I'm on my way to Somerset right now. I'm staying at a hotel there tonight, and maybe for longer, too."

"Oh James, you always work so hard. Have you got everything you need?" his **housekeeper** asks in a motherly voice.

"Yes, don't worry about me," he says. "I've got my **emergency** overnight bag. If the **investigation** goes on for long, I'll come home and get some fresh clothes."

"Alright, James. Good luck with the case. You can tell me all about it when you get home!" Miss Paddington ends the call.

Der **M3 motorway,** die Autobahn M3, verläuft durch die englischen Grafschaften Hampshire und Surrey südwestlich von London.
Das Tempolimit auf Autobahnen ist 70 miles per hour, ca. 113 km/h.

Exercise 10: Correct the mistakes. Lesen Sie weiter und korrigieren Sie die sechs Fehler!

DI Joe Bradley standing in the middle of a scrapyard in Basingstoke. He sighs. Why does Hudson always gives the most interesting jobs to Jarvis? Next to him stands a 14-years-old boy wearing lot of hair gel and rings threw his eyebrows. He is busy writing a message on his handy.

1. ____________________ 4. ____________________

2. ____________________ 5. ____________________

3. ____________________ 6. ____________________

"Shane, stop that now," says Bradley impatiently. "Show me exactly where you found the car."
"Over there, mate," replies the boy. "Next to the wrecks."
Bradley and the boy walk over to a pile of wrecked cars at the side of the yard. Here three forensic officers in protective clothing are searching for clues.
"What did you do next?" asks Bradley.
"The car looked great," says Shane. "And the door wasn't locked. So I said to my mates, 'Let's take her for a spin!'"
"So you drove out through the gates over there?"
"Past the train station and onto the M3!" says the boy proudly.
"Did you see anyone else in the scrapyard?"
Shane shakes his head. "It was very late. The place was empty."
"Hey, you! How long will this take?" An old man with white hair and a wrinkled face comes over to Bradley. "I don't like this. There are police all over my yard!" He takes his cigarette out of

his mouth and **spits** on the ground angrily.
Bradley sighs again. "I already told you, Mr Dawkins. This is a **crime scene** now. Did you see who left the car here?"
"No, I never saw a red Toyota. It wasn't here when I left on Friday evening to go to the Dog and Duck.[i] And it wasn't here on Monday morning when I came back to work. "
"You left the gates open all weekend, didn't you? Don't you ever **lock up**?" asks Bradley.

impatiently	ungeduldig
⚡ **mate**	Kumpel
pile	Haufen
protective clothing	Schutzbekleidung
Let's take her for a spin.	Lass uns eine Spritztour machen.
proudly	stolz
wrinkled	runzelig
to spit	spuken
crime scene	Tatort
to lock up	abschließen
factory	Fabrik
security guard	Sicherheits-bediensteter
meanwhile	währenddessen

"There's nothing here to steal," replies Dawkins.
"Wait here, Shane. I'm going to have a look around," says Bradley. He walks out of the scrapyard and along the street outside. Next to the scrapyard is a small **factory**. Bradley walks up to the entrance and waves at a **security guard** behind the gate.
"Detective Inspector Bradley," he shouts and holds out his ID card. "I'm investigating a crime at the scrapyard next door. Can I ask you a few questions?"

Meanwhile in Edgbaston, an expensive part of Birmingham, DI Jarvis walks up the path to the Suttons' home. With her is a young police officer from the Birmingham Constabulary. She rings the doorbell and waits, but there is no answer.

i: Englische Pubs haben oft eher traditionelle Namen wie **The Crown,** oder **The King's Head,** aber es gibt auch lustige Beispiele wie **The Pig and Whistle, The Hairy Lemon** oder **The Mad Dog.**

Exercise 11: Translation quiz. **Übersetzen Sie und enträtseln Sie das Lösungswort!**

1. Notfall _ _ _ _ _ _ _ □ _
2. Haufen _ _ □ _
3. stolz _ _ _ □ _
4. Nachricht _ □ _ _ _ _ _

Lösung: □□□□

"Shall I break the door down, Inspector?" asks Constable Cavanagh in an excited voice.

"You watch too many action films, I think!" says Jarvis, amused. She takes out her phone and dials the mobile number for Mr Sutton, Penny's husband.

"Neil here," says a deep voice.

"Mr Sutton, this is Detective Inspector Jarvis from Scotland Yard. I need to contact your wife **urgently**. Can you tell me where she is?"

"How should I know where Penny is? She hasn't spoken to me for over two weeks," he replies in a loud and angry voice.

"So you don't live together?"

"No. She **kicked me out**! She says we need some time apart." ℹ

"Well, I'm afraid your wife is missing," Jarvis tells him **gently**. Sutton doesn't reply.

"Mr Sutton? Are you still there?" Jarvis asks.

"Penny... missing?" he says quietly.

"We need your help to find your wife. I'm standing outside your house right now. Can you come and let us in?"
"Yes, of course," says Mr Sutton. "I'll be there in ten minutes."

urgently	dringend
to kick sb. out	jmd. rausschmeißen
gently	sanft
surrounded by	umgeben von
oak	Eiche
to gasp	nach Luft schnappen, kurz einatmen
to wonder	sich fragen
to sign	unterschreiben

Hudson looks at his watch. It's 1:30 p.m. It was a three-hour journey from London to Shepton Mallet. He parks his car outside the White Hart Hotel, an old black and white building **surrounded by** large **oak** trees. Next to it is a pretty little pub with roses around the door. Hudson walks into the hotel's reception area.
"How can I help you, sir?" asks Michele, the receptionist, politely.
"Hudson, Scotland Yard," he says, holding out his ID card. I'm investigating the case of a missing person – Penelope Sutton."
Michele **gasps**. "Mrs Sutton, you say? She's missing?"
Hudson nods. "Tell me everything you know."
"She stayed here last Saturday night, in room 14. But she went home very early on Sunday morning, even before I was on duty."
"What time do you start work?" asks Hudson.
"7 a.m.," replies Michele.
"That is very early for a Sunday morning. I **wonder** why she left so soon. Did she say anything to you the day before?"

False friend alarm!
apart bedeutet „auseinander" – NICHT „apart"!
Andere falsche Freunde sind:

familiar	vertraut (nicht „familiär")
brave	mutig (nicht „brav")

"No," says Michele, "but I found this on my desk." She passes him a little hand-written note. Hudson reads it: *Emergency at work. Must leave early.* The note is **signed** Penelope Sutton.

"And the chambermaid found this in her room." Michele hands him Penny's mobile phone.
"Thank you," says Hudson. He puts the note and the phone in his pocket. "Can I have the keys to her room, please?"
"Oh, we have a new guest staying there at the moment," Michele replies. "But I'll ask him for you. I'm sure it will be okay."
"Excuse me," says a voice behind him. "I heard you say that you are looking for Penny. Is she in trouble?"
Hudson turns and sees a woman of about forty with short red hair.
"Claire Hockey," she says and holds out her hand. "I was at school with Penny."

upset	aufgebracht

Hudson shakes her hand. "Is there a quiet place where we can talk?" he asks.
Claire leads him into the empty breakfast room.

An hour later, Hudson is sitting alone in the hotel lounge drinking a cup of tea. I didn't find any clues in room 14, he thinks sadly. The chambermaid did her job too well. But Miss Hockey was helpful. He reads the notes he made during his talk with Claire:
school open day... met old friends, e.g. Jennifer Blacksmith, Margaret Taylor, headmistress Veronica Musty
– I will have to talk to all of them, he thinks –
Penny upset about a phone call... strange man watching school through binoculars... Drives off in dark-coloured coupé...
That sounds very suspicious...
Miss Hockey last saw Penny outside Queen's Arms where she was meeting her friend, Fiona Lambert, at 7 p.m.
So I've got a lot of people to interview, thinks Hudson. I'll start with Miss Musty at the school.

Exercise 12: Opposites. Verbinden Sie die Gegenteile!

1. ☐ rudely
2. ☐ happily
3. ☐ badly
4. ☐ aggressively

a) sadly
b) politely
c) gently
d) well

Mr Sutton **unlocks** the front door of his house in Edgbaston. "Please wait here, sir, while we search the house," says Jarvis. He nods and stands outside alone, looking **miserable**.

"You start upstairs and I'll do the ground floor," Jarvis tells Cavanagh as she picks up a pile of post and newspapers from the mat inside the front door.[i]

She walks from room to room looking for clues. Everything is very **neat and tidy**. There's no **sign** of a fight. Jarvis sees a large collection of CDs sorted in alphabetical order. B for Bizet... C for Chopin... They really like classical music, she thinks.

to unlock	aufschließen
miserable	elend
neat and tidy	ordentlich, picobello
sign	Zeichen, Hinweis
windowsill	Fensterbank
wooden	aus Holz
court	*hier*: Gericht

Next she goes into the kitchen. It's a sunny room with flowers on the **windowsill**. Jarvis finds two letters on the big **wooden** table. She picks one up and reads:

Invitation to Shepton Mallet School Open Day, July 18th

She then looks at the other letter. It's from the **court**.

In Wohnhäusern wird die Post meistens durch einen Schlitz in der Eingangstür geliefert.

A date has been set for the case of Wiley **versus** *Wiley – August 3rd, 2015.*

Jarvis puts both letters in her pocket.

"Cavanagh, how are you doing?" she shouts.

The constable comes down the stairs carrying a plastic **evidence** bag. "I found a pink toothbrush in the bathroom," he says proudly.

versus	gegen
evidence	Beweis
liar	Lügner
appointment	Termin
to get one's hands on sb.	jmd. in die Finger kriegen
CU (see you)	wir sehen uns
outgoing calls *pl*	ausgehende Anrufe

"Good. I'll send that to Dr Barrington straight away. Let's go."

As they leave they see Mr Sutton still waiting on the doorstep.

"Do you know anything about this, Mr Sutton?" asks Jarvis and shows him the letter about the open day.

"Yes," he says, looking very pale. "Penny told me about her school open day last time I saw her. But I really have no idea why she didn't come home. Detective, will you please let me know if there is any news?"

"Of course, sir. And please call me at this number if your wife contacts you." Jarvis gives him her card.

"Do you think he kidnapped her?" asks Cavanagh when the two officers are in their car.

"No, he really does look very worried about her, doesn't he?" Jarvis replies.

"Maybe he's just a good **liar**. I saw a film once..."

"Yes, thank you, Cavanagh! Let's go now please!"

And so they drive towards the city centre and Corbett & Co Lawyers Ltd.

bloody bedeutet zwar "blutig", es ist aber auch ein häufig verwendetes Schimpfwort, abgeleitet vom Ausruf „By my Lady!" (Jungfrau Maria). Deshalb sollte man ein blutiges Steak als „rare steak" und nicht als „bloody steak" (verdammtes Steak) übersetzen!

Exercise 13: Contracted forms. **Lesen Sie weiter und ergänzen Sie die Kurzformen!**

My **appointment** with Miss Musty is in 90 minutes, thinks Hudson. So **1.** I have ________________ got time to have a look at the village. While **2.** he is ________________ walking, he listens to the voice mail on Penny's phone.

"You bloody[i] bitch! **3.** You are ________________ ruining my life!" says a man's voice.

Charming! thinks Hudson and clicks to the next message.

4. It is ________________ from the same number.

"If I **get my hands on you**, **5.** you will ________________ wish you were dead!"

Very interesting indeed, thinks Hudson. He takes out his own phone and calls Scotland Yard.

"Harvey, I want you to trace a mobile phone number. It's 0776 2341 4297. Thanks, bye."

He pauses under an oak tree to look at Penny's text messages. There are three from Saturday evening, all from a sender with the number 085 7825 6679. He reads them carefully:

8 p.m.: `1985: A pack of lies!`

8:25 p.m.: `Ask HM`; and finally at 8:45 p.m.:

`CU at QA in 10 minutes.`

"Harvey, it's me again. I need you to trace another number, too."

Next he checks Penny's **outgoing calls**. She only made one call last Saturday, at 8:35 p.m. Hudson redials the number.

"Sunshine Retirement Home, Sarah speaking," says a friendly woman's voice.
"Detective Inspector Hudson here. Did you receive a call from a Mrs Sutton on Saturday evening?"
"Yes, she wanted to know our visiting hours for the next day."
"Who did she want to visit on Sunday?" asks Hudson.
"I don't know, she didn't say. And she never came."

DI Jarvis is sitting in Penny's boss's office in central Birmingham.
"No, I'm sorry, Inspector, I don't know where Penelope is. She hasn't come to work since last Friday," says a **bald** man with a grey **moustache** and a **bow tie**.
"This is serious, I'm afraid, Mr Corbett. Mrs Sutton may be in danger. If you know anything at all, please tell me. Did she have any personal problems?" Jarvis asks.
"Well, I heard that she and her husband are **separated**. But I don't know all the **gossip**. Maybe you should ask Mrs Lovett, our secretary. She always knows everything that's going on."

bald	kahlköpfig
moustache	Oberlippenbart
bow tie	Fliege
separated	getrennt
gossip	Klatsch
enemy	Feind
confidential	vertraulich
forehead	Stirn
divorce	Scheidung
to get in touch	Kontakt aufnehmen

"Yes, I'll speak to her later. What about work? Did Mrs Sutton have any problems there? Was anyone aggressive towards her?"
"You know, lawyers always have **enemies**. It's part of the job," he replies. "But I never thought Penelope was in danger."
"What can you tell me about this?" asks Jarvis, putting a letter on the table. "Wiley versus Wiley".
"I can't tell you about our clients, Inspector. That's **confidential** information."

After a few more minutes, Jarvis says goodbye and walks out of Mr Corbett's office. She feels frustrated.

I need to find out more about the Wiley case, she thinks.

In the reception area, Cavanagh is drinking coffee with Mrs Lovett, the secretary, a smartly dressed blonde. Mrs Lovett gives Jarvis a friendly smile.

"Your colleague here told me you're trying to find Penelope?"

Jarvis nods. "Yes, that's right."

"Let me know if I can help in any way," continues Mrs Lovett.

Jarvis smiles back and goes outside to phone Hudson.

"Hello, sir, it's Jarvis here. I've just spoken to Mrs Sutton's boss. But he won't give me any information about the Wiley case."

"Maybe he will when you tell him this," replies Hudson. "Harvey has traced the number of the aggressive phone calls. They came from Mr Ted Wiley."

"Bingo!" says Jarvis. "I'll talk to Corbett again right away!"

She goes back inside. The secretary and Cavanagh both look up.

"I need to speak to your boss again, Mrs Lovett."

"I'll see what I can do," she replies and picks up her phone. "Mr Corbett, the Police Inspector is still here. She needs to talk to you again." She smiles at Jarvis. "You can go in now, dear."

"Mr Corbett, we've got some new information. We now know that Mr Wiley sent Mrs Sutton some very aggressive messages. We're worried about her. We must speak to Wiley as soon as possible. Now what can you tell me about that case, Wiley versus Wiley?"

Corbett sighs and rubs his **forehead**. "OK, I'll tell you everything I know. What's important now is that you find Penelope quickly."

He takes a deep breath and goes on. "Wiley's wife, Brenda, is Penelope's client. Mrs Wiley wants a **divorce**, but her husband doesn't. He's a violent man and he beats her."

"Thank you, Mr Corbett. How can I **get in touch** with the Wileys?"

intercom	Gegensprechanlage
recently	in letzter Zeit
it's not like her	es ist nicht ihre Art

"One moment. Mrs Lovett?" Corbett speaks into an intercom. "Please find the address for Mr and Mrs Wiley. Goodbye, Inspector Jarvis. And good luck!"

In the reception area Mrs Lovett gives Jarvis the address of the Wileys' house in Dudley, a town 10 miles south of Birmingham.

"But you won't find Mrs Wiley there," she tells Jarvis. "Penelope told me she moved out three weeks ago."

"Do you have any idea where she is?" asks Jarvis.

"Yes," says Mrs Lovett with a smile. "Brenda Wiley is staying at her sister's house in Solihull. Here's the address."

"Where do you think Mrs Sutton might be?" asks Jarvis.

"Well, I know Penelope is having some problems with her husband, Neil. They're a lovely couple, but they've had some very bad arguments recently. Have you spoken to him yet?"

"Yes, we have. He says he has no idea where his wife is."

"I hope she's okay. It's not like her to miss work without calling me. I'm very worried about her, Inspector."

Exercise 14: Relationship matching. Ergänzen Sie die fehlenden Begriffe!

assistant boss husband colleague

1. DI Jarvis is DI Bradley's ________________.
2. Mr Sutton is Penny's ________________.
3. PC Cavanagh is DI Jarvis's ________________.
4. Mr Corbett is Penny's ________________.

3 The Teacher's Pet

"This is Mr Brown," says the factory manager in Basingstoke. "He was here at the weekend. Talk to him."
DI Bradley turns to a young man with long hair and a beard.
"So you're the night-watchman, Mr Brown?"
"Yeah, that's me. It's a good job – no early mornings," he grins.

night-watchman	Nachtwächter
CCTV (closed-circuit television)	Überwachungs-kamera

"Did you see anything strange at the scrapyard at the weekend?"
"No. I'm not paid to watch the scrapyard. That would cost extra!"
Bradley sighs. He leaves the factory and walks up and down the street to clear his mind. I'm getting nowhere, he thinks. He stops and looks around him. Then he sees it – a CCTV camera on the factory wall! It's pointing towards the street outside the factory, the same street that leads to the scrapyard.

"I've got the contact information you wanted for Jennifer Blacksmith, Margaret Taylor and Fiona Lambert, sir," says PC Harvey. "Blacksmith lives in Bath and Taylor in London. Mrs Lambert's address is in Shepton Mallet, not far from the school."
She gives him the addresses and phone numbers.
"Thank you, Harvey," says Hudson and smiles. She's doing well. I'm glad I gave her this chance to show that she's good at her job.
"And I traced the text messages that Mrs Sutton received, too. They were from Fiona Lambert."

Hudson looks at his watch. Still 30 minutes before I meet Miss Musty. Time to visit Mrs Lambert. He opens a map of Shepton Mallet on his mobile phone and walks towards Fiona's house.

Meanwhile at the White Hart Hotel, Fiona knocks on Claire's door.

ϟ What's up?	Was ist los?
to be in a terrible hurry	es schrecklich eilig haben
Never mind.	Macht nichts.
weeds	Unkraut
to mow the lawn	Rasen mähen
to move out	ausziehen
state	Zustand

"What's up, Fiona? You're really pale. Are you ill?"
Fiona shakes her head. "Is it true about Penny?" she asks. "That she's disappeared and the police are looking for her?"
"Yes, she didn't come to breakfast on Sunday. She checked herself out really early. She was in a terrible hurry, it seems. She even left her phone behind," says Claire.

Exercise 15: Translation. **Übersetzen Sie die folgenden Sätze!**

1. What's up?

____

2. She's doing well.

____

3. Never mind!

____

4. I'm getting nowhere!

____

"Where's her phone now?" she asks, going even paler.
"The Inspector from London has got it. He's probably checking all her calls," Claire tells her friend.

Hudson arrives at Fiona's house in Shepton Mallet. He rings the doorbell and waits. There's no one home. **Never mind,** I'll try again later. But now it's time for my meeting with Miss Musty, the headmistress of Shepton Mallet School.

At the same time in Dudley, DI Jarvis and PC Cavanagh arrive at Mr and Mrs Wiley's house. All the curtains are closed and there is no sign of life. Jarvis knocks on the door but there's no answer. "Damn, there's no one home," she says. "Let's check the back." Behind the house is a small garden. The grass is long and full of **weeds**. Over in the next garden, a man is **mowing his lawn**. "Hello!" shouts Jarvis. "Do you know where Mr Wiley is?"

Exercise 16: Verb forms. Lesen Sie weiter und setzen Sie die korrekte Verbform ein!

The man **1.** turn off ________________ his lawnmower and **2.** walk ________________ towards her.
"Ted? No idea," he **3.** reply ________________. "I haven't seen him since last Thursday. And Brenda **moved out**, poor woman. That's why the garden **4.** be ________________ in such a bad **state**."
"Thank you. Okay, Cavanagh, let's **5.** go ____________ and talk to Mrs Wiley," says Jarvis.

At 4:30 p.m. on Tuesday, Hudson walks up the path to Shepton Mallet School, a huge stone building with a big garden around it. A traditional public school,[i] thinks Hudson.

A man with thick grey hair and work clothes walks past him slowly, pushing a **wheelbarrow**.

"Good afternoon," says Hudson politely.

The man stares at him but he doesn't reply.

> Eine **Public School** oder **Independent School** ist in Großbritannien eine Privatschule, die also nicht durch staatliche Stellen, sondern stattdessen durch oft horrende Schulgebühren sowie durch Spenden und Vermächtnisse finanziert wird.

"Hello, you must be Inspector Hudson," says Miss Musty as she comes out to greet him. She looks very smart in her green **silk** blouse and skirt. "Don't worry about Henry. He's been working at the school for a long time. He's a very good gardener but not a good talker," she says and laughs. "Let's go inside."

She leads Hudson into the school and along a corridor. They walk past a room where a woman with curly grey hair and glasses is busy typing a letter.

"Mrs Motherwell, please bring us some tea," says Miss Musty to her secretary. She takes Hudson into her office next door.

"Please take a seat," says Miss Musty. "How can I help you?"

"I am trying to find a missing person – a Mrs Penelope Sutton," Hudson explains.

Miss Musty **looks blank**.

"Her **maiden name** was Braithwaite," Hudson adds.

"Ah, Penny! Yes, she was a pupil here back in the 80s. I taught her French. She had a terrible accent! She was here on Saturday for the open day... What do you mean, 'a missing person'?"

"No one has seen Mrs Sutton since Saturday, I'm afraid. I need to find out exactly what she did that day."

"Of course, Inspector. I'll do my best to help you. Poor Penny! I wonder where she is." Miss Musty looks very worried.
"Tell me, how was Mrs Sutton when you saw her?"
"She was fine. She's a **successful** lawyer now. I'm so proud of her. She seemed happy. No, wait a minute. I remember there was something... a phone call. Yes, she went outside to answer her phone. And when she came back she was very pale and quiet."
Ted Wiley and his **nasty** phone calls, thinks Hudson.
"Who did Mrs Sutton talk to at the Open Day?" he asks.
"Well, we were standing in a little group and chatting. Margaret Taylor was there...Jennifer, too...and Claire, Claire Hockey."
"Were they good friends of Mrs Sutton?" Hudson asks.
"No, not really. Margaret was the head girl when Penny was 11 years old. Jennifer and Penny were quite good friends. They both slept in the same **dormitory** and played in the school netball[i] team. Claire was in the same class as Penny but she wasn't really her friend. She hung around with Fiona mostly."
"Do you mean Fiona Lambert?" asks Hudson with interest.
"That's right," Miss Musty sighs. "Fiona was a **nightmare**!"
"What do you mean?" Hudson asks.
"She was very aggressive and difficult to teach," says Miss Musty.
Hudson writes all of this in his notebook.
"Miss Musty, how long have you lived in Shepton Mallet?"
"Over 30 years, Inspector," she answers.

wheelbarrow	Schubkarre
silk	Seide
to look blank	verständnislos schauen
maiden name	Geburtsname
successful	erfolgreich
nasty	böse
dormitory	Schlafsaal
nightmare	Albtraum

Netball ist ein basketballähnliches Mannschaftsspiel, das im englischsprachigen Raum v.a. Frauen spielen. Netball ist oft Teil des Sportunterrichts.

"So you probably know most of the villagers, then."
She nods.
"Could you look at this, please?"

resident	Bewohner
tongue	Zunge
tray	Tablett

Hudson shows her a message that PC Harvey has just sent him. It's a list of the residents of the Sunshine Retirement Home.
"Is there anyone on this list who Penny knew well?"
"Let me see... yes, Miss Sharp. She was headmistress when Penny was a girl. 'Sharp' is the perfect name for her. She has a very sharp tongue. All the girls were frightened of her – so were the teachers!"
Hm... headmistress, thinks Hudson. I wonder if Miss Sharp is the 'HM' in the text message that Penny received.

Exercise 17: Match up the words. Bilden Sie zusammengesetzte Begriffe!

1. ☐ retirement — **a)** person

2. ☐ maiden — **b)** school

3. ☐ public — **c)** name

4. ☐ missing — **d)** home

Jarvis and Cavanagh are sitting on a sofa in a house in Solihull, 10 miles south-east of Birmingham. Mrs Wiley's sister brings them some tea and biscuits on a tray.
"Thanks very much," says Cavanagh happily.
He takes a handful of biscuits and starts to eat. Jarvis gives him a sharp look.

"Mrs Wiley," she says, turning to the small, **shy** woman sitting opposite her. "Can you tell us where your husband might be?"
Mrs Wiley looks at her nervously but doesn't answer.
Jarvis **notices** a **bruise** above her left eye. Poor woman, she's too afraid to talk to us, she thinks.
"We've just been to your house in Dudley, but your husband isn't at home. We need to speak to him quickly. It's about a crime."
Mrs Wiley looks up.
Jarvis goes on, "Penelope Sutton is missing."
Mrs Wiley gasps. "Mrs Sutton!" she **whispers**.
"She's your lawyer, isn't she?" Jarvis asks gently.
Mrs Wiley nods.
"When did you see her last?" Jarvis asks.
"She came here on Thursday morning. She told me the court has **set a date** for the **trial**," replies Mrs Wiley.
"Did you know that your husband was **threatening** Mrs Sutton on the phone?"
Mrs Wiley just shakes her head sadly.
"Well, I wouldn't be surprised if Ted has done something to **hurt** Mrs Sutton," says Mrs Wiley's sister angrily. "He is a **good-for-nothing**. Look at what he has done to poor Brenda!"
"Lucy, please!" whispers Mrs Wiley.
"Come on, Brenda. Tell the police where that bastard is hiding. It's time he was **put behind bars**!" She puts her arm round her sister.

shy	schüchtern
to notice	(be)merken
bruise	blauer Fleck
to whisper	flüstern
to set a date	einen Termin festlegen
trial	Gerichtsverfahren
to threaten	drohen
to hurt	wehtun
ϟ good-for-nothing	Taugenichts
ϟ to put sb. behind bars	jmd. hinter Gitter bringen

"Well, he might be at the **allotment**," says Brenda Wiley in a **shaky** voice. "He sometimes goes there to be alone."
"To **get drunk**, you mean!" says her sister.
"The allotment?" asks Jarvis. Brenda Wiley is silent and looks miserable. She has already said more than she wanted to.

allotment	Schrebergarten
shaky	zitternd
to get drunk	sich betrinken
registration number	Autokennzeichen
ordinary	normal, gewöhnlich
to get on with sb.	mit jmd. auskommen
to bully	mobben, schikanieren
to sleepwalk	schlafwandeln
awful	furchtbar
to bury	begraben

Her sister Lucy answers for her. "I'll give you the address."
"One more thing," says Jarvis. "What kind of car does he drive?"
"A Honda coupé," answers Lucy again. "About two years old, black. Shall I give you the **registration number**?"
Jarvis nods. "Yes, please."

"Tell me more about Fiona Lambert, Miss Musty," says Hudson.
"I heard that she got divorced last year, and that she's looking for a new job. She still lives in the village, you know."
"But this is a boarding school, isn't it? I thought the pupils came from other towns further away."
"Yes, mostly. But we also have some day girls who live locally. They come to school at 9 a.m. and at 3:30 p.m. they go home, just like at an **ordinary** school. Fiona was a day girl."
"Did she come to the open day?"
"I'm not sure. I didn't see her. But there were a lot of people on the lawn, so it's possible that she was there."
"How did she **get on with** Penny?" he asks.
Miss Musty pauses to think before answering. "Fiona and Penny were complete opposites. Penny was very hardworking and po-

lite. I remember Fiona always called her 'Perfect Penny, the teacher's pet'."
"Do you know why Fiona was so angry with Penny?" asks Hudson.
"Yes," Miss Musty sighs. "Penny once told us that she saw Fiona **bullying** another girl. Fiona got into big trouble for that."
So Fiona hated Penny. So why those text messages? wonders Hudson. He takes Penny's phone out of his pocket and reads:
`1985: A pack of lies!`

Exercise 18: Question words. Lesen Sie weiter und ergänzen Sie die fehlenden Fragewörter!

what what what who why

"Miss Musty, 1. ______ do you remember about the year 1985?"
Miss Musty puts down her tea cup and rubs her forehead.
"1985 was a very sad year for all of us at Shepton Mallet School."
"2. ______? 3. ______ happened?" asks Hudson.
"There was a tragic accident. One of our girls was **sleep-walking** in the upstairs corridor. She fell down the stairs and broke her neck. It was **awful**! She is **buried** in the village churchyard."
Hudson sits forward in his chair. "4. ______ was she?"
"Her name was Rebecca Bracknell. Poor little Becky."
"5. ______ can you tell me about her?" he asks.

"She was a very special child, a **loner** and a day dreamer," she continues. "She wasn't like the other girls, so they **made fun of** her. You know how **cruel** children can be! I remember once a girl put a dead rat in Becky's desk. It nearly **scared her to death**."
"Were you Rebecca's teacher, Miss Musty?"
"I only taught her French. Miss Foster was her class teacher."
"Miss Foster?" Hudson raises his eyebrows.
"Emily Foster. In 1985 she and I were the only young members of **staff**. All the other teachers were at least 50. That seemed old to us back then," she laughs. "Emily and I were good friends. She told me once that she was very worried about Becky. She wanted to put a stop to the bullying, but the girl was too scared to say who it was. When Becky died, Emily was very upset. She didn't want to stay here any longer. She left the school and went to live with some **relatives** in Australia. After that we lost contact, I'm afraid."

loner	Einzelgänger
to make fun of sb.	sich über jmd. lustig machen
cruel	grausam
to scare sb. to death	jmd. zu Tode erschrecken
staff	Personal
relative	Verwandte
curious	neugierig
marble	Marmor
gravestone	Grabstein

"Do you have any idea who was bullying Becky?" asks Hudson.
Miss Musty sighs deeply. "Yes, Penny told us... it was Fiona."

At 5:30 p.m. Hudson is leaving the school when his phone rings.
"Hello, this is Jennifer Blacksmith. Constable Harvey called me and told me to ring this number," says a woman's voice.
Well done again, Harvey, thinks Hudson.
"Thank you for calling, Mrs Blacksmith. I've got a few questions about the school open day last Saturday. You spoke to Penelope Sutton, didn't you? Did you notice anything unusual?"
"No, nothing, Inspector. Is Penny in trouble?"

"I'm afraid she's missing," Hudson replies.
"Oh dear, how terrible!" says Jennifer, shocked.
"Can you think of anything that might help us to find her? Did she say anything strange? Was she worried or scared?"
Jennifer thinks for a moment. "No, we just made small talk really – nothing important," she says. "Then she went outside to take a call. I don't know anything more than that, I'm afraid."

Exercise 19: Choose the correct alternative. Unterstreichen Sie die richtige Variante!

1. Hudson is leaving the school when his phone is ringing / rings.
2. Thank you for call / calling.
3. We both loved / were loving netball when we were at school.
4. I don't know anything more as / than that.

After his talk with Jennifer, Hudson walks back to Fiona's house. I am curious to meet her now, he thinks. But when he arrives at her house there is still no one home. He takes out Penny's phone and rings Fiona's number. No answer!
I must talk to her as soon as possible, but how can I find her?
He decides to take a walk to clear his head. The road from the school leads to the church. He opens a little wooden gate and goes into the churchyard. It is very quiet and peaceful here. He looks around until he finds what he is looking for – a marble gravestone with the words: Rebecca Bracknell 1974 – 1985. There are fresh flowers lying on the grave.

I wonder who put these there? Hudson thinks as he stands looking at the grave. Miss Musty told me that Fiona bullied Rebecca. And Rebecca died. Could there be a connection?
Suddenly he feels a vibration in his pocket. It's Penny's phone. He takes it out and sees that there's a new message:
`51° 11′ 23″ North, 2° 32′ 50″ West.`

Exercise 20: Unscramble the words. Lesen Sie weiter und bringen Sie die Buchstaben in die richtige Reihenfolge!

Those are geographical coordinates, thinks Hudson in **1.** sripuser ____________________. It's from the same **2.** munreb ____________________ as the other **3.** xett ________________ messages. That means it's from Fiona Lambert. But why would Fiona send Penny a **4.** gasseem ________________ like this?

Hudson opens the GPS function on his own phone and types in the coordinates. It's really close by, he thinks. What's going on?
Hudson follows the route along a path to a field behind the church. On one side of the field is a small wood with oak trees. There's no sign of Fiona. Hudson walks to the middle of the field where the coordinates meet.
There he finds a large concrete paving slab with the words "Somerset District Council" carved on it. On top of it someone has left a mobile phone. He picks it up and sees that it is flashing "new message". He opens the message and nearly drops the

phone in shock. The message is addressed to himself!

Inspector, long time no kill! Dig deep and solve a crime!

Is someone watching me? thinks Hudson.

He looks around but the field seems to be empty.

connection	Verbindung
concrete paving slab	Betonplatte
to carve	meiβeln
to drop	fallen lassen
to dig	graben
to solve	lösen

Exercise 21: Word spiral. Finden Sie die Begriffe in der Wortspirale!

1	2	3	4	5	6
20	21	22	23	24	7
19	32	33	34	25	8
18	31	36	35	26	9
17	30	29	28	27	10
16	15	14	13	12	11

1-7: an English sport for girls

7-12: the opposite of big

12-20: a critical situation

20-25: a colour

25-30: to think about a question

30-36: the girl that Fiona bullied

Suddenly there is a noise in the little wood at the side of the field. Hudson stares into the woods, but two **magpies** come flying out from between the trees.

Just birds, thinks Hudson and breathes out again. He bends down and examines the paving slab closely. It seems to be a **cover** to something. There are deep **scratches** around the slab. It looks as if someone moved it **by force**.

magpie	Elster
cover	Abdeckung
scratch	Kratzer
by force	mit Gewalt

Time to call the Somerset police, he thinks and dials the number that Harvey gave him earlier.

"Hello, this is Inspector Hudson from Scotland Yard. I need someone to help me move a heavy object."

4 Caught on Film

"Bradley, tell me what you found out in Basingstoke," says Sir Reginald on Tuesday at 7 p.m. in his office at Scotland Yard.
Bradley proudly holds out the video tape from the CCTV camera.
"This film shows the road leading to the scrapyard. I'm sure it will show us who drove the Toyota there last weekend."
"Very good," says Sir Reginald. "So now all you have to do is watch the film carefully, **frame by frame**, for the whole time from Friday evening till Monday morning."
Bradley sighs deeply.
"Yes, that does sound like a lot of work, doesn't it, Bradley? I'm going to give you an assistant to help."
"Thank you, sir!" says Bradley with a grin.

frame by frame	Bild für Bild
ϟ Phew!	Uff!
sleeve	Ärmel

Exercise 22: Fill in the blanks. **Lesen Sie weiter und ergänzen Sie die fehlenden Adjektive!**

deep closer heavy dark hard terrible

"**Phew**, that was **1.** ________ work!" says young PC Baker from the Warminster police with his **sleeves** rolled up. He and his colleagues are working in the field behind the church in Shepton Mallet, moving the **2.** __________ slab that Hudson found. They all wipe the **sweat** from their foreheads.

"God, what a **3.** __________ smell!" Baker says, holding his hand in front of his nose.

The others do the same. Then they step forward to have a **4.** __________ look. They see a hole going **5.** __________ into the ground.

"It looks like an old **well**," says Hudson. "It's really **6.** __________ down there. I can't see the **bottom**. Has anyone got a **torch**?"

PC Stewart comes forward and holds his torch over the well. It looks **ghostly** in the torchlight.

"Can you see anything?" asks Inspector Matthews.

"No," replies Hudson. "Someone will have to go down there."

"How deep do you think it is?" asks Matthews.

sweat	Schweiβ
well	Brunnen
bottom	Boden
torch	Taschenlampe
ghostly	unheimlich

Hudson picks up a stone and throws it into the well. They wait a couple of seconds, then they hear a splash as the pebble hits the water at the bottom of the well.

"It's too deep for us," says Hudson. "This is a job for the police **diving squad**."

I have a very bad feeling about this, he thinks to himself.

In Ashwick, four miles from Shepton Mallet, Dr Willerby looks at his watch. His next patient is very late. He presses the button on his intercom.

diving squad	Polizeitaucher
to cancel	absagen
progress	Fortschritt
anxious	besorgt, ängstlich
armed	bewaffnet
body	*hier*: Leichnam
to cordon off	absperren
council	Gemeinderat
villager	Dorfbewohner

"Mrs Cranmore, has Mrs Lambert **cancelled** her appointment?"

"No, doctor. Maybe she forgot," answers the receptionist.

What a shame, thinks Willerby. We were making good **progress**.

"Jarvis? It's Hudson. Where are you exactly?" Hudson sounds **anxious**.

"Just outside Dudley, sir. Cavanagh and I are on our way to Ted Wiley's allotment. We think he's hiding there."

"Wait where you are. I'm sending a team of **armed** officers to help you," says Hudson in a serious voice. "Be careful, Jarvis. Wiley may be very dangerous. We have just found a **body**. I think it's Penelope Sutton."

Hudson ends the call and looks at his watch. It's 8:30 p.m. He turns to the forensic team, who are working around the well.

"It's getting dark now, so I think we should stop for today. **Cordon off** the area round the well and put a night-watchman on guard."

They nod.

"Inspector Matthews, who owns this field?" Hudson asks.

"It belongs to the **council**, Inspector. The **villagers** come here to walk their dogs."

"Right. I'm going to take the body to London for examination. I need Dr Barrington to identify her as soon as possible," says

Hudson. Turning back to the forensic team he continues, "I would like you to go on looking for clues here tomorrow morning. See if you can find any traces of blood around the well or any signs of a fight. And Inspector Matthews, tell your officers to go door-to-door questioning the villagers. Find out if anyone saw anything suspicious. Please report to me immediately if you find anything."

> Bei Adressen steht im Englischen die Hausnummer vor dem Straßennamen.

Why did Fiona lead me here in such a mysterious way? thinks Hudson, puzzled. What does she have to do with Penny's death? It's very important that we find her quickly.
"Constable Baker, you watch Mrs Lambert's house. It's 45 Oaktree Lane.(i) Call me as soon as you see her. I need to talk to her urgently."

Exercise 23: Opposites. **Finden Sie die Gegenteile im Text und schreiben Sie sie auf!**

1. top ________________	**4.** safe ________________
2. early ________________	**5.** life ________________
3. funny ________________	**6.** search ________________

Meanwhile, in a quiet area just outside Dudley, a team of armed policemen arrive at a group of small allotments. Each one has a small garden hut and a fence around it. It's late on Tuesday evening and the allotments seem to be empty.
"Wiley's is over there," Jarvis whispers, pointing to the middle of the allotment area.

The armed police move[i] slowly and silently towards it. They check that there is no sign of Wiley outside, then they open the gate to his allotment and **creep up to** the hut. Two men with guns stand by the window and another two men guard the door.
"Wiley, are you in there?" shouts an officer.
There's no reply.
"We're coming in!"

puzzled	verblüfft, verwirrt
to creep up to	sich anschleichen an
to catch one's foot	mit dem Fuß hängenbleiben

The men kick the door hard and it flies open. The hut is full of beer bottles and cigarette packets, but Mr Wiley is not there.
"Listen!" says Cavanagh. "I can hear a car!"
They all look through the window and see a black Honda coupé stop next to the allotment gate. A man gets out and walks towards the hut. He is carrying a six-pack of beer.
"Stay where you are and put your hands up!" shouts an officer, running out of the hut and pointing his gun at him.
The man drops his beer in shock and runs as fast as he can. He jumps over the fence into the next allotment.
"Catch him!" shouts Jarvis.
She and Cavanagh jump over the fence and run after him. The next fence is higher. The man tries to jump over it, but it's too high for him and he **catches his foot** on the top. He cries out as he falls face-down on the grass.
"Quick, let's get him!" shouts Jarvis.

> Einige Sammelbegriffe verlangen ein Plural-Verb, wenn man darunter eine Gruppe von Menschen versteht, u.a.
> **police, press, public, staff und team:**
> z.B. *The team are playing well today.* or *The staff are unhappy with the changes.*

She and Cavanagh run to where the man is lying. He tries to get up but the two police officers push him down.

Exercise 24: Unscramble the text. **Lesen Sie weiter und bringen Sie die Sätze in die richtige Reihenfolge!**

a) "Sir, we've got Wiley," says Jarvis on the phone, **out of breath**.

b) "It's him," she says, holding out a bank card with the name Ted Wiley on it.

c) "Good work!" says Hudson. "Bring him to Scotland Yard. I'm on my way back to London, too. We can question him together tomorrow morning."

d) Cavanagh kneels on his back while Jarvis **handcuffs** him and searches his pockets.

1	2	3	4

On Wednesday at 9:30 am, Hudson meets Dr Barrington in his forensic **lab** in London.
"You look tired, Tony," comments Hudson.
"Yes, I am. I worked all night, James. You said it was important to get quick results," replies Barrington.
"Thank you, Tony. So show me what you have found."
The two men walk towards a table. A dead body is lying on the table under a sheet. Hudson **shudders**. This is the part of his job that he really doesn't like. Barrington lifts the sheet.
"As you can see, the body is very **swollen**. She's been in the water for several days. However, I didn't find any water in her lungs, so she was dead before she was put into the well."

"So she didn't drown," comments Hudson.
"No, the cause of death was this," says Barrington.
He turns the woman's face to one side. On the back of her head Hudson sees a deep cut.
"Someone hit her very hard with a sharp object. Then they threw her body into the well."
"What about the time of death?" asks Hudson.

out of breath	atemlos
to handcuff sb.	jmd. Handschellen anlegen
lab	Labor
to shudder	schaudern
swollen	angeschwollen
to drown	ertrinken
cause of death	Todesursache
sample	Probe
doubt	Zweifel
leather	Leder

"I'd say she died at the weekend, Saturday or Sunday."
"What about the DNA samples we gave you? Do they match?" i
"Yes, James. The dead woman's DNA matches the blood in the car and the sample we found on Mrs Sutton's toothbrush."
"So there is no doubt, Tony. This is Penelope Sutton."
"That's right. But there's something else that I don't understand."
Barrington takes Hudson to the other side of the lab, where Penny's things are lying on a table: her black pencil skirt, white silk blouse, blazer, handbag and a shoe. Barrington picks up the shoe and holds it out to show Hudson.
"This is the wrong size. Mrs Sutton's feet are size 4. This shoe is size 5½ – much too big."
"You mean it's not Mrs Sutton's shoe?" asks Hudson, puzzled.
"Look at it, James. It's very good quality leather, but it's been in the water for a very long time, maybe 20 or 30 years."
"Where are Mrs Sutton's shoes, then? Are they still in the well?"

Das Wort **match** wird sowohl als Substantiv als auch als Verb verwendet, mit unterschiedlicher Bedeutung.

match	Streichholz, Partie (beim Sport)
to match	(zusammen)passen

mood	Laune

Hudson takes out his phone to call Inspector Matthews in Shepton Mallet. Matthews answers immediately.

"Sir, I was just about to call you," he sounds out of breath. "The divers have found something!"

"A pair of shoes?" asks Hudson.

"Yes! But that's not all. There's another body in the well!"

"What?" Hudson looks at Barrington and then at the old shoe in his hand. "Matthews, send the body and everything else you've found here as soon as possible." And to Dr Barrington he says, "Tony, I'm afraid I've got more work for you."

Exercise 25: Word order. Lesen Sie weiter und bringen Sie die Wörter in die richtige Reihenfolge!

1. Scotland Yard | Hudson | next | back | to | drives

   ____

2. room | he | Jarvis | interview | outside | meets | an

   ____

3. brightly | sir! | says | she | morning

   ____

4. morning | morning? | Wiley | this | Jarvis | Mr | is | how

   ____

"He's is in a very bad **mood** after spending a night in a police cell. He's shouting and swearing[i] at everyone."

"Great! Just what I need," says Hudson sarcastically. "I've got a search warrant for Wiley's house in Dudley," Jarvis tells Hudson. "I'm driving back there after we have questioned him."
"Good. But before we go in, I have to make a call. Wait here."

in person	persönlich
↯ pig	*hier*: Bulle
to mind one's own business	sich um seine eigenen Angelegenheiten kümmern
stern	streng

Hudson goes into his office. "Mr Sutton? It's Inspector Hudson from Scotland Yard. I'm afraid I have some very bad news."
"It's Penny, isn't it? Have you found her? Is she okay?" Neil Sutton asks anxiously.
"We have found her. I'm sorry to say..."
"She's dead, isn't she?" Sutton interrupts him. "Oh my God–"
"Mr Sutton, are you still there?" Hudson waits a moment and then continues gently. "Mr Sutton, when could you come to London? I'd like to speak to you **in person**."
Sutton answers in a quiet voice. "I...I'll take the midday train. I can be there in about 3 hours."

"You bloody **pigs** are all the same!" shouts Ted Wiley as Hudson and Jarvis enter the room. "Arresting people for no reason."
Jarvis looks at Hudson. "See what I mean, sir?"
"There I was, **minding my own business**," Wiley continues. "And suddenly my allotment is full of police."
"Mr Wiley, I want to talk to you about Penelope Sutton," says Hudson in a **stern** voice.

> Das Verb **to swear** hat zwei Bedeutungen, die man nicht durcheinander bringen sollte! Es heißt „fluchen" aber auch „schwören".

"That bloody bitch! She's ruining me, you know! Brenda met that woman and now she wants a divorce! Well, she can forget it, the stupid cow!"

Hudson bangs his **fist** on the table. "That's enough, Wiley! Mrs Sutton is dead. And you are in big trouble. We know that you threatened her. We found your messages. Now tell me exactly where you were last weekend."
Wiley stares at the table. "I won't say a word without my lawyer."

fist	Faust
witness	Zeuge
identity parade	polizeiliche Gegen-überstellung
height	Größe, Höhe
to recognize	wiedererkennen

Just then someone knocks on the door and enters.
"I came as quickly as I could," says the man in a blue suit and a bright red tie. "Bruce Appleton's my name. I'm Mr Wiley's lawyer." He takes a seat next to Ted Wiley.
"So, now that your lawyer is here, let's go on," says Hudson. "Where were you at the weekend, Mr Wiley?"
"I told you already. I was on my allotment, minding my own business." Wiley is still angry, but he is also scared now.
"Any **witnesses**?" asks Jarvis.
"Yeah, my neighbour was there on Saturday morning. And on Sundays the allotments are very busy, so many people saw me."
"What about Saturday afternoon and evening? Did anyone see you there then?" she asks.
"No, but I swear I never touched Mrs Sutton!" Wiley shouts at Jarvis. "God, you women are all the same!"
Jarvis remembers the bruise above Brenda Wiley's eye. "Do you have a problem with women, Mr Wiley?" she asks in a cold voice.
"Don't answer that," says Appleton to his client. "You've said enough already."
"Mr Wiley, have you ever been to Shepton Mallet?" asks Hudson.
"Shepton what?" replies Wiley. "Never heard of it."
"Well, I've got a witness who saw a man watching the school in Shepton Mallet on Saturday. She is on her way here now," says

Hudson to Appleton. "I'm arranging an identity parade. I'm sure you don't have a problem with that, do you?"
Appleton shakes his head.

Exercise 26: Definitions. **Verbinden Sie die Wörter mit ihren Erklärungen!**

1. ☐	The police need this to search your house.	a) bruise
2. ☐	A person who sees a crime.	b) lawyer
3. ☐	A blue mark on the skin.	c) witness
4. ☐	You need one if you are in trouble with the police.	d) warrant

At 3 p.m. Harvey tells Hudson that Miss Hockey has arrived.
"Thank you for coming here so quickly, Miss Hockey," Hudson says as he takes her into a room with a big window on one wall.
"We can see through this window into the next room. But the people on the other side of the glass cannot see us," he explains.
"Please take a seat and try to relax. Harvey, send in the men."
Through the window, Claire sees six men standing in a line. The men are all about 40 years old and medium height with dark hair – just like her description of the man with the binoculars. She looks from one face to the next and sighs.
"I'm sorry, Inspector. I don't recognize any of them."
Hudson sighs, too. "Okay, Miss Hockey. That's all for now."
Claire walks along the corridor to the exit. As she is leaving, a man comes in and bumps into her. He doesn't say sorry or even look at her. He just walks on along the corridor, lost in thought.

How rude! thinks Claire, watching him go. Wait a minute, I've seen him somewhere before!

Exercise 27: Fill in the blanks. Lesen Sie weiter und vervollständigen Sie die Wörter!

"Please take a **1.** *s* ________, Mr Sutton," says Hudson minutes later in his **2.** *o* ________. "Can I get you a coffee or a glass of water?"
Sutton **3.** *s* ________ his head.
Hudson takes a deep **4.** *b* ________ and goes on.
"As I said on the phone, we have found your wife. I am very sorry, but it seems she was the victim of a violent **5.** *c* ________."

"Are...are you sure it's Penny?" Mr Sutton asks Hudson.
"Yes, I'm afraid so."
Sutton puts his head in his hands.
"Our forensic expert has tested her DNA. So it's not necessary for you to identify her."
"But I want to see her," Sutton says in a quiet voice.
"Of course, Mr Sutton," says Hudson kindly. "I'll drive you to the forensic lab."
On the way to the lab, Mr Sutton is very quiet and lost in thought. Then suddenly he says miserably, "You must find the person who did this terrible thing to my Penny!"
"I will certainly do my best," Hudson answers. "When did you last see your wife?"

"Two weeks ago," Sutton answers. "I came to the house to get some books. And we had a talk."
"What did you talk about?"
"Nothing important. She told me about the school open day."
"I'm sorry, Mr Sutton, but I have to ask you this... I'm sure you understand... Where were you last weekend?" asks Hudson.
"I had a lot of work, so I spent the weekend sitting at my computer in my flat. I'm renting it at the moment, just until Penny and I get back together... Oh God, I keep forgetting that she's dead!"

rude	unhöflich
necessary	notwendig
to rent	mieten
to complain	sich beschweren
to escape	fliehen, flüchten
prime suspect	Hauptverdächtiger

"Do you have any witnesses for last weekend, Mr Sutton?"
"No, no one." Mr Sutton puts his hand over his eyes.

"How did it go, sir?" Jarvis asks Hudson an hour later at Scotland Yard.
"It wasn't easy," says Hudson sadly. "Mr Sutton was very upset."
"Hm. Appleton wants to see you, sir," Jarvis says and takes him into the next room.
"Ah, there you are, Inspector," Wiley's lawyer says. "I really must complain. You are keeping my client here against his will. And you have no evidence against him."
"It's true that our witness can't identify him. But he threatened Mrs Sutton and he has no alibi for the time of the crime. Plus he tried to escape arrest. Wiley is still a prime suspect."

Das Verb **to keep** übersetzt man mit „be-/erhalten", aber in Kombination mit einer ing-Form bedeutet es „immer wieder". *I keep forgetting it* heißt also: Ich vergesse es immer wieder.

"Inspector, you know you can only hold a suspect for a maximum of 96 hours. After that you have to let him go."
Well, I should get moving then, thinks Hudson **grimly**.

In another room at Scotland Yard, DI Bradley and his assistant are examining the CCTV film from Basingstoke.
"Look, sir!" says young PC Smith excitedly. "I've found something. Saturday evening, 11 p.m."
He and Bradley watch as a Toyota drives past the camera in the direction of the scrapyard.
"**Rewind** it," says Bradley. "Good, stop right there."
Smith puts the film on pause. Together they stare at the screen.
"Can you **magnify** it a bit more. Good. Look at that."
They see two people in the car, a driver and a passenger.

Meanwhile Hudson walks down the corridor towards the kitchen. He passes the waiting room and is surprised to see Claire Hockey sitting there. She stands up when she sees him.
"Miss Hockey, why are you still here?"
"I've seen him again! The man with the binoculars," Claire says **breathlessly**. "He was here. He walked past me."
"Okay, let's go to my office." Hudson leads her to his room where Claire gives him a description of the man.
"Black trousers and a yellow sweatshirt," Hudson repeats slowly. "3:30 p.m., you say, just as you were leaving."
Claire nods. "Yes, exactly."

grimly	grimmig
to rewind	zurückspulen
to magnify	vergrößern
breathlessly	atemlos
neither ... nor	weder ... noch
APB (all points bulletin)	Fahndungsaufruf
noisy	laut
wallet	Portemonnaie

The man she saw was Mr Sutton, thinks Hudson. What was he doing in Somerset? And why did he lie to us? And what about our other missing witness?
Hudson leaves the room and dials Sutton's number. No answer. He dials Matthews' number again. "Hudson speaking. Have you found Fiona Lambert yet?"
"No, sir. There is no sign of her, **neither** here **nor** in the village."
Hudson goes to the team room. "Harvey, please put out 2 **APBs**: Neil Sutton and Fiona Lambert, our two missing witnesses."
Or suspects? he thinks.

In a **noisy** pub in Birmingham, Neil Sutton sits alone at the bar. "Give me another whisky," he says to the barman.
Just then, Sutton's phone rings. He switches it off. He takes a photo out of his **wallet** and looks at it sadly. Penny, my darling! What went wrong? he sighs, banging his fist on the table.

Exercise 28: Translation. Übersetzen Sie die folgenden Sätze!

1. Ich verbrachte das Wochenende an meinem PC.

____

2. Sie versucht zu fliehen.

____

3. Er beschwert sich immer wieder.

____

4. Ich miete zur Zeit eine kleine Wohnung.

____

5 The Missing Link

"Come and sit down, James," Miss Paddington tells Hudson on Wednesday evening. "I've made lamb stew for dinner."

"Mmm... it smells delicious!" Hudson smiles as he sits down at the dining table. "It's so good to come home, Miss Paddington, even if it's just for a short break."

"This new case sounds hard. I can't wait to hear about it," says Miss Paddington.

She always enjoys listening to Hudson talk about his work. And she often has some helpful ideas, too. She puts some food on his plate and pours him a glass of wine.

link	Verbindung
to sip	nippen
coincidence	Zufall
thoughtfully	nachdenklich
bloodstain	Blutfleck
track	Spur

James **sips** his wine and starts to talk. "A woman called Penelope Sutton has been murdered. She was in Somerset for an open day at her old school, Shepton Mallet Boarding School."

"Wait a second, James. Shepton Mallet, you say? I've heard of that school before. Wasn't there a scandal there back in the 80s?"

"Yes, that's right. A pupil fell down the stairs and broke her neck."

"Oh dear. I remember reading about it in the newspaper," says Miss Paddington. "And now an ex-pupil has died at the open day? What a **coincidence**!"

"I don't really believe in coincidences," Hudson says **thoughtfully**.

"I know," says Miss Paddington. "That's one reason why you are such a good detective, James."

> **Lamb stew,** oder **Irish stew,** ist ein traditionelles irisches Eintopfgericht. Es besteht aus Lammfleisch, Kartoffeln, Zwiebeln, Lauch und Petersilie. Oft werden auch Karotten und Pastinaken hinzugefügt.

After dinner, Hudson lies on his bed and closes his eyes. But he can't stop thinking about the case. He picks up Fiona's phone and reads again the text messages she sent to Penny on Saturday:
1985: A pack of lies!; Ask HM;
and finally **CU at QA in 10 minutes.**
QA could be the Queen's Arms pub next to the hotel, thinks Hudson. I must go there when I'm back in Shepton Mallet.
He clicks to the strange message Fiona sent him on Tuesday:
Long time no kill! Dig deep and solve a crime!
I wish I could solve this crime, he thinks grimly.

Exercise 29: Match-up. Welche der folgenden Begriffe gehören zusammen? Ordnen Sie zu!

1. ☐ sip	**a)** down the stairs
2. ☐ solve	**b)** a drink
3. ☐ fall	**c)** smell
4. ☐ delicious	**d)** a crime

It's 8:30 a.m. on Thursday morning. Hudson is parking his car opposite Tony Barrington's forensic lab when his phone rings. "Good morning! Matthews here. My men have found bloodstains and some interesting tracks leading to the well. We've

sent some samples and pictures to forensics, but I'd like to show you in person. Will you be coming back to Shepton Mallet soon?"
"Good work, Matthews. Yes, I'm coming back this afternoon," Hudson replies as he walks towards the lab. "After I've looked at that other body you sent me."
"**Rather you than me**, Inspector!" says Matthews.

Rather you than me!	Lieber Sie als ich!
sight	Anblick
to swallow	schlucken
skull	Schädel
blow	Schlag
asap	schnellstmöglich
mess	Unordnung

"Hello again, James," says Barrington. "We're meeting quite often these days, aren't we?"
"Yes, Tony. Too often," says James, looking at the long table. Once again there's a body lying under a green plastic sheet.
"Are you ready, James? This is not a pretty **sight**," Barrington says and he pulls back the sheet. On the table is a skeleton.
Hudson **swallows**. "Oh God," he whispers.
"Yes, there's not much left[i] of her, is there? I'd say she's been dead for about 30 years. I can see from the skeleton that this was a young woman – about 25 years old. Her feet are size 5½, just like that old shoe I showed you last time."
"What was the cause of death?" asks Hudson, looking at Barrington so that he doesn't have to look at the body.
"Look at the back of the **skull**," the forensics expert replies. "She died from a **blow** to the head. Just like Mrs Sutton did."
"Do you have any idea who she was?" Hudson asks. "None at all," says Barrington. "But clearly there is a connection between the two dead women."
"Yes," Hudson agrees. "And it's my job to find out what it is."

left hat mehrere Bedeutungen. Als Verb ist es die Vergangenheitsform von **to leave** (verlassen, zurücklassen).
Als Adjektiv bedeutet es „links" aber auch „übrig", wie in diesem Fall.

Exercise 30: Correct the mistakes. **Lesen Sie weiter und korrigieren Sie die sechs Fehler!**

"Listen, everyone. I've got some knew work for you," Hudson tells his team soon afterwards at Scotland Yard. "I want you too check the cases off all missing persons in the Somerset area in the 1980s and 1990s."

"That's a long time ago," comments PC Harvey.

"You're write, Harvey. Long time no kill, just like Fiona Lambert wrote in her message to me. We must find she asap. Where on earth can she be?"

Hudson takes Fiona's phone out of his pocket and hands it to Harvey. "Check all Mrs Lambert's incoming and outgoing calls and text messages and let me no if you find anything interesting."

1. ____________ 4. ____________

2. ____________ 5. ____________

3. ____________ 6. ____________

Meanwhile in Dudley, Jarvis and Cavanagh are searching Mr Wiley's house. It's a terrible mess. In the living room they find broken beer bottles all over the floor. Jarvis bends down and picks up a business card from the floor.

⚡ So what?!	Ja und?!
sober	nüchtern

"Penelope Sutton, Corbett & Co Lawyers Ltd.," she reads. "It's Mrs Sutton's card. And here's the number that Wiley phoned when he made those aggressive calls."

Just then, Cavanagh's phone rings. "Cavanagh here... Hi, Bill... Fine, thanks... Yes... yes... really? Okay, I'll tell her."

He turns to Jarvis. "My colleagues at the station in Birmingham arrested a man for drink-driving last night."

"So what?" says Jarvis impatiently. "We're looking for a murderer. We haven't got time for drink-drivers."

"It's Mr Sutton, Inspector!" Cavanagh explains. "They put him in a cell overnight. He's sober now and ready for questioning."

"Okay. Sorry, Cavanagh," says Jarvis. "We'll go and talk to him as soon as we're finished here. Wiley and Sutton, what a pair! Penny was not very lucky with men, was she?"

An hour later, Jarvis sits down opposite Neil Sutton in an interview room at Birmingham police station. Sutton's hair is a mess and he has dark rings under his eyes.

"Mr Sutton, I'm Inspector Jarvis, a colleague of James Hudson. You spoke to him yesterday, I believe."

Sutton nods.

"Tell me, where were you last Saturday after 4 p.m.?"

"I was at home, working. I already told Inspector Hudson everything I know. Why are you asking me all this again?"

"Mr Sutton, you didn't tell us the truth, did you? We've got a witness who saw you in Shepton Mallet on Saturday afternoon at around 3 o'clock and again that evening at 6:30."

Sutton is silent for a minute. His shoulders are shaking.

"Okay. It's true. I…I was at the school. I was watching Penny."

"You were watching your wife?" asks Jarvis. "Why?"

"I thought she was having an affair," says Sutton unhappily. "She told me she was going away for the weekend to visit her old school. But I didn't believe her. I thought she was meeting a man."

"So you followed her there? All the way to Somerset?"

Sutton nods.

"Did your wife see you? Did you speak to her?"

"No. But one of the other guests saw me watching the school. So I drove away quickly. I was back home by 9 p.m."

"Do you have any witnesses for that?" asks Jarvis.

Sutton shakes his head miserably.

"Mr Sutton, you wouldn't be the first jealous husband who killed his wife," Jarvis says sharply.

"Oh God, Penny!" Sutton cries. "I made a terrible mistake!"

Exercise 31: True or false? Welche Aussagen sind korrekt? Markieren Sie mit richtig ✔ oder falsch – !

1. The police have found two dead bodies. ❒
2. Dr Barrington knows who the second dead woman was. ❒
3. DI Jarvis finds the murder weapon in Wiley's house. ❒
4. Mr Sutton lied to the police. ❒

Back at Scotland Yard, DI Bradley points at the computer screen. "Look at this, sir. Here you can see the Toyota as it drives past the factory on the

Woman bedeutet „Frau", **wife** bedeutet „Ehefrau", z.B. *Please meet my wife,* und nicht *Please meet my woman!*

instead	stattdessen
reluctantly	widerwillig
to commit a crime	ein Verbrechen begehen

way to the scrapyard. Smith, pause the film right there... What do you think of that, sir!" says Bradley, proudly.

"Well, I can see two people in the car. But I can't see their faces. Can you magnify it a bit more, Smith?" asks Hudson. "Yes, that's better. Hmm, the passenger is looking at the driver so we can't see his face – just the back of his head. And he is blocking our view of the driver, too. Damn! We can't see the driver's face at all. Just the hands on the steering wheel. But Smith, let's have a close-up of the driver's hands... Now, that's more interesting!"

On the screen they see that the driver's fingernails are painted.

"Our driver is a woman!" says Hudson.

I wonder if it is Fiona Lambert. He calls Inspector Matthews in Shepton Mallet.

"Matthews, Hudson here. Please tell me you've found Lambert."

"Sorry, sir. There's still no sign of her," Matthews replies.

Hudson sighs deeply. Just then there is a knock on the door and WPC Harvey walks in.

"I've checked all the messages on Mrs Lambert's phone," she says. "I'm not sure, but I think this might be important."

She clicks on the voice mail and hands Hudson the phone. He puts it to his ear and listens:

"Hello Mrs Lambert. It's Irene Cranmore, Dr Willerby's receptionist. I'm afraid we will have to change the time of your appointment next week. Please call me back."

"I found Dr Willerby's practice, sir," Harvey says. "It's in Ashwick, about 5 miles from Shepton Mallet. He's a psychologist."

"That means Fiona Lambert had psychological problems. How interesting. I'm going back to Somerset now. I'll visit the doctor as my first priority. Good work, Harvey!" says Hudson.

Exercise 32: Opposites. **Lesen Sie weiter und unterstreichen Sie die Gegenteile der angegebene Wörter!**

stands up | square | soft | leaves | thin

At 2 p.m. Hudson arrives at Dr Willerby's office in Ashwick. The doctor is sitting in an armchair next to a couch. He watches Hudson carefully through his thick, round glasses as the inspector walks past the couch and chooses a hard wooden chair **instead** and sits down.

"Dr Willerby, I'm trying to contact a patient of yours – Fiona Lambert. I need to talk to her urgently."
Willerby doesn't answer. He just watches Hudson's face.
My God, I'm not here for therapy! thinks Hudson.
At last the doctor replies. "What makes you think that Mrs Lambert is my patient, Inspector?"
"It's very simple. There's a message from your receptionist on her voice mail," answers Hudson smiling.
"Oh... alright, it's true," Willerby says **reluctantly**.
"Why is she coming here?"
"You know I can't tell you that, Inspector." Now Willerby smiles.
Hudson tries again. "Listen, a woman is dead and a murderer is running free. Mrs Lambert is connected to the crime in some way and I have to find her. Do you know where she is?"
"No. All I can say is she missed her appointment on Tuesday and I haven't heard from her since," says the doctor. "Inspector, I've known Fiona Lambert for a very long time. And I have no reason to believe that she would **commit a** violent **crime**."

Exercise 33: Word forms. **Ergänzen Sie das jeweilige Substantiv!**

1. arrive ____________________
2. choose ____________________
3. think ____________________
4. reply ____________________
5. die ____________________
6. connect ____________________

Shortly afterwards in Shepton Mallet, Hudson walks up the path behind the church on his way to meet Inspector Matthews.
"Excuse me," he says as he walks past a group of villagers who are trying to see what is going on.
"It's no good, son. The police won't let you through," an elderly man tells him.
Hudson sees that Matthews' men have cordoned off a large area around the well, including part of the wood. PC Stewart is on guard, making sure that no one enters the crime scene. He stands back to let Hudson pass.
"Hudson, good to see you," says Inspector Matthews. "Let me show you what we have found."
Matthews leads the way towards the edge of the field near the wood.
"How did the door-to-door questioning go?" Hudson asks as they walk across the field.
"Well, there was a lot going on at the weekend because of the school open day. The village was full of strangers. But no one

saw anything suspicious around this field. Now here we are, Hudson. Look at these tracks," he says, pointing at the ground. "Car tyres. And the forensic team found traces of blood here, too. And look here."
Inspector Matthews points at another track going across the field to the well. "As you can see, it's from just one wheel. But it's too wide for a bicycle."
"You're right, Matthews. I wonder what made this track."
"Excuse me, sir," says young PC Baker. "I really like gardening. I've got some lovely roses in my garden."
"Baker, get back to work. Can't you see we're busy?" Matthews says angrily.
"But, sir! This track is just like the mark that my wheelbarrow makes in the mud."
"He's right, you know," says Hudson. "A wheelbarrow. There must be lots of them in this village. Matthews, you'll have to send your men round the village again. Tell them to make a list of everyone who owns a wheelbarrow. And find out if someone's wheelbarrow is missing."

elderly	älterer
edge	Rand, Kante

Hudson walks a few steps towards the churchyard and takes Fiona's phone out of his pocket. He reads her message again:
`Dig deep and solve a crime!`
Why did Fiona lead me here? Hudson asks himself. And why did she send me this strange message? Why didn't she contact me directly? What does she have to do with Penny's death? And who is the other dead woman? So many questions but no answers! The link between Penny and Fiona lies far in the past. Perhaps I need to dig deeper into the past to find a clue, he thinks.
He has an idea. He gets in his car and drives off to the Sunshine Retirement Home on the other side of the village.

Exercise 34: Translation. Lesen Sie weiter und übersetzen Sie die deutschen Begriffe ins Englische!

"Miss Sharp is over there, sitting by the **1.** Fenster ________________," says Sarah, the **2.** Empfangsdame ________________.
Hudson walks towards a small, white-haired lady in a **rocking chair**. There is a radio on the **3.** Fensterbank ________________. Miss Sharp is listening to the **4.** nachmittags ________________ talk show on BBC Radio 2.

So this is the woman who was so strict that all the pupils and teachers were scared of her, Hudson thinks.
"May I speak to you, Miss Sharp?" he asks politely.
"Pssst," she replies. "Be quiet. I'm missing my programme."
"Miss Sharp, I'm Inspector Hudson from Scotland Yard."
But she ignores him, so Hudson walks over to the radio and turns it off. Miss Sharp looks up angrily.
"I'm here on important police business," Hudson continues.
"Alright, young man. Tell me what this is about," she says in a voice that makes Hudson feel like a schoolboy again.
"Yes, Miss Sharp. A **former** pupil of Shepton Mallet School has been murdered – Mrs Penelope Sutton. Maybe you remember her as Penny Braithwaite."
Miss Sharp frowns as she tries to remember. "Ah, Penny, a

> Die British Broadcasting Corporation, kurz **BBC**, ist eine britische Rundfunkanstalt, die mehrere Hörfunk- und Fernsehprogramme betreibt.

good girl, very polite. Someone murdered her, you say. How terrible!"
"Last Saturday she phoned the retirement home. I think she wanted to talk to you. Do you have any idea what she wanted?"

rocking chair	Schaukelstuhl
former	ehemalig
to reach for sth.	nach etw. greifen
to come to no good	böse enden

"Penny wanted to see me? That's unusual! Not many of my ex-pupils or staff have been to visit me, you know."
I'm not surprised, thinks Hudson.
"So you don't know what it was about?" he asks again.
Miss Sharp shakes her head and **reaches for** her radio.

Exercise 35: Synonyms. Finden Sie die Synonyme im Text und schreiben Sie sie auf!

1. frightened ______________________
2. significant ______________________
3. strange ______________________
4. go on ______________________

"Wait, Miss Sharp. There's something else," Hudson says. "I need to find another ex-pupil – Fiona Lambert. What can you tell me about her?"
Miss Sharp sighs. "I always knew Fiona would **come to no good**!"
"What do you mean?"
Miss Sharp closes her eyes for a moment to think. "Fiona was a rebel. Of course, she had a difficult home life, which is probably why she was so much trouble..."

She pauses, lost in thought. "I remember it all quite clearly. Fiona's father was dead. Fiona's mother wanted her to go to Shepton Mallet School, but it's quite expensive, you know. The poor woman was always working, trying to **earn** the money to pay the **school fees**. "

to earn	verdienen
school fees *pl*	Schulgebühren
grades *pl*	*hier*: Noten
comprehensive school	Gesamtschule
relationship	Beziehung
physically	körperlich
letter of resignation	Kündigungsbrief
manners *pl*	Benehmen

"How did Fiona get on at Shepton Mallet School?" Hudson asks.

"It was difficult for her," Miss Sharp tells him. "She felt quite bitter about the other girls, because most of them came from rich families. But she wasn't stupid. Her **grades** were quite good... to begin with. Then suddenly, around the end of 1985, they started to get worse and worse. And after that she was a nightmare for the teachers. They couldn't control her at all. In the end I decided to speak to her mother. I told her that maybe Fiona would be happier at the local **comprehensive school**. So in 1986 she left."

"And what about Fiona's **relationship** to Penny?" Hudson asks.

"Well, the class teacher Emily Foster was very worried about one of the girls in the same class as Fiona and Penny, because someone was bullying her. Miss Foster told me she wanted to find out who the bully was. But no one would tell her – no one except Penny. She was braver than the others. She told her teacher that it was Fiona. After that Fiona hated Penny."

"Was Fiona ever **physically** aggressive towards Penny?"

worse and worse bedeutet „immer schlimmer". Diese Struktur kann man mit allen Adjektiven verwenden, z.B. *She understood more and more.* Sie verstand immer mehr.

Miss Sharp thinks hard about this. "I can't remember. The class teacher would know more about that than I do."

"Miss Foster?" asks Hudson. "How can I contact her?"

Miss Sharp looks very angry. "I don't know and I don't want to know! She suddenly left the school back in 1985, but she didn't even tell me she was going! She just wrote a **letter of resignation** and left in the middle of the night – went to live on her brother's farm in Australia. No respect! No **manners**!"

"Did she leave a contact address in her letter?" asks Hudson.

Miss Sharp frowns again. "You are asking a lot of difficult questions, young man. I'm 86, you know! I can't remember everything. Why don't you read the letter yourself? It should still be in the school archives somewhere."

"Yes, I'll do that. Thank you very much for your time, Miss Sharp."

Hudson gets into his car and drives straight to Shepton Mallet School.

So what is the evidence so far? he thinks as he drives along. Fiona has psychological problems. As a child she hated Penny. Now Penny is dead and Fiona has disappeared. All the evidence points towards Fiona. But how can I find her? And why do I have the feeling that Miss Foster may be the missing link?

6 Lost Friends

At 5 p.m. Hudson walks up the path towards Shepton Mallet School once again. It's very quiet and there is no one in sight. He rings the doorbell. A minute later Miss Musty opens the door.
"Ah, Inspector," she says with a warm smile. "Do come in."
"Thank you, Miss Musty. I'd like to ask you some more questions."
"Of course. Come this way," she says and she leads him along the corridor and up the stairs to her office on the first floor.

Exercise 36: Choose the correct alternative. Lesen Sie weiter und unterstreichen Sie die richtige Variante!

"It's very **1.** quiet / quite here today," comments Hudson as he takes a seat.
"Yes, the summer holidays have started. There's only me and my secretary **2.** hear / here now, finishing **3.** some / any paper work."
"Miss Musty, you told **4.** my / me before about Miss Foster who worked here in the 1980s. Have you got her address or phone number?"
"No, I'm afraid not," she says **5.** sad / sadly. "We lost touch when she left. We haven't spoken since 1985."

only child	Einzelkind
shelf	Regal
filing cabinet	Aktenschrank
record	*hier*: Akte
envelope	Umschlag

"I see. Please tell me about your time working together."

Miss Musty pauses to think. "Emily and I were good friends. She was like a sister to me. We were about the same size, you know. So we often borrowed each other's clothes and shoes!"

"If you were such good friends, why did you lose touch? Didn't you ever try to contact her at her brother's farm in Australia?"

Miss Musty looks puzzled. "Her brother's farm? But Emily hasn't got a brother! She's an only child."

"Did she tell you that?" asks Hudson.

"Yes, she said her parents are already dead. The only other relatives she has are some cousins who live in Brisbane."

"Miss Sharp told me that when Emily went she left a letter behind. Have you read it, Miss Musty?"

"No, I haven't. It was addressed to Miss Sharp, not to me," she replies. "Emily didn't leave any message at all for me."

"I would like to look at the letter," Hudson continues. "Miss Sharp said it must be in the archives. Can you find it for me?"

Miss Musty stands up and walks past a shelf of sports trophies. Then she opens a door to a small room full of filing cabinets.

"Oh dear, I have no idea where the records for 1985 are. Mrs Motherwell would know, but she has left work already today."

"I'll help you," says Hudson.

And together they search through the files.

"Inspector, I think I've found it," Miss Musty says fifteen minutes later and hands Hudson an old brown envelope with Miss Sharp's name on it.

Borrow und **lend** bedeuten beide „leihen, ausleihen". Aber Vorsicht! **Borrow** benutzt man, wenn man sich etwas ausleiht. **Lend** verwendet man, wenn man etwas verleiht. z.B.
*Can **I** borrow your car? = Can **you** lend **me** your car?*

Hudson opens the old envelope and pulls out a piece of paper.

I have decided to give up teaching and go to help my brother on his farm in Brisbane.

"It's signed 'Emily Foster', but she doesn't give her brother's address."

"Brother? I don't understand!" Miss Musty says, surprised.

There's something strange about this letter, thinks Hudson. I think I have seen that writing before. How can that be?

"Thank you, Miss Musty. I'd like to take this with me," he says and puts the letter in his pocket.

As soon as he is outside the school he calls Harvey. "Hudson here. I want you to find a farm in the Brisbane area of Australia. The farmer's name is Foster."

Exercise 37: Where does it happen? Verbinden Sie die Ereignisse mit den Orten.

1. ☐ The teenagers crash the car in ...	**a)** Birmingham.
2. ☐ Penny worked at a law company in ...	**b)** Shepton Mallet.
3. ☐ Hudson is staying at the White Hart Hotel in ...	**c)** Dudley.
4. ☐ The police arrest Mr Wiley on his allotment in ...	**d)** Brixton.

An hour later, Hudson and Miss Musty meet again, this time at the police station in Warminster.

"Inspector Hudson, I really must complain! Why have you brought Henry here? What has he done?" Her **cheeks** are red with anger.
"It's always the same," says Mrs Motherwell, who is standing next to her with tears in her eyes. "People don't understand Henry. They are afraid of him because he's **handicapped**. But I swear **he wouldn't hurt a fly**."
So that's why he won't answer any of my questions, thinks Hudson. He looks at Henry, who is sitting at a table and staring out the window in silence.
"Come with me, please, and I'll explain," Hudson says, and he leads the two women into another room.
"One of our officers tried to question Henry at his **cottage**. But when Constable Baker asked to see his wheelbarrow, Henry ran inside and locked the door. Do you have any idea why?"

cheek	Wange
handicapped	behindert
He wouldn't hurt a fly.	Er kann keiner Fliege etwas zuleide tun.
cottage	Häuschen, kleines Landhaus
shed	Schuppen
in tears	in Tränen aufgelöst
to promise	versprechen

Both women look puzzled and shake their heads.
"I'd like to see that wheelbarrow. Can you tell me where it is?"
"It's in the school's garden **shed**. I'll show you," Miss Musty says.
"How long are you going to keep my brother here?" asks Mrs Motherwell **in tears**.
"No longer than necessary, I **promise**," answers Hudson.
"Baker, can you call the police psychologist? Tell him I need him to help me question a witness. Ask him to meet me here in an hour," Hudson says as he leaves the station with the two women.

Exercise 38: Translation. **Lesen Sie weiter und fügen Sie die richtige Übersetzung ein!**

It's 8 p.m. when Hudson parks the car at the **1.** Rand ____________ of the field **2.** hinter ____________ the church in Shepton Mallet. He and one of his passengers **3.** aussteigen ____________ of the car.
"Thank you for coming, Dr Willerby," says Hudson. "Our police psychologist is **4.** beschäftigt ____________ and I don't **5.** warten wollen ____________ any longer."

"I'm happy to help, Inspector," replies the doctor. "So you think the killer used a wheelbarrow to move the body."
"Yes, I think he did. Look, here are the tracks."
"You said "he". Are you sure it was a man?" asks Willerby.
"Probably. Whoever put the body in the well was strong enough to move the heavy concrete cover," Hudson replies. "I went to the school to examine Henry's wheelbarrow, but it has disappeared. I think he knows something about this and I want to know what."
Hudson opens the car door to let the other passenger out.
"Come with me, Henry," Dr Willerby says. "We want to show you something."
He holds Henry's arm and leads him across the field towards the well. As they come closer to the well, Henry gets very nervous. He tries to pull his arm away, but the doctor **holds on tight**.
"Don't worry, Henry. No one is going to hurt you," he says calmly.
"Did you come here last Saturday night, Henry?" Hudson asks.

Henry tries desperately to get away.

"That's enough for today, Inspector," says Dr Willerby firmly. "He's clearly frightened and he doesn't understand what's going on. I think you should let him go home now."

"Okay," Hudson agrees reluctantly. "But we must try to talk to him again tomorrow."

to hold on tight	fest halten
desperately	verzweifelt
firmly	fest
headache	Kopfweh
tiled	gefliest
shape	Form
to get rid of	loswerden

Exercise 39: Unscramble the adjectives. Bringen Sie die Buchstaben in die richtige Reihenfolge!

1. mrif __________

2. sovreun __________

3. rgtnso __________

4. httgi __________

Fiona wakes up with a terrible headache. She's lying face down on a cold tiled floor. She tries to move, but her hands and feet are tied tightly.

Where am I? she thinks in panic.

She rolls onto her back and tries to focus her eyes. It's very dark except for the moonlight shining through a window. She sees the shapes of two people, but she can't see their faces.

"What are we going to do now?" whispers one of them. "There are police all over the village! We have to get rid of her quickly. We can't leave her here any longer. Come on, help me move her."

On Friday morning in the hotel breakfast room, Hudson is looking at Penny's phone and thinking. 'CU at QA in 10 minutes'...

Did Fiona mean the Queen's Arms? I should go there straight away.

underage	minderjährig
landlord	*hier*: Wirt
to be deep in conversation	ins Gespräch vertieft sein
The time is up.	Die Zeit ist abgelaufen.
to insist	auf etw. bestehen

He finishes his breakfast quickly and walks to the pub next door. The Queen's Arms doesn't open until 11 a.m., but a bald man with a beer belly is already cleaning the tables in the beer garden.

"Morning, I'm Inspector Hudson from Scotland Yard."

The man looks up in surprise. "Is this about those underage drinkers[i] at the weekend?" he asks nervously.

"No, it isn't," says Hudson. "Can we go inside to talk?"

"Yes, of course. My name's Lewis. I'm the landlord here," he says and he leads the way into the pretty little black and white building.

The two men sit at the bar.

"Would you like a beer?" Lewis asks.

"No thanks, I never drink on duty," Hudson replies. "Mr Lewis, I'd like to ask you some questions. Did you see this woman in the pub on Saturday evening?" He holds out a photo of Penny Sutton.

Lewis looks at it carefully. "Yes, I remember her. A pretty woman."

"Right," says Hudson. "Was she here alone?"

"No, they were sitting over there in the corner." He points to a table on the other side of the room."

In Großbritannien ist der Verkauf und Konsum von Alkohol in der Öffentlichkeit für alle unter 18 Jahren verboten. Jedoch darf man ab 16 in Restaurants und Bars Bier, Wein oder Cider (Apfelwein) zu einer Mahlzeit trinken, wenn eine Person über 18 Jahren die Bestellung aufgibt.

"They?" asks Hudson.
"Yeah, the woman in the photo and Fiona from Oaktree Lane."
"Did you notice anything unusual. Did they have an argument?"
"No, they were deep in conversation for a while. And then they got up and left together."
"What time was that?" asks Hudson.
"About 10 p.m.," says Lewis. "I haven't seen either of them since."

Exercise 40: Mixed verb forms. Lesen Sie weiter und setzen Sie die Verben in der richtigen Form ein!

be have leave miss ring think

Hudson is just 1. ______ the pub when his phone 2. ______.
"This 3. ______ Jarvis speaking. We 4. ______ a problem. Ted Wiley is 5. ______."
"Wiley? I 6. ______ he was safe in our police cell."

"We had to let him go yesterday evening, sir," Jarvis explains. "The time was up and Appleton insisted."
"Damn lawyers!" says Hudson angrily. "So where is Wiley now?"
"We don't know. Lucy Johnson called the police station last night."
"That's Brenda Wiley's sister, right?" asks Hudson.
"Yes, sir. She said Wiley was banging on the door of her house and swearing. But when our officers arrived, he was gone. We've checked his house and his allotment, but he's disappeared."

"So one of our prime suspects is running free," Hudson says.
"I'm afraid so, sir," Jarvis replies miserably.
Just then Hudson's phone beeps as a text message arrives from Harvey at Scotland Yard:
I've got news! Please call me back.
"Jarvis, I've got to make another call. I'll speak to you later."
Hudson calls Harvey.
"Inspector, I've found out something!" Harvey sounds excited. "I tried to trace Miss Foster in Brisbane, but there was no sign of her or her brother and his farm."

habit	Gewohnheit

"Is that your news?" asks Hudson, disappointed.
"No, sir. There's more. What I *did* find were Miss Foster's cousins. They live on the coast in a little town called Castaway Beach, south of Brisbane. I spoke to them, and guess what? They told me that their cousin Emily doesn't have any brothers or sisters. And they haven't heard from her for 30 years!"
"It sounds as if Miss Foster never went to Australia," says Hudson thoughtfully. "Thank you, Harvey. That's very interesting."
Next he dials the number of the forensic lab in London.
"Tony, Hudson here. Can you to send me a photo of a piece of evidence?"

It's 10 o'clock and Hudson is sitting in Miss Musty's office again.
"This is becoming a **habit**, Inspector," Miss Musty says. "Mrs Motherwell, could you bring us some tea, please?"
The secretary nods and walks off towards the kitchen.
"Is this about Henry?" she asks after Mrs Motherwell has left.
"No, Miss Musty. I want to talk to you about your old friend, Miss Foster. You told me that you were very close, almost like sisters."
"Yes, we were," she replies sadly. "I missed her when she left."

"You told me you shared each other's clothes," Hudson continues. "Do you recognize this shoe?"
Hudson holds out his phone. On it he has several photos of the shoe that the divers found in the well.
Miss Musty looks at them carefully for some time.
Then she whispers, "That's my shoe!"
Hudson's phone rings. Damn! he thinks.
"Excuse me just a moment, Miss Musty," he says and goes outside to take the call.
"Matthews here. Inspector, I've got Dr Willerby with me. We're at the cottage to pick up Henry for questioning. But he's gone."
"Okay, tell your men to search the area and find him. I'm in the middle of something important. I'll be there later."
He rings off[i] and goes back into Miss Musty's room.
"Where did you find my shoe?" she whispers in shock.
"Miss Musty, as you know we are investigating a murder."
"Yes, I know. Poor Penny," she replies.
"We found this shoe at the crime scene. It was at the bottom of a well," Hudson tells her and watches her face carefully.
Miss Musty frowns. "How did it get there? I don't understand."
"When did you last see this shoe?" he asks.
"In 1985. Emily wanted to go to a party in Warminster," Miss Musty remembers. "She borrowed my best shoes. That was about two weeks before she went to Australia. She forgot to give them back to me when she left. I was quite angry about that."
"We have been trying to find Miss Foster in Brisbane. It seems she never went to Australia at all," Hudson says gently.
"Well, where is she then?" Miss Musty is confused and upset.

Phrasal Verbs
Das Verb **to ring** wird mit verschiedenen Präpositionen verwendet:

to ring sb. up	jmd. anrufen
to ring back	zurückrufen
to ring off	den Hörer auflegen

"I'm sorry to have to tell you this," says Hudson quietly. "We found a second body at the crime scene, together with your shoe. It seems there was another murder... about 30 years ago."
Miss Musty looks at him open-mouthed. Then she covers her face with her hands and starts to cry.

Exercise 41: Match-up. Verbinden Sie die Begriffe!

1. ☐	prime	a) evidence
2. ☐	close	b) suspect
3. ☐	piece of	c) scene
4. ☐	crime	d) friend

Just then Mrs Motherwell walks in and puts the tea tray on the table. She gives Hudson a cold look and leaves the room.
Hudson pours the tea and hands a cup to Miss Musty.
"I think you are hiding something," says Hudson sternly. "If you and Emily were so close, why didn't you stay in contact? Didn't you think it was strange that you never heard from her again? Why don't you tell me the whole truth?"
Miss Musty sighs. "Emily and I had a bad argument... about what happened to Becky."
She closes her eyes for a moment to remember. "I can see it all clearly, as if it were yesterday. It's 1985. I'm coming back to the school after an evening out with Larry, my boyfriend. We've been to the cinema in Ashwick to see 'Back to the Future'. I say good-bye to Larry outside the school gate and then I start walking up the path. Suddenly I see Henry. He comes running out of the school. He seems frightened and he runs home to his cottage. I

think, how strange. What has he been doing in the school at this time of night? And I'm surprised to see that all the lights are on in the entrance hall. Everyone usually goes to bed early in a boarding school, Inspector." She pauses.

to protect	schützen
reputation	Ruf
to persuade sb.	jmd. überreden

"What happened next?" Hudson says gently.

"I open the front door and go in. There's a group of teachers and girls standing at the bottom of the stairs. And someone is lying on the floor covered with a sheet. Emily is talking to the police on the telephone. She was always good in an emergency. She says, 'Come quickly! One of our girls has fallen down the stairs. I'm afraid she is dead!'"

"Was it Rebecca Bracknell?" asks Hudson.

She nods.

"Do you think Henry had something to do with Rebecca's death?"

"No," she replies. "He's completely harmless. But I thought it was strange how he reacted, so I decided to tell Miss Sharp."

Hudson nods. He remembers Fiona's text messages: '1985: A pack of lies' and 'Ask HM'.

"Please go on, Miss Musty."

"So I go to see Miss Sharp. I'm a bit scared of her, but I tell her about Henry and ask her if we should tell the police."

"What did she say to that?" Hudson asks.

"She said, 'No, we don't need to talk to the police again. You know that Henry is harmless. Rebecca's death was a terrible accident. We don't want even more scandal about the school.'"

"So she wanted to **protect** the school's **reputation**," says Hudson. "Did you agree to that?"

"Well, I wasn't sure about it at first. It didn't seem right, not telling the police. But she **persuaded me**."

"How did she do that?" Hudson asks with interest.

"I remember she said that I was doing a great job and she offered me the post of **deputy** headmistress."

"So you kept your mouth shut and she gave you a promotion."

deputy	Stellvertreter

Exercise 42: Translation quiz. Übersetzen Sie die Begriffe und finden Sie das Lösungswort!

1. Tablett _ _ □ _
2. Wahrheit _ _ □ _ _
3. überreden _ _ _ □ _ _ _ _
4. Unfall _ _ _ _ _ _ _ □
5. Ruf □ _ _ _ _ □ _ _ _ _
6. harmlos _ _ _ _ □ _ _ _
7. Lügner _ □ □ _

Lösung: □ □ □ □ □ □ □ □ □

7 The Sports Trophy

Fiona **is blindfolded** now and her arms are still tied behind her back. She tries to move her hands but her fingers just **scratch** the floor underneath her. She gives a little scream when a **splinter** goes under her nail. The floor is no longer tiled. It feels like wood.

Where am I now? What's going on? She tries to shout for help but her mouth is still **gagged**.

to be blindfolded	die Augen verbunden haben
to scratch	kratzen
splinter	Splitter
gagged	geknebelt

Exercise 43: Unscramble the words. Lesen Sie weiter und bringen Sie die Buchstaben in die richtige Reihenfolge!

"You **1.** dlot __________ me that you and Miss Foster had an **2.** matgeunr __________ about Becky," Hudson asks Miss Musty. "Tell me more **3.** utboa __________ that."

"It was shortly after Becky **4.** eidd __________," Miss Musty says. "Emily seemed **5.** tuspe __________.

tap	Wasserhahn
hosepipe	Wasserschlauch
attached	befestigt
ϟ to get somewhere	vorankommen (mit etw.)
handle	Griff
to fetch	herbeiholen
to pull oneself together	sich zusammenreißen

She told me that on the evening of the accident, from her bedroom window she saw Henry running across the garden. She thought she should tell the police."

"And what did you say to her?" Hudson asks.

"I said, 'No, don't do that! Think of the scandal!' Then I told her to talk to Miss Sharp about it," replies Miss Musty. "That's when Emily got really angry with me. 'All you care about is your career,' she shouted. But she did what I asked. She went to see Miss Sharp... And I never saw her again."

Hudson's phone rings.

"Hudson, it's me again," says Inspector Matthews.

"Have you found Henry yet?" Hudson asks.

"No, but we've found the wheelbarrow. Stewart found it at the school. The forensic team are checking it right now. I'm here with them. It looks as if someone washed it recently."

"Someone who has something to hide. Where exactly are you?"

"Just outside the back of the school building," Matthews replies.

"I'm in the headmistress's office. I'll come and meet you in two minutes." Hudson turns back to Miss Musty who is looking very pale. "I'm afraid you were wrong about Henry," he tells her. "We must find him as soon as possible."

"This is where I found it, sir," PC Stewart says minutes later.

He points to a wheelbarrow which is standing in front of a door in a wall. Hudson sees a tap on the wall, with a garden hosepipe attached to it. They walk over to the forensic officers who are busy examining the wheelbarrow.

"We think someone used that hosepipe to clean it," Stewart says.

"So we won't find much then," says Hudson, disappointed.
"I wouldn't say that, sir," answers a young woman in white overalls. "Look here. They forgot to wash the bottom. This looks like a bloodstain to me. By the way, my name's Nancy."
"Good work, Nancy! Now we're finally **getting somewhere**."
Behind the wheelbarrow there is a wooden door. Hudson tries to turn the **handle** but the door is locked.
"I'll **fetch** the keys," he says and walks back inside to Miss Musty's office.
She is still sitting at her desk looking very pale.
"Miss Musty, I know this is a shock for you, but I think a criminal is hiding somewhere in the school and I need your help. Please give me the keys for the building."
Miss Musty **pulls herself together**. "Yes, of course, Inspector. Mrs Motherwell has them in her desk."
They walk to the secretary's office next door. The room is empty.
"She's left already. Never mind, I know where she keeps them."

Exercise 44: Translation. Übersetzen Sie die Sätze!

1. By the way, my name's Nancy.

____

2. Pull yourself together!

____

3. Now we're finally getting somewhere.

____

4. I'll fetch the keys.

____

Miss Musty opens a drawer and hands Hudson a heavy **key ring**.

key ring — Schlüsselbund

"Come with me and show me which key fits which door."
Minutes later Hudson unlocks the door behind the wheelbarrow. It opens onto a dark corridor. Near the end of the corridor there is another door.
"This leads to the girls' shower room," Miss Musty explains. "How strange! The shower room key is missing."
"Henry! Are you in there?" Hudson shouts and he bangs his fist on the locked door.
There is no answer.
"Baker, Stewart. Help me open this door."
The two young officers run at the door and hit it with their shoulders. It moves a little but doesn't open. They run at it again. This time there is a loud bang and the door flies open.
"Look at that!" Baker says, rubbing his shoulder.
In one corner the white floor tiles are covered in blood.
"Get the forensic team in here," Hudson says.
Seconds later Nancy appears.
"Inspector Hudson, we've found some more blood outside," she says. "And a track going across the garden."
"Show me," Hudson orders. "And ask your team to examine this room. I want to know if Fiona Lambert has been here."
Outside Nancy points to some marks in the wet grass. They lead from the school, across the garden and into a field behind it.
"What's over there?" Hudson asks Miss Musty.
"That's the school sports ground," she replies.
"Okay, men, come with me. You too, Miss Musty. I may need your help again. Matthews, where is Dr Willerby now?"
"He's waiting in the car over there," Matthews points to a police car in the school car park.
"Good, bring him along, too. He may be useful."

Exercise 45: Prepositions. **Lesen Sie weiter und unterstreichen Sie alle sechs Präpositionen!**

Together they follow the track past the tennis courts[i] and towards the hockey pitch.[i] Next to it Hudson sees a small wooden building.
"The girls keep their tennis rackets and hockey sticks in there," Miss Musty explains.
"Is there another way in, besides that door?" Hudson asks.
"No, Inspector, but there's a large window at the back."

"Baker, Stewart, cover the back window. Matthews, you and I will try the front door. Miss Musty, Dr Willerby, please wait here."
Hudson and his men move carefully towards the building.
"Henry, are you there?" shouts Hudson as he walks forward.
"Stay where you are!" a woman's voice shouts back. "Leave us alone or Fiona dies!"
"Oh my God, that's Mrs Motherwell!" Miss Musty exclaims as she recognizes her secretary's voice.
"Yes, and she's got Fiona – just as I thought," says Hudson.
He and Matthews stand still. "I just want to talk to you, Mrs Motherwell," Hudson says in a calming voice. "You are only making the situation worse for yourself... and for Henry."

Der Begriff „Platz, Spielfeld" wird verschieden übersetzt, je nachdem welche Sportart gemeint ist:

tennis **court**	Tennisplatz
football **pitch**	Fußballplatz
golf **course**	Golfplatz

So ähnlich ist es auch bei Schlägern:

tennis **racket**	Tennisschläger
hockey **stick**	Hockeyschläger
golf **club**	Golfschläger

equipment	Ausrüstung
throat	Hals
to collapse	zusammenbrechen
relieved	erleichtert
wicked	böse
responsible	verantwortlich

"Don't talk to me about Henry!" she screams hysterically. "I've spent my whole life trying to protect him from people like you – people who don't understand what a lovely, gentle person he is."

Hudson slowly takes another step forward. Through the window at the front of the shed he sees a room full of sports **equipment**. Mrs Motherwell is standing in the middle with her arm around Fiona's neck. She is holding a knife to her **throat**.

"Please don't do anything stupid, Mrs Motherwell. Put the knife down and let's talk about this."

"There's nothing to talk about. This has all gone too far. I've done my best for Henry, but it's no good..."

A crash of broken glass interrupts Mrs Motherwell. She turns round in surprise and sees Baker pointing a gun at her through the back window.

"Put your hands up!" he shouts.

Mrs Motherwell screams and drops her knife to the ground.

"Quick, Matthews," says Hudson.

Together they run in and grab Mrs Motherwell from behind, holding her arms tightly.

"Miss Musty, call an ambulance," Hudson shouts over his shoulder as Fiona **collapses** on the floor.

"Dr Willerby, come quickly!"

The doctor runs into the shed and kneels on the floor next to his patient.

In the corner of the room, Henry stands watching in silence as the policemen put handcuffs on his sister. He looks strangely relaxed... even **relieved**.

Exercise 46: Find the opposites. **Finden Sie die Gegenteile im Text und schreiben Sie sie auf!**

1. calmly ____________________
2. intelligent ____________________
3. aggressive ____________________
4. intact ____________________
5. loosely ____________________

"Where's Henry?" Mrs Motherwell asks as Hudson and Matthews sit down opposite her in the Warminster police station. Her voice is shaky and her eyes are red from crying.

"He's alright," Hudson replies. "Dr Willerby is taking care of him. Mrs Motherwell, we've got a lot of questions for you. Let's start with Fiona Lambert. Why did you kidnap her?"

"I just wanted to frighten her so she wouldn't go to the police. It worked before."

"What do you mean, 'It worked before'?" asks Matthews.

"Back in 1985...," she bites her fingernails for a moment. "Fiona was a **wicked** girl, you know. She was **responsible** for Rebecca's death. That's what I told her when she came to see me... when she told me that terrible story..."

"I've read about the case," Matthews interrupts. "The police said it was an accident. How can Fiona be responsible?"

"Fiona bullied Rebecca. The poor girl was traumatized. That's why she started sleepwalking. That's why I told Fiona she was a murderer!" Mrs Motherwell's voice is louder now and there is a wild look in her eyes.

Now Hudson interrupts. "What terrible story did Fiona tell you?"

hooded	mit Kapuze
car jack	Wagenheber
ridiculous	lächerlich
mad	verrückt
to trust	vertrauen
How dare you!	Was erlauben Sie sich!

"One afternoon she came to see me. She was very frightened. This is what she told me."
Mrs Motherwell takes a deep breath and suddenly she is back in the past. "It's a dark, rainy evening and Fiona is hiding in the wood behind the church. She often goes there to smoke so the teachers don't see her. Suddenly she sees Henry pushing his wheelbarrow and Miss Sharp is with him. Fiona recognizes her **hooded** raincoat. They walk to the middle of the field. Miss Sharp gives Henry a **car jack** and he uses it to move a heavy stone. Then he and Miss Sharp lift something out of the wheelbarrow... a body! They throw it into the well." She laughs. "**Ridiculous**! My sweet brother and the headmistress throwing a body into the well! I told Fiona she was **mad**. 'You dreamt it!' I said."
Hudson picks up his phone. "Baker, go to the Sunshine Retirement Home in Shepton Mallet. Please get Miss Sharp and bring her in for questioning."
Hudson turns back to Mrs Motherwell. "Why did Fiona come to you? Why didn't she go straight to the police?"
"Fiona was only 11. She wanted to talk to someone she **trusted**."
"And she trusted you?" asks Hudson.
"Yes, I was the only person at the school that she trusted – me and her friend Claire. So she came to tell me first."
"And you told her she was a wicked girl and a murderer, right?"
"Right!" Mrs Motherwell replies with a nasty smile.
"So you bullied Fiona to stop her telling the police about Henry?" Hudson asks. "And you were protecting Miss Sharp, too?"
"Heather Sharp is my friend," she replies loudly. "She was the only one who gave Henry a chance."

"Tell me about Miss Foster. Did Henry and Miss Sharp kill her?"
"Of course not! How ridiculous! Henry wouldn't hurt a fly. And Heather was a very strict headmistress but not a killer."
"So who killed the teacher then?" Matthews asks.
Mrs Motherwell does not answer.
"Emily Foster was Rebecca's class teacher, wasn't she?" Hudson asks.
Mrs Motherwell sits in silence and doesn't react.

Exercise 47: Correct the mistakes. Lesen Sie weiter und korrigieren Sie die sechs Fehler!

"This is what I thing," says Hudson, watching Mrs Motherwell careful. "Miss Foster new something about who Rebecca died. Perhaps it wasn't a accident. Perhaps Henry killed the girl and her teacher found out. That's why Miss Foster had to died. Right?"

1. ________________
2. ________________
3. ________________
4. ________________
5. ________________
6. ________________

"**How dare you!**" Mrs Motherwell shouts. "You're just like she was. Stupid young woman... saying such bad things about Henry!"
"What did Miss Foster say about Henry?" Hudson asks quietly.
"She comes to the office one evening and says she wants to talk to Miss Sharp, but Heather is out. She seems upset so I ask her

to sit down and tell me what's wrong. 'It's Henry. I saw him on the night of the accident,' she says. 'I think he hurt Becky. I'm going to tell the police.' 'Please don't do that!' I **beg**. But she won't listen to me. 'I'm not waiting any longer,' she says... and she leaves."

to beg	(an)flehen
briefcase	Aktentasche
Board of Directors	Aufsichtsrat
trial period	Probezeit
to confess	gestehen

"But Miss Foster never went to the police, did she?" Hudson asks. "You stopped her, didn't you? You killed her and hid her body. Then you wrote a letter to say that she had gone to Australia."

"That's a lie! I never did any of that!" she shouts, hysterical now.

Hudson opens his **briefcase** and takes out two pieces of paper. He puts them on the table in front of her.

"This is Miss Foster's resignation letter," he says pointing at an old piece of writing paper. "And this is the note that Penny left at the hotel last week to say that she had to go back to work. Matthews, what do you think about that?"

"It's the same handwriting," Matthews answers.

"Exactly. And this...," Hudson takes a third piece of paper out of his pocket, "...is a shopping list I found lying on your desk this afternoon, Mrs Motherwell. It's the same handwriting, too. You wrote all of these notes, didn't you?"

For a moment there is silence in the interview room. Hudson and Matthews hold their breath, waiting. Then at last she starts to talk.

"It's a warm June evening in 1985. Heather invites Henry and me to her office for a glass of sherry. We're celebrating Henry's new job as school caretaker. She says the **Board of Directors** are happy to give him a six-month **trial period**. All he has to do is

work hard and stay out of trouble. We drink to that. Then Henry and I stand up to leave. I open the office door and that little girl is standing there. She's sleepwalking again. She wakes up suddenly. She's frightened and she doesn't know where she is. When she sees a tall man standing in front of her, she opens her mouth to scream. 'Calm down girl, it's only Henry!' I say and I step towards her. But she steps backwards. And then she's falling... Heather runs out of the office and sees Rebecca lying at the bottom of the stairs. 'Go home at once!' she says to Henry and he runs off to the cottage."
"So Rebecca's death really was an accident, then?" Hudson asks.
"Of course it was. But Heather knew that people would suspect Henry if he was at the scene. That's why she sent him home. But it didn't help. There are so many stupid people in the world."
"Like Emily Foster, you mean?" Hudson asks.
Mrs Motherwell nods.
"So either you killed her or Henry did," Hudson continues. "Which of you is the killer? Tell me the truth, Mrs Motherwell."
She puts her head in her hands. "Emily made me really angry, you know. 'Why do so many people think badly of my brother? He's a sweet and gentle man,' I say. But she won't listen to me. She tries to leave. What could I do? I try to hold her back but she hits me hard. Then she breaks away and tries to run out of the room. It all happens so fast. I don't have any time to think. I just know that I have to stop her. So I pick up a tennis trophy from the shelf next to me and I hit her on the back of her head. She falls down dead."

"Well done, Hudson. She's **confessed** to everything," Matthews says half an hour later in the corridor. He and Hudson watch as two officers lead Mrs Motherwell away.
"Thanks, but I'm afraid that's not the end of my day's work."

They walk towards the reception desk where someone is complaining in a loud, angry voice.
"Why am I here, young man? Explain at once!"
"Ah, Miss Sharp, thank you for coming," Hudson says politely. "I'd like to talk to you about your friend Mrs Motherwell."
"Good luck, Inspector," says Matthews as Hudson takes Miss Sharp into an interview room.

Exercise 48: True or false? Welche Aussagen sind korrekt? Markieren Sie mit richtig ✔ oder falsch – !

1. Miss Foster told Miss Sharp about Henry. ❐
2. Mrs Motherwell didn't like Miss Sharp. ❐
3. Henry killed Rebecca Bracknell. ❐
4. Miss Sharp tried to protect Henry. ❐

"Thank you for your help, doctor," Hudson says to Willerby two hours later outside Fiona's room at the hospital. "She wouldn't talk to me until you came. But now we know the whole story."
"She has a phobia about **people in authority**, like teachers or policemen," the doctor explains. "That's probably why she sent you those messages about the well. She couldn't tell you directly."
"Did you know about the body in the well? Did Fiona tell you about it during her therapy?" Hudson asks.
"Yes, she did. But I never believed her. I thought she **made** the story **up** because she hated that school so much. I never believed she was telling the truth." He **looks ashamed**.
"Excuse me, Dr Willerby. I have to make a call," Hudson says. He walks a few steps away and dials Matthews' number.

"Hudson here, I've just finished talking to Mrs Lambert."

"How is she?" Matthews asks.

"Just a few cuts and bruises, nothing serious. And she has told me everything. For 30 years she tried hard to forget about 1985. She really believed what Mrs Motherwell told her – that she was responsible for Becky's death. But when she saw Penny at the open day, all the **memories** came back. And when Claire told her that Penny was a successful lawyer, Fiona thought, 'Perhaps Penny can help me to **uncover** the past'. But she knew that Penny hated her when they were young, so she couldn't talk to her directly. Instead Fiona sent her a message. And then another one. And after that she felt braver and asked Penny to meet her at the pub."

people in authority	Autoritätspersonen
to make sth. up	eine Geschichte erfinden
to look ashamed	beschämt aussehen
memories *pl*	Erinnerungen
to uncover	aufdecken

"So they met at the Queen's Arms?"

"That's right," Hudson says. "Fiona was scared that Penny wouldn't believe her. But Penny was very interested in the story. She asked Fiona to show her where it had happened, so they left the pub. And because it was raining they took Penny's car. At the field near the well, they sat in the car while Fiona described what she had seen."

"How did Penny react to that?" Matthews asks.

"She wanted to go to the school straight away and tell Miss Musty. That's when Fiona lost her nerve. She said, 'No! I don't want anything to do with that school again.' So Penny decided to go there alone and Fiona went home on foot. That was the last time she saw her. Fiona had no idea what had happened to Penny."

debriefing session	Abschlussbesprechung
to confirm	bestätigen
to feel sorry for sb.	mit jdm. Mitleid haben

"Good morning, everybody," says Hudson on Monday at Scotland Yard. "Team, I'd like you to meet Inspector Matthews, Constable Baker and Constable Stewart. They have been working with me in Shepton Mallet."
The policemen from Somerset and London shake hands.
"Now, let's get started with the **debriefing session**," says Hudson.
"I've got a question, sir," says DI Jarvis. "Was Rebecca Bracknell's death an accident, like Mrs Motherwell said?
"Yes, Miss Sharp **confirmed** Mrs Motherwell's story."
"What did Mrs Motherwell do after she killed Miss Foster?" asks Bradley.
"Well, she had to get rid of the body somehow. So she told Henry to fetch his wheelbarrow and together they took it to the well."
"But why did Fiona think it was Miss Sharp who threw the body in the well?" asks DI Jarvis.
"That evening it was raining," Hudson explains. "So Mrs Motherwell put on her friend's raincoat which was hanging in the office. And that's what Fiona saw – someone wearing Miss Sharp's raincoat."
"Didn't Mrs Motherwell tell Miss Sharp what had happened?"
"No, she didn't," Hudson replies. "All these years Miss Sharp really believed that Emily Foster had gone to Australia."
"And what about Penny Sutton?" Jarvis asks. "She went to the school to talk to Miss Musty about Fiona's story, didn't she?"
"Yes, but that night she met Mrs Motherwell before she had a chance to speak to Miss Musty," Inspector Matthews explains.
"Yes," says Hudson. "For 30 years Mrs Motherwell hid Miss Foster's death. So when Penny Sutton turned up[i] at the school asking questions, she had to kill her, too."

"So she hit Penny on the head and put her body in the boot of her own car?" Bradley asks.
"Yes, exactly," Hudson says. "Then she parked Penny's car next to the field, and Henry took Penny to the well in his wheelbarrow."
"But why did Mrs Motherwell kidnap Fiona?" asks Jarvis.
"When I arrived in the village looking for Penny, Fiona wanted to contact me," Hudson explains. "Remember how she led me to the well? Mrs Motherwell found out about it and wanted to stop her."

Exercise 49: Which term is correct? Welcher der Begriffe ist korrekt? Unterstreichen Sie!

1. car shoe | car boot | car space
2. handcuffs | handgloves | hand shells
3. key bundle | key band | key ring
4. hockey stock | hockey stick | hockey bat

"Now I've got some questions for you," Hudson says. "Jarvis, what's the news about Mr Wiley. Is he still missing?"
"No, sir, we found him yesterday back at his allotment. He's very sorry for everything and wants to make a new start with his wife."
"Oh dear, I hope Brenda Wiley doesn't say yes," Hudson says.
"Don't worry, sir. Mrs Wiley has a new lawyer now. It's Penny's boss, Mr Corbett. The court case is next Thursday."
"Good luck to her," says Hudson. "And what about Mr Sutton? I feel quite sorry for him."

Phrasal Verbs

Das Verb **to turn** wird mit verschiedenen Präpositionen verwendet:

to turn up	auftauchen
to turn off	ausschalten
to turn over	umdrehen
to turn into	sich verwandeln in
to turn down	ablehnen

funeral	Beerdigung
prison	Gefängnis
cheeky	frech

"Yes," says Jarvis. "Poor Sutton... his wife's death and then the murder investigation. He's staying with his sister in Manchester until after the funeral."

"I've got a question, too," says Inspector Matthews. "Mrs Motherwell left Penny Sutton's car at the scrapyard, didn't she?"

"Yes, that's right," answers Bradley. "And Henry was the man I saw on film sitting next to her on the passenger seat."

"But how did they get home from Basingstoke without a car?"

"The train station is just a mile from the scrapyard," Bradley explains. "So they walked there and waited for the first morning train back to Warminster."

"Any more questions?" Hudson asks.

"Just one," says WPC Harvey. "What will happen to Henry if his sister goes to prison?"

"I was worried about that, too," Hudson admits. "But Miss Musty says she will take care of Henry. And you know what? I think he may even be happier without Mrs Motherwell."

Ein **pink elephant** meint entweder etwas ganz außergewöhnliches oder bezeichnet Halluzinationen, die man unter Drogeneinfluss hat.

He looks around the room at his colleagues. "That was a difficult case, but together we solved it. You all did some very good work. So I'm taking you all out for a nice pub lunch at the Pink Elephant!" (i)

"But sir, you never drink on duty!" says Harvey with a cheeky grin.

"There's always a first time," Hudson replies with a laugh.

Death Wasn't the Deal

Tracy Bowens

Der windige Finanzberater Tobias James wird erdrosselt in seiner Londoner Stammkneipe „Aristotle's" aufgefunden. In derselben Nacht stirbt auch Michael Finn, einer der Barkeeper. Die Polizei geht von einem Selbstmord aus und ermittelt nur im Mordfall James. Doch hat Finn sich wirklich selbst umgebracht? Und wie hängen die beiden Fälle miteinander zusammen? Zunächst fehlt den Ermittlern jede Spur, aber nach und nach decken sie ein tödliches Geflecht aus Geldgier, Lügen und Erpressung auf …

B1

1 Murder in the Air

"I wouldn't do that if I were you," Tobias James warned Ian Brown, one of his long-time clients.
"I've listened to you long enough. It's time for me to start running my own affairs," replied Ian Brown angrily.
The line went dead.
A feeling of panic **struck** Tobias. Who else would Ian **persuade** to leave Future Trends Limited, the London financial services firm Tobias had started five years ago? His fingers raced through the contacts stored in his **PDA**.
Tobias was just about to make another call when his office door flew open. Paul Windsor, another long-time client, stormed in. Tobias's secretary, Sarah, **rushed** in after him.

to strike	*hier*: ergreifen
to persuade	überzeugen
PDA	Organizer (Personal Digital Assistant)
to rush	eilen
scum	Abschaum

"I'm sorry, Mr James. I told Mr Windsor that you weren't available."
"It's okay, Sarah. I can talk to Mr Windsor now."
Sarah left the office, closing the door behind her.
Tobias rose from behind his desk. He tried to shake Paul's hand.
"Paul, what can I do for you?"
Paul pushed him in the chest.
"You **scum**. You know what you can do for me. You can get my money back."
Tobias raised his hands.

bailout	Notverkauf
platter	Servierplatte
to slam	(zu)schlagen

"Whoa, Paul! Calm down. What are you talking about?"
Paul pushed Tobias again.
"You know exactly what I'm talking about. I told you to sell my shares and you didn't do it straight away. I've lost thousands because you were waiting to collect your commission."
"Paul, Paul, calm down, please. I know how you feel. I felt awful when I saw that we had sold too late. But it was bad timing. That's all," Tobias said calmly.
"Liar. How stupid do you think I am? You and your risk-taking. If you had followed my orders I would have made money. I know exactly what happened. You thought that the share prices would rise with the news of the bailout. Plus you probably got some kind of commission based on those shares. When you got my order you sat on it for as long as you could. When you finally sold the shares it was too late. You bastard. I'll have your head served on a platter."
Paul Windsor hurried out of the office, slamming the door behind him.

Exercise 1: Odd one out. Welches Wort ist das „schwarze Schaf"? Unterstreichen Sie das nicht in die Reihe passende Wort!

1. wait rush run hurry
2. stomach heart lung toe
3. scum kind immoral bad
4. client customer buyer owner
5. bailout destruction aid money

Sarah watched Paul walk around the corner towards the lifts. When she could no longer see him, she rose and went to Tobias's office. Sarah tapped on the door, then opened it slightly. The distinctive smell of cigar smoke **lingered** in the air. Tobias was sitting at his desk, pressing keys on his PDA. His tie was **crooked** and his shirt **wrinkled**.

to linger	verweilen
crooked	*hier*: zerknittert
wrinkled	faltig
reputation	Ruf
scapegoat	Sündenbock
rumpled	zerknittert
to have a bad temper	schlecht gelaunt sein

"Is it that bad?" Sarah asked.
"Why do you ask?"
"You've been smoking a cigar. You know you aren't supposed to smoke in the office," she replied.
"You know me and my risk-taking. Damn it, Sarah. They all made money because of me during the good times. Did they question any of my decisions then?" Tobias asked.
"No. Everyone knows your **reputation**."
"Exactly. And now they are blaming me for all of their losses."
"It's human nature to look for a **scapegoat**."
"At least you understand me. Sarah, will you marry me?"
"I think you already have too many women in your life. Which reminds me. Both your wife and Arabella Hornsby called," Sarah replied.
"I don't have time to call them back now. I'm meeting Ethan Smith for dinner. Maybe I can manage to keep at least one client today."
"Well, you can't go looking like that."
Tobias inspected his **rumpled** shirt.
"You're right. I didn't know Paul **had** such a **bad temper**. I have another shirt in the cupboard."
"Maybe you should wear another tie, too. That one never seems to bring you much luck."
"You can say that again," Tobias agreed.

Exercise 2: Unscramble the words. Bringen Sie die Buchstaben in die richtige Reihenfolge und bilden Sie sinnvolle Wörter!

1. His tie was okcdero *crooked*.
2. His shirt was kwdirnel ______________.
3. The smell of cigar smoke glendrie ______________ ______________ in the air.
4. People know your pretnituao ______________.
5. Paul has a bad mretep ______________.
6. It's human nature to look for a tcagsopae ______________.

Five minutes later, Tobias walked out of his office wearing a fresh shirt and a different tie. He **stuffed** the tie he had been wearing earlier into his coat pocket.
"How's that?" he asked.
"Much better," Sarah replied.
"Look, I'll probably call in at Aristotle's, you know, in Soho, after seeing Ethan. Do you want to meet me there?"
"Thanks, but no thanks."
"If it's my wife you're worried about, there's no need," Tobias said.
"Is that why you're planning to go home wearing the same tie that you had on when you left the house this morning?"
"Just to be on the safe side. You know how **suspicious** you women are. Well Sarah, my dear, if you change your mind..."

to stuff	stopfen
suspicious	argwöhnisch, misstrauisch

"Don't hold your breath," Sarah replied.

Exercise 3: Prepositions. Lesen Sie weiter und fügen Sie die passende Präposition in die Lücken ein!

at by into near of at

It was ten-thirty **1.** ______ the time Tobias walked **2.** ______ Aristotle's, a stylish, expensive restaurant and bar **3.** ______ Soho Square. Tobias hadn't **expected** to see such a large crowd **4.** ______ that time of night. He recognized Michael Finn, one **5.** ______ the barmen, who was taking a picture of some customers. Tobias **grabbed** a stool **6.** ______ the other end of the bar where Stewart Adams, another barman, was cleaning glasses.

"Good evening, Mr James. What can I get you?" Stewart greeted Tobias.

"A whisky and coke, Stewart."

"You seem to be in a good **mood**."

"I've just had a very successful meeting," Tobias replied.

"You're one of the lucky ones. I hear that the Canary Wharf cafés have turned into

Don't hold your breath.	Da kannst du lange warten.
to expect	erwarten
to grab	schnappen, greifen
mood	Laune

recruitment centre	Jobbörse
at first hand	*hier*: mit eigenen Augen
sip	kleiner Schluck
rumour has it...	Es geht das Gerücht herum ...
back-up plan	Plan B
up one's sleeve	im Ärmel
immortalized	verewigt
regular	*hier*: Stammgast
You don't say!	Allerdings! Sie sagen es!
to stand out from	sich abheben von

recruitment centres. Here you go, Mr James, your whisky and coke."

"I've seen it **at first hand**. It's a little like speed dating." Tobias took a **sip** of his drink. "I never thought I would see such a thing in London's financial district. You know some of the financial industry's biggest players are located on Canary Wharf."

"**Rumour has it** that even the British government is recruiting," the barman said.

"Things would have to be really bad before I think about becoming a school teacher."

"So you have a **back-up plan up your sleeve**, Mr James?"

"You could say that."

Laughter broke out at one of the tables behind Tobias.

"Aristotle's seems to be doing well," Tobias continued.

"Thanks to Michael."

"What do you mean?"

"The customers love his portraits. Everyone wants to be **immortalized** by his paintbrush. We are keeping our **regulars**, and we're getting new customers."

"**You don't say**. People really don't mind him taking pictures of them and then painting their portrait?" Tobias asked.

"On the contrary, Mr James," the barman told Tobias. "They love it. Michael's our secret weapon. He makes us **stand out from** the other restaurants and pubs around town."

"This is a damn good area to be in for that sort of thing. You have all those theatre-goers coming here."

to groan	ächzen
to be in charge	zuständig sein

"You financial types seem to like it, too," Stewart joked.
Just then, Tobias's mobile phone rang. He glanced at the display and decided not to answer the call. He pressed the off-button.
Suddenly, a hand landed on his back.
"Tobias, old boy! What are you doing here?"
Tobias tried not to groan as he turned around.
"Wallace. Good to see you. How's your company treating you?"
"Can't complain. And how's your company doing?" Wallace asked.
"I'm still in charge," Tobias replied.
"You know you can give it up and come to work for us any day."
"Thanks, Wallace. I'll remember that."

Exercise 4: True or false? Welche der folgenden Aussagen sind wahr? Markieren Sie mit richtig ✔ oder falsch – !

1. Tobias also lost Ethan Smith as a client. ❒
2. Sarah plans to meet Tobias at Aristotle's later in the evening. ❒
3. Tobias was successful in the past. ❒
4. The Canary Wharf cafés are hiring people from the financial industry. ❒
5. Tobias is happy to see Wallace. ❒
6. Tobias didn't sell Paul's shares quickly. ❒
7. Paul Windsor is one of Tobias's long-time clients. ❒
8. Sarah is Tobias's wife. ❒
9. Tobias changes his shirt and tie at the office. ❒
10. Tobias smoked a cigarette after Paul left. ❒

to approach	sich nähern
It's on me.	Das geht auf mich.
to slap	einen Klaps geben
knot	Knoten
to snatch	schnappen
to wrap	wickeln

Tobias and Wallace talked until Stewart reminded them that closing time was **approaching**. Tobias was about to pay when Wallace placed enough money on the bar to cover both of their bills.

"**It's on me**. Keep the change, Stewart."

Tobias **slapped** Wallace on the back.

"Thanks, mate."

"Remember what I said, Tobias. If you ever get tired of working for yourself, you know where to come."

"I'll remember."

Tobias watched Wallace leave the bar. Then he got up.

"Night, Stewart."

"Good night, Mr James."

Tobias started to leave. He fished in his pocket for his keys. Soft silk slid through his fingers.

"My tie. I might as well change it here. That's better than doing it in the car."

Tobias went into the toilets. They were empty. Standing in front of the mirror, he pulled the tie he had worn earlier in the day from his pocket and placed it on the shelf. The toilet door opened. Tobias looked in the mirror at the person who had just entered. Tobias laughed.

"I was wondering when I was going to hear from you. But I must say that I didn't expect to see you here. I'm surprised that you can still afford to come to places like this."

Tobias loosened the **knot** of the tie he was wearing.

"In case you've come to beg me, forget it. I'm not going to change my mind."

Without saying a word, the person standing behind Tobias

snatched the tie on the shelf and quickly wrapped it around Tobias's neck. Tobias raised both hands to his throat. Desperately, he tried to dig his fingers in the space between the tie and his throat. But the tension got tighter and tighter. Tobias's breathing became more laboured. He gasped for what little bit of air he could get. And then a final pull of the tie ended the life of Tobias James.

throat	Hals, Kehle
tension	Spannung
laboured	mühsam, schwerfällig
to gasp	japsen
to apologize	sich entschuldigen
staff	Belegschaft

Exercise 5: Match up the translations. Welche Übersetzung ist richtig? Ordnen Sie zu!

1. ☐ mate	a) stöhnen
2. ☐ bill	b) verewigen
3. ☐ groan	c) an einen Ort strömen
4. ☐ gasp	d) Kumpel
5. ☐ snatch	e) nach Luft schnappen
6. ☐ flock	f) Seide
7. ☐ immortalize	g) schnappen
8. ☐ silk	h) Rechnung

It was midnight before the last group of customers left Aristotle's. Michael Finn apologized to the staff members.

"Sorry," he said as they grabbed their coats. "I had to take a photo of that group near the door. It'll be a great painting."

to get on. with sth	mit etw. weitermachen
to yell	brüllen
dumb	dumm
to inquire	nachfragen

Several waiters and waitresses waved their hands as if to say that there was no need to apologize. Frederic Molly, the restaurant manager, was the only one who spoke.

"No apologies needed. You and that camera are keeping us in business. Hey, Ross." He turned his attention to one of the waiters. "Did you check the toilets?"

"Not yet."

"Well **get on with it**."

"Okay, Mr Molly." Ross **yelled** to one of the other waiters. "Wait for me, Eddie."

"Hurry up then," Eddie replied.

Ross ran to the toilets. He entered the women's [i] toilets first. After giving it a quick check, he ran to the men's toilets. He opened the door.

"I'm leaving," Ross heard Eddie yell.

"Wait, wait. I'm coming, Eddie."

This is the **dumbest** job ever, Ross thought. There's never anyone in here. Ross turned around without inspecting the toilets. Outside, his colleagues were standing on the pavement, smoking.

"Everything okay in there?" Frederic **inquired**. His voice was filled with doubt.

"You checked both toilets?"

Ross lit a cigarette. "Yeah, sure."

> Wird an ein englisches Substantiv ein Genitiv-s angehängt, um ein Besitzverhältnis anzuzeigen, so benötigt man einen Apostroph: **Eddie's colleagues are waiting for him.** Im Deutschen hingegen nicht: **Eddies Kollegen warten auf ihn.** Steht das Substantiv im Plural, dann steht der Apostroph nach dem Genitiv-s: **My parents' house.** Ist jedoch die Pluralform eine unregelmäßige, wie bei *men* und *women*, so steht der Apostroph vor dem Genitiv-s: **women's toilets, men's toilets**

Exercise 6: Unscramble the phrases. Ordnen Sie die Wörter zu sinnvollen Sätzen!

1. British recruiting government the is

___

2. a seem in to you good be mood

___

3. smoking have a you been cigar

___

4. a human scapegoat for nature it look to is

___

5. had very I meeting a have successful just

___

6. meeting Ethan dinner I Smith am for

___

It was one o'clock in the morning when Olivia Waters finally decided to get out of bed.

"I'm sure I heard a scream," she had told Andrew, her husband. Andrew had rolled over.

"Michael's probably just got home. Maybe he got lucky and picked up a girl."

Men, Olivia thought.

estranged wife	Noch-Ehefrau
bead of sweat	Schweißperle
survey	überwachen
hot flush	Hitzewallung

"It wasn't that sort of scream."

Now that she was up, Olivia felt silly.

What if Andrew was right? Maybe Michael is with his **estranged wife**. What's her name? Kathy. That's it. Kathy Finn. She has paid more visits lately.

Olivia pressed her ear against the wall. I can't hear a thing. Maybe they went to sleep. **Beads of sweat** broke out on her forehead. Olivia went to the window. She opened it and **surveyed** the ground below. Damn these **hot flushes**, she thought.

Then a figure on the ground caught her attention. She placed her hand over her mouth.

Oh my God, Olivia thought. She ran to the bedroom.

"Andrew. Call the police. There's a dead man in the garden. I think it's Michael Finn."

Exercise 7: Match up the phrases. **Verbinden Sie und bilden Sie sinnvolle Sätze!**

1. ☐ Olivia Waters	**a)** standing on the pavement.
2. ☐ Kathy Finn has	**b)** no need to apologize.
3. ☐ He was	**c)** works at Aristotle's.
4. ☐ There was	**d)** paid more visits lately.
5. ☐ There's a dead man	**e)** got out of bed.
6. ☐ Andrew	**f)** is Olivia Waters's husband.
7. ☐ Michael Finn	**g)** in the garden.

2 Discovery at Aristotle's

Detective Inspector Roberta Nettles rushed into the lift of the police station just as the clock **struck** ten. Hurry up, she thought as the lift moved upwards. The doors opened on the third floor. Roberta rushed out, almost colliding with a **pale** woman with bloodshot eyes and brown hair.

"Excuse me," Roberta apologized.

The woman dabbed her eyes with a tissue and disappeared behind the lift doors.

Roberta made a cup of coffee and grabbed a biscuit. On her way to her desk she **pumped** her colleague, Sam Meadows, **for information**.

"Who was that?"

Sam looked up from his computer screen. "Who?"

"The weeping woman?"

"Oh her. Kathy Finn. Her husband killed himself last night. Or so they say."

to strike	*hier*: schlagen (Uhrzeit)
pale	blass
to pump so. for information	etw. aus jmd. heraus-quetschen

Roberta took a bite of her biscuit.

"Ouch, that's tough. You don't think it was a suicide?"

Sam was just about to answer when Detective Chief Inspector Oscar Peters, Roberta's boss, walked out of his office.

"Don't get too comfortable, Roberta. We're going to Aristotle's. There's been a murder."

Roberta gulped down some coffee and handed her cup to Sam.

swiftly	flink, schnell
to occure	passieren, vonstattengehen

"Here."

"Sounds more fun than writing up a suicide," Sam commented.

Roberta felt the adrenaline running through her veins as she ran after Oscar.

Oscar drove swiftly to Soho Square. When he and Roberta arrived, they saw a few bystanders gathered behind police tape. Reporters and cameramen were positioning themselves near the front door of the restaurant. They wanted to get the best pictures. One of them ran up to Oscar.

"Chief Inspector Peters. Is it true that the murder actually occurred last night?"

Exercise 8: Choose the correct verb forms. Lesen Sie weiter und ergänzen Sie die passende Verbform!

Oscar did not slow down. He gently **1.** push ____________ the reporter aside.

"We'll be **2.** make ______________ a statement to the press later this afternoon."

"If it's true, how are you going to **3.** round up ________________ suspects? You don't even **4.** know ___________________ who was in the restaurant last night."

Roberta saw that Oscar was frustrated. She **5.** place ___________________ herself between Oscar and the reporter. "You heard Chief Inspector Peters. You'll get your questions answered at the press conference later this afternoon."

The reporter **6.** scribble ___________ notes on his pad.

An officer who was guarding the door **7.** see ______________ Oscar and Roberta approaching. He stepped aside.

"You'll find the victim in the men's toilets, sir."

Oscar nodded his thanks. Roberta followed him into the restaurant. Hysterical **shrieks** came from the dining room. A tall, well-built policeman in his mid-thirties was talking to a woman holding a pair of plastic gloves. She started to say something but then waved the gloves in the air as she tried to fight back tears. The policeman **patted** the woman on the shoulder.

"You've been very helpful. Excuse me."

Rising from his chair, he greeted Oscar and Roberta. He shook Oscar's hand and then smiled as he shook Roberta's.

"DCI Peters. Roberta."

Oscar spoke first.

"Edmonds. Good to see you."

shriek	Schrei
to pat	tätscheln

Another weeping woman, Roberta thought, looking at the woman with the plastic gloves.

"Who's she?"

"The cleaning lady. She found the body this morning. With one of the other staff members."

Oscar looked at the woman and then turned his attention back to Police Constable Edmonds.

"Why did it take them so long to find the body?"

to estimate	schätzen
cubicle	Kabine
to have a knack for sth.	eine Vorliebe für etw. haben
to be related to	in Verbindung stehen mit
to solve	lösen

"Apparently, one of the waiters didn't check the toilets very carefully last night," PC Edmonds replied.

"And none of the customers had to use the toilets last night?" Roberta inquired.

"The time of death is **estimated** at close to closing time. The toilets have two **cubicles**. The victim's feet were against the door, so it was hard to open. Our guess is that anyone trying to use the blocked cubicle simply thought it was in use and went to the other one."

Oscar looked around.

"Who's here now?"

"The forensic team is in the toilets, sir. More staff members are being questioned[i] in the kitchen."

"And who's the victim?" Roberta asked.

"Tobias James," Constable Edmonds said.

"The Tobias James?" Roberta asked in surprise.

"The one and only," Edmonds replied.

Oscar looked at PC Edmonds and then at Roberta.

"Wait. What am I missing here? Is this Tobias James famous?"

Roberta answered.

"In the financial world he is. He seemed to **have a knack** for adding to the family **fortune**."

Oscar felt stupid.

"James. **He's related** to Sir Stanley James. That's all I need. This is going to be a high-profile case. They are going to want us to **solve** this murder quickly. I think it's time that I take a look at Mr Tobias James."

"The toilets are over there, sir."

"Thanks, Edmonds."

Mit der Passiv-Konstruktion **to be + being + Partizip II** drückt man aus, dass etwas gerade geschieht (Verlaufsform): **He is reading. The book is being read.**

Exercise 9: Questions. Bilden Sie vollständige Fragesätze und fragen Sie nach den unterstrichenen Informationen!

1. Tobias James was killed around 11:30 p.m.

   ____

2. His body was found in the toilets.

   ____

3. The cleaning lady found his body.

   ____

4. The inspector drove to Aristotle's.

   ____

5. We're going to Aristotle's to investigate the death of Tobias James.

   ____

6. It look them so long to find the body because the toilets hadn't been checked carefully.

   ____

   ____

ajar	angelehnt, halboffen
to dust for fingerprints	Fingerabdrücke sichern

The door to the toilets was ajar. Oscar recognized various members of the forensic team. They were searching the crime scene for evidence. Not much use dusting for fingerprints, he thought even though he knew it was standard procedure. Plenty of people have passed through here.

Exercise 10: Synonyms. **Lesen Sie weiter und unterstreichen Sie die Synonyme der unten stehenden Begriffe im folgenden Abschnitt!**

clue | forensic doctor | could | if not

Unless, that is, they find the fingerprints of a known **perpetrator** already in our database. That might give us a lead. The head medical examiner, Morris Turner, had just finished examining the **corpse** when Oscar and Roberta approached him.
"Chief Inspector, Roberta," he greeted them.

Oscar stared at the dead body sprawled halfway in and halfway out of the cubicle. Tobias James's finely tailored suit, manicured nails and gelled blond hair echoed Roberta's previous description.
"Hello Morris," Oscar said. "What do we have here?"
Morris bent down and pointed to Tobias James's neck.
"Death by strangulation. I would say that the murder weapon was a soft piece of material. Something like silk. Maybe a tie or a scarf."

"He wasn't killed as he was coming out of the cubicle, was he?" Roberta inquired.
"No. It seems as if he was killed over there, near the sinks. Someone dragged his body over here and stuffed it into the cubicle. Look, you can see black scuff marks."

perpetrator	Eindringling
corpse	Leiche
sprawled	ausgestreckt
gelled	gegelt (Haar)
sink	Waschbecken
scuff mark	Abnutzungs-spur

zip-locked	mit Reißverschluss
to hunt	jagen

"From his shoes," Roberta guessed.
Morris confirmed her theory.
"Exactly."
"PC Edmonds said that the time of death was around closing. That would place it at around 11:30 p.m., is that right?" Oscar asked.
Morris rose.
"I would say so."
"Excuse me, sir." PC Edmonds was standing behind Oscar and Roberta. "More staff members from last night have arrived."
"Thank you, Edmonds. Roberta, why don't you and Edmonds go and interview them?" Oscar said.
After they had left, Morris told some members of his team to cover Tobias James's body with a sheet. Morris and Oscar moved closer to the sinks. They were careful not to destroy possible evidence.
"What about his personal belongings?" Oscar asked Morris.
Morris turned to one of his assistants.
"Jones, can you bring us the victim's personal belongings?"
"Yes, sir."
Jones returned carrying a plastic, **zip-locked** bag. He handed it to Morris. Oscar put on a pair of plastic gloves and then took the bag from Morris. It contained a leather wallet, keys and a PDA.
Oscar took the PDA out of the bag.
"Modern technology is great, Morris. We used to have to **hunt** for phone records. Now we can get a lot of the information we need with the press of a few keys. I wonder what this little thing can tell us."
Morris watched Oscar study the PDA's display.
"Anything interesting?"
"Seems as if he missed a call from someone named Arabella. Based on your estimated time of death, he was still alive when she called."

factual	sachlich
to consider sth. to be sth.	etw. für etwas halten
to know the drill	wissen, wie etw. läuft
scoop	Knüller
to release	hinausgeben, freigeben
sealed	versiegelt
tousled	verwuschelt (Haar)
lad	Junge, Bursche
to summon back	zurückrufen
at the top of one's game	in Bestform
to trail off	verstummen

"If he was here, maybe he didn't hear the phone ring," Oscar said.
"Or maybe he didn't want to talk to her. And it looks as if he was quite interested in his bank account. It seems to be one of the last websites he accessed."
"His business was finance." Morris's tone was factual.
Oscar dropped the PDA into the plastic bag. He passed the bag to Morris.
"What are you going to do with all of those reporters out there?" Morris asked.
"I've already told them that we're holding a press conference later this afternoon. At the time I didn't know why they considered this case to be a scoop."
"Tobias James made a name for himself," Morris commented.
"So I hear. Look, you know the drill. Make sure none of the details concerning Tobias James's death are released to the press."
"My lips are sealed."

Roberta listened to Ross, the youth sitting in front of her. His breath smelled of cigarette smoke. His hair was tousled and he looked tired. Poor lad, Roberta thought. He had probably just gone to bed when his boss summoned him back to Aristotle's.
"I'm not in trouble with the police, am I?"
Roberta realized that this was at least the third time he had asked that question. Funny how murder touches the lives of people. This poor lad was just a waiter trying to earn a bit of extra money. Now he was involved in a murder investigation.

Exercise 11: Idiomatic expressions. **Welche Bedeutung haben die folgenden Sätze? Kreuzen Sie an!**

1. It was a scoop.
   a) ❐ It was a way to get ice cream.
   b) ❐ It was an important news story.

2. Morris confirmed her theory.
   a) ❐ Morris proved her theory to be true.
   b) ❐ Morris said that she was wrong.

3. You can see black scuff marks.
   a) ❐ You can see a drawing on the floor.
   b) ❐ You can see marks made by someone's shoes.

4. The door was ajar.
   a) ❐ The door was slightly open.
   b) ❐ The door was closed.

5. Maybe they will find the fingerprints of a known perpetrator.
   a) ❐ Maybe they will find the prints of a famous person.
   b) ❐ Maybe they will find the prints of a known criminal.

The barman, Stewart, had seemed truly sorry that Tobias James was dead.
"He was an intelligent man. Always at the top of his game. I enjoyed talking to him." Stewart's voice had trailed off, as if he were remembering some of their discussions.

to tip	*hier*: Trinkgeld geben
to be echoed	widerhallen

"Did you see him talking with anyone else last night?"
"Yes. Wallace, a friend of his, came over to the bar. They talked about work. I remember Wallace telling Mr James that he could always come and work with him if he ever needed to."
"Oh, was Mr James having financial problems?"
"He spoke about a deal or two that had gone wrong. But that's normal business these days."
"He still **tipped** well?"
"He was never mean. He was a good customer," Stewart had replied.

Exercise 12: Choose the correct alternative. Unterstreichen Sie die richtige Variante der Verbformen!

1. If I hear from Michael Finn, I will / will have call you.
2. If only I had / will checked the toilets.
3. If Tobias hasn't / hadn't gone to the toilets, he would still be alive.
4. I will call you if I would remember / remember something.
5. If I were you, I wouldn't / will sell.
6. If I had win / won a lot of money, I would invest it in property.

Stewart's words **had been echoed** by Frederic.
"I've been managing this place for five years. Tobias James was one of our best customers. This is a sad day indeed."
Sad for whom, Roberta wondered. Tobias James and his family or you and your business?
Frederic had asked, as if reading her mind, "Will I be able to open for business tonight?"

Roberta had told him that it would be one or two days before Aristotle's could open again. She had then changed the subject. "Are all the staff members here who were working last night?"

to mumble	murmeln

"Everybody except for Finn. Michael that is. He's our other barman."
"Finn," Roberta had **mumbled**. "I've heard that name before. Is he famous?"
"Not yet, but he will be one day. You may have seen one of his paintings in the dining room."
"Maybe so. I'll take a look on the way out. Where is he?"
"Don't know. I phoned him but there was no answer."
"One more thing. We'll need a list of the customers who were here last night. Can you get that for me?" Roberta had asked.

Exercise 13: Possessive apostrophes. Bilden Sie Possessivkonstruktionen und fügen Sie den Apostroph – falls nötig – an der richtigen Stelle ein!

1. Roberta / Notizblock ____________________
2. Mr. James / Geldprobleme ____________________
3. Stewart / Worte ____________________
4. ihr Ehemann / Tod ____________________
5. seine Kunden / Besuche ____________________
6. Wallace / Freund ____________________

"I'll do my best," Frederic had responded.
Ross's voice reminded her that he was still there. "If only I'd checked the toilets carefully last night. Then we would have

with ease	mit Leichtigkeit
to commit	begehen
to exclaim	ausrufen
widow	Witwe
steering wheel	Lenkrad
to nod	nicken
fit	Anfall
unlikely	unwahrscheinlich

found his body last night."

Roberta tried to make Ross feel better.

"That probably wouldn't have made much difference."

"But it would have been better if someone had found the body during opening hours, wouldn't it?"

Roberta saw Oscar walk into the kitchen. She closed her note pad.

"Thank you, Ross. Here's my card. Feel free to call me if you think of anything else. You've been very helpful."

She joined Oscar by the kitchen door.

"Where to now?"

"I think it's time we visited Mrs Tobias James. I wouldn't want her to hear of her husband's death from those reporters out there."

The Jameses lived in Notting Hill. Oscar navigated the London traffic **with ease** until he and Roberta reached Notting Hill Gate. Cars clogged the street. The traffic jam did not bother Oscar. It gave him the opportunity to think.

"What do you think happened to Michael Finn?" he asked.

"I wish I knew. I feel that I'm missing something."

"Something to do with Michael Finn?"

"I know I've heard that name before." Suddenly she remembered. "He **committed** suicide," she **exclaimed**.

Oscar took his eyes off the road and looked at Roberta.

"What?"

"This morning. Actually, he committed suicide last night. But this morning I ran into his **widow** at the police station."

Oscar tapped the **steering wheel** with his fingers.

"Suicide, eh? Do you think there's a connection between his suicide and Tobias James's death?"

Exercise 14: Prepositions. **Lesen Sie weiter und fügen Sie die passenden Präpositionen ein!**

about at for in of to with

Roberta thought **1.** ______ a minute. "You mean do I think Michael Finn killed Tobias James and then committed suicide?"

Oscar **nodded** without taking his eyes off the road.

"No, I don't think so. Everyone **2.** ______ Aristotle's seemed **3.** ______ like Tobias James, or at least his money. Michael Finn didn't even seem to have much contact with Mr James last night. Why would he kill Mr James and then commit suicide?"

"Guilt? Things like that happen all the time. Michael Finn killed Tobias James in a **fit** **4.** ______ rage. Then he went home. He couldn't live with what he had done. So he killed himself," Oscar said.

"Your theory might work if Michael Finn and Tobias James had contact **5.** ______ each other outside the bar. It is very **unlikely** that they did. What reason would he have for killing Tobias James **6.** ______ a fit of rage? His tip wasn't big enough?"

Oscar laughed at Roberta's sarcasm. "My theory is still something to think **7.** ______."

maid	Dienstmädchen
to take a puff	einen Zug nehmen, paffen
tray	Tablett

When Oscar and Roberta finally reached the Jameses' house, they were greeted by a **maid**. The investigators showed her their police badges.

"Is Mrs James in?" Oscar asked.

The maid was shocked to see the police standing at the front door. "Yes, she is. Please follow me."

The maid took Oscar and Roberta to the library.

"Please wait here. I will tell Mrs James that you wish to speak to her."

A few minutes later, two women entered the library. A tall, blond woman in her late forties stepped forward.

"Elisabeth James." She waved her hand towards the shorter, dark-haired woman standing behind her. "This is my friend, Tina Cutter. Please have a seat."

Oscar and Roberta sat down.

"Mary, will you bring some tea for our guests, please?" Elisabeth called the maid as she turned to Oscar and Roberta. "You do want tea, don't you?"

Oscar and Roberta accepted.

"What can I do for you?" Elisabeth inquired.

Oscar spoke carefully: "We have some bad news about your husband. I'm sorry to say that… he's dead. He was killed last night."

Tina let out a small shriek. Elisabeth stood up. She walked to the fireplace, reached for a pack of cigarettes and pulled one out. Oscar rose to light it for her.

"Thank you." She **took a puff**.

"So, Tina," she said, looking at her friend, "that explains why Tobias didn't come home last night."

Mary entered carrying a **tray** with a teapot and four cups. She placed it on the table.

"Thank you, Mary," Elisabeth said.

Exercise 15: Match up the translations. Welche Übersetzung ist richtig? Ordnen Sie zu!

1. ☐ dab	a) hinkritzeln
2. ☐ hot flush	b) schriller Schrei
3. ☐ scribble	c) Noch-Ehefrau
4. ☐ estranged wife	d) abtupfen
5. ☐ shriek	e) Geliebte
6. ☐ mistress	f) Hitzewallung

Tina Cutter dried her eyes with the palm of her hand. Then she spoke for the first time.

"Elisabeth was worried when Tobias didn't come home last night."

"Did you call the police?" Roberta asked.

Elisabeth shrugged her shoulders. She took another puff of her cigarette.

"Why should I have called the police? Tobias is, I mean was, a grown man. He could do whatever he wanted to do."

Oscar and Roberta exchanged glances. Elisabeth walked from the fireplace to the sofa and sat down next to Tina.

Tina grasped Elisabeth's free hand.

"Did Tobias die in a car accident?" she asked.

"No. He was murdered," Oscar responded.

palm of one's hand	Handfläche
to shrug	mit den Schultern zucken
glance	Blick
to grasp	ergreifen

mistress	Geliebte
to dump so.	jmd. den Laufpass geben
to claim	behaupten
to make up	Frieden schließen
to squeeze	drücken
merely	lediglich
to be cut from a different cloth	aus einem anderen Holz geschnitzt sein
enemy	Feind

"Ha," Elisabeth laughed. "If you're looking for suspects, I suggest that you start with Tobias's **mistress**. Oh, excuse me, I mean ex-mistress. She's called Arabella Hornsby."

"Why do you recommend that we speak to Ms Hornsby?" Roberta asked.

Elisabeth took another puff of her cigarette before she replied. "Arabella appeared last night on our, I mean my, doorstep. She told me that she was Tobias's mistress and that he had just **dumped** her. Apparently he had **claimed** that he could no longer pay for her flat and support her expensive lifestyle. She declared that no one treated her like that. She planned to make Tobias pay for what he had done to her. Based on that, I would say that she's an obvious choice, wouldn't you?"

Roberta studied Elisabeth while she spoke.

"How did her statement make you feel?"

"You mean hearing that she was his mistress?" Elisabeth James asked. "The news (i) didn't surprise me. It was Tobias's style. All of his friends had a mistress. So it was only natural that he had to have one, too. I think it made him feel powerful. When he didn't come home last night, I thought they had **made up**. That's why I didn't call the police."

Elisabeth looked at Tina and **squeezed** her hand.

Achtung! Einige Wörter im Englischen haben keine Singularform, sie stehen immer im Plural, verhalten sich aber grammatisch wie Singularformen: **Nachrichten – news: This is good news** (Pl.). Genau umgekehrt verhält es sich mit dem Beispiel **Polizei – police:** Das Wort *police* im Englischen steht immer im Plural: **The police are coming.**

"Sorry, Tina. You know I wasn't talking about Daniel."
Tina merely smiled weakly.

Exercise 16: Fill in the blanks. **Setzen Sie das richtige Wort ein!**

puff sealed top made hold gulped knack cloth

1. They had a big fight yesterday, but now they've ______ up.
2. He's different from the others. He's cut from a different ______.
3. Sarah said she might come, but don't ______ your breath.
4. He's doing really well. He's at the ______ of his game.
5. I won't tell anyone. My lips are ______.
6. Roberta ______ down her coffee quickly.
7. He's very good at making money. He has a ______ for it.
8. Elisabeth took another ______ of her cigarette.

Elisabeth's attention returned to Oscar and Roberta.
"Daniel, Tina's husband, is cut from a different cloth."
"Did your husband have any other enemies?" Oscar asked.
"I'm sure there are a lot of people who aren't happy with the

stock market	Aktienbörse
piercing	durchdringend

financial advice my husband gave them. They've lost fortunes on the **stock market**. His secretary would know more. I suggest you talk to her."

Full of suggestions, aren't you, Oscar thought.

He gave Elisabeth a **piercing** stare. She stared back, waiting for him to ask her another question. Instead, Oscar rose from the chair.

"Thank you, Mrs James. I think that's all for now."

Elisabeth James saw the two inspectors out and watched them get into their car.

Back in the car, Oscar and Roberta decided to pay a visit to Tobias's secretary before stopping for lunch.

"What did you think of Mrs Tobias James?" Oscar asked Roberta.

"Her husband's death didn't seem to upset her very much."

"Did you notice anything else?"

"She wasn't very curious about how he died," Roberta replied.

"Exactly. I wonder if she is as untouched by her husband's love affair as she claims to be."

Exercise 17: Synonyms. Lesen Sie weiter und unterstreichen Sie die Synonyme der folgenden Wörter!

belongings | went into | called | looked around | remarked | detested | angry

The two investigators found Tobias's secretary packing his personal items. She looked up as they entered the office. There were tears in her eyes. She stuffed a tissue into her pocket before speaking to them.

"You must be Chief Inspector Peters and Inspector Nettles."
"You're well informed, Mrs...," Oscar said.
"Just call me Sarah," the secretary said. "Mrs James phoned. She said you would be coming." Roberta inspected the office.
"Did she also ask you to pack up her husband's belongings?"
"Yes, she did. I am to send the things to their, I mean her, house when I've finished." Sarah sniffed.
Poor woman, Roberta thought. She reached into her handbag and pulled out a packet of tissues. She gave one to Sarah.
"Mrs James is very efficient," Roberta commented.
"Oh yes, she is," Sarah replied. "She and Mr James made a formidable couple."
"Do you know of anyone who hated Mr James enough to kill him?" Oscar asked.
"Paul Windsor was probably mad enough to kill him yesterday," Sarah said. She immediately covered her lips with her fingers. "Oh, I probably shouldn't have said that. I don't want to cause trouble for Mr Windsor."

"The truth isn't going to cause problems for anyone," Roberta commented.
Sarah leaned against the desk.
"Mr Windsor and Mr James had a terrible argument yesterday. Here, in the office."

Roberta retrieved her note pad from her handbag.
"What was the fight about?"
"Good investments gone bad."
"Do you know Arabella Hornsby?" Roberta asked.
Sarah's eyes narrowed. "Yes, she's a client."
Roberta and Oscar exchanged glances.
"Do you know if Mr James was meeting anyone at Aristotle's last night?" Oscar asked.
"No. He was simply going to stop by after dinner. But both Mrs James and Ms Hornsby knew he would be there."
"Oh really," Oscar and Roberta said in unison.
"Yes, both of them phoned. They called earlier, but Mr James didn't have time to talk to them. He instructed me to tell them where they could find him if they called again."
"Who did he have dinner with?" Oscar asked.
"Ethan Smith. Mr James was very happy with the outcome of their meeting. I can give you his number and address if you'd like. You probably want the same for Mr Windsor and Ms Hornsby."

Exercise 18: Question tags. Fügen Sie das jeweils richtige Frageanhängsel an!

1. You will be able to help me, *won't you* ?
2. You didn't see the killer, ________________?
3. You held onto my shares, ________________?
4. He has left the office, ________________?
5. She found the body, ________________?
6. We won't be able to open tonight, ________________?
7. You don't think he killed himself, ________________?

to retrieve	herausholen
to narrow	sich verschmälern
unison	Einklang
outcome	Ausgang, Ergebnis
sitting room	Wohnzimmer

Oscar smiled. "Thank you. That would be very helpful."

Tina Cutter had cried all the way home. Now, at home in her **sitting room**, she couldn't stop thinking about Tobias.

Tobias, dead. How will Daniel take the news? Oh my God. Does he even know? She picked up the phone.

"Daniel. It's me." She tried to sound calm.

"Tina. What's wrong? Are you okay?"

Her voice shook.

"Yes. Yes, I'm fine. Daniel, it's Tobias."

"What about him?" her husband asked.

Tina paused. Daniel's tone had changed. Should I even be telling him this over the phone?

"Tina, are you still there?"

Too late. I have to tell him.

"Daniel, Tobias is dead."

Tina heard a noise on the other end of the line and then the line went dead.

Exercise 19: Rhymes. **Finden Sie Begriffe im vorangehenden Abschnitt, die sich auf die Übersetzung der folgenden Wörter reimen!**

fein | schütteln | zeigen | stoßen | seufzen | Knochen

1. ____________ 4. ____________

2. ____________ 5. ____________

3. ____________ 6. ____________

3 Death for No Reason

pale	bleich
desperate	verzweifelt
sympathetically	*hier*: mitleidig
to tremble	zittern
to sniffle	die Nase hochziehen
to lead	führen, begleiten
to blow one's nose	sich die Nase putzen

Jennifer York was deciding what to eat for lunch when a woman dressed in black walked through the door of Shipman Investigations (i). She looked very **pale** and quite **desperate**. Jennifer felt extremely sorry for the sad woman and smiled at her **sympathetically**, but she didn't quite know what to say.
"May I help you?" she asked as if she were speaking to a child.
The woman's voice was **trembling** when she spoke.
"I came to see Henry Shipman."
"Please have a seat, Mrs..."
The woman **sniffled**, and Jennifer was afraid that she was going to cry. She **led** the woman to a chair and sat down on a chair in front of her.
"I'm sorry," the woman said while **blowing her nose**. "My name is Kathy Finn. My husband died last night. An officer at the police station said that Mr Shipman might be able to help me."

> **i** Wenn etwas gerade vor sich geht und dann ein anderes Ereignis eintritt, so wird dies im Englischen mit folgender Konstruktion ausgedrückt: **Past Progressive + when + Simple Past.**
> Das plötzlich eintretende Ereignis unterbricht das vorher schon länger anhaltende:
> **Jennifer *was deciding* what to eat, *when* (suddenly) a woman *walked* through the door.**

Exercise 20: Choose the correct verb forms. Lesen Sie weiter und setzen Sie die Verben in Klammern in die richtige Zeitform!

Henry Shipman **1.** read ______________ and listening to classical music when Jennifer **2.** knock ______________ on the door of his office.

"Come in," he shouted.

"I'm sorry to bother you, but Mrs Finn would like **3.** talk ______________ to you."

Henry turned down the volume. "Who's Mrs Finn and what's it about?"

"She's the woman **4.** sit ______________ in the waiting room. She **5.** want ______________ to talk to you about the death of her husband."

"Sounds interesting. Please send her in," Henry said.

Jennifer **6.** return ______________. Kathy Finn stood next to her.

Henry rose. "Mrs Finn. First let me **7.** tell ______________ you how sorry I am to hear about your husband's death."

"Thank you," Kathy replied.

"Now, how can I help you?" Henry asked Kathy Finn.
Kathy pulled at the tissue in her hand.
"The police think that my husband killed himself. But that's not true, my husband wasn't depressive.
"The police must think there was a reason."
"The two of us were separated, but we were about to get back together. My husband also had a history of financial problems. But **recently** he was making a lot of money selling his paintings. He was paying off his debts."
"Did you tell this to the police?"
"Yes, but the investigator in charge didn't listen to me. One officer, Sam Meadows, suggested that I come and see you. He said you could help me," Katy Finn explained.

recently	kürzlich, in letzter Zeit
hallway	Diele, Hausflur
to hug	umarmen

Sam's a good policeman, Henry thought. If he doesn't think Kathy's husband killed himself, he probably didn't.
"Did Sam Meadows tell you why he didn't believe that your husband killed himself?" he asked Mrs Finn.
"He said that there was no note. People who kill themselves usually leave one."
"The investigator in charge would have noticed the same thing. Were there signs of a robbery? Did anyone visit him?"
"No. It seems as if my husband was alone in the flat when he died." Kathy Finn ran her hands through her hair.
"I know it sounds strange, but I know my husband didn't kill himself. He didn't jump out of the window. Please help me. If you don't, nobody else will."
Henry looked at Kathy's sad face. This woman needs to know the truth. I can't send her home without helping her.
"Do you have the key to your husband's flat?" he asked.
"Yes."

Henry got up.
"Jennifer, I'll be out of the office for a few hours. Mrs Finn and I are going to pay a visit to her husband's flat," he said as he and Kathy Finn walked into the waiting room.

Exercise 21: True or false? Welche der folgenden Aussagen sind wahr? Markieren Sie mit richtig ✔ oder falsch – !

1. Kathy Finn was Michael's ex-wife. ❒
2. All of the policemen think that Michael killed himself. ❒
3. Henry Shipman knows Sam Meadows. ❒
4. Sam Meadows believes that Michael Finn didn't kill himself. ❒
5. Michael Finn's financial situation was improving. ❒
6. Kathy Finn is very sad about her husband's death. ❒
7. Elisabeth James thinks that Arabella Hornsby might have killed Tobias. ❒

Olivia Waters was about to go to the market when she saw Kathy Finn and Henry Shipman in the hallway. She hugged Kathy Finn. "I'm sorry about Michael. He was a good neighbour."
"Thank you," Kathy Finn responded.
Olivia Waters looked at Henry. I hope she hasn't already got a new boyfriend, she thought. Maybe that's why Michael killed himself. This one is more handsome than Michael. He seems to have more muscles, too. The grey in his brown hair makes him look very important.

to lower	senken
lock	Schloss
paper clip	Büroklammer
to bend	biegen
to pick	*hier*: knacken (Schloss)

Olivia introduced herself to Oscar.
"Hello, I'm Olivia Waters. I live here, next door."
"Olivia found Michael's body," Kathy added.
"I discovered his body by accident," Olivia explained. "I heard a scream and got out of bed. Then I saw his body in the garden. It was terrible."
"You said you heard a scream," Henry said. "Did Michael have a guest yesterday evening?"
Olivia remembered what her husband had said. He had thought that Michael might have had a girl with him. But I can't tell them that, Olivia thought.
"No, I don't think so," she said.
"You don't think so?" Henry repeated Olivia's words.
"I can't say for sure. We, my husband and I, were in bed when Michael came home."
"You didn't see anyone in the garden?" Henry asked.
He definitely asks a lot of questions, Olivia thought. He must be a policeman.
"No, just poor Michael. I told the other policemen the same thing. I'm sorry I can't be of more help."
Suddenly Olivia's eyes got bigger.
"You don't think Michael killed himself, do you?"
"No, I don't," Kathy answered. "I've asked Mr Shipman to help me find out the truth about Michael's death."
Olivia was happy to hear that the man was not Kathy's new boyfriend. She looked at her watch.
"I must get to the market. But, if you ask me, Michael didn't kill himself. He was looking forward to being with you again, Kathy."
Kathy lowered her head. Olivia hugged Kathy again before she walked down the hallway.

Exercise 22: Indirect speech. Setzen Sie die Sätze in die indirekte Rede!

1. I'm sorry to hear about Michael's death.

   She said she was sorry to hear about Michael's death.

2. I heard a scream.

   She said ______________________________

3. I'll let you know if I think of anything else.

   She said ______________________________

4. What do you mean?

   She asked ______________________________

5. I don't think anything is missing.

   She said ______________________________

6. Where did you go yesterday?

   She asked ______________________________

After Olivia Waters had gone, Kathy turned to the door of Michael's flat. She placed the key in the **lock**, but Henry stopped her before she could unlock the door.
"Wait."
He took a **paper clip** out of his pocket and **bent** it. Slowly, he placed it in the lock. The door opened.
"This is an easy lock to **pick**," he said.
"Do you think a robber picked the lock on the night of Michael's death?" Kathy asked.

"If Michael didn't kill himself, he was either killed by a thief or by someone he knew."
Kathy **shivered**. "I can't think of anyone who would have killed Michael."

to shiver	frösteln, schaudern
possession	Besitztum
canvas	Leinwand, Gemälde

"Then he might have surprised a thief."
Henry looked around the one-bedroom flat. There was not much furniture, a laptop computer and a digital camera sat on a table near the door. Henry guessed that the table served as both a desk and an eating area. There was also a sofa and a coffee table in the room.
There's not much here to steal, Henry thought. Maybe Kathy knows more about her husband's **possessions** than I do.
"Kathy, why don't you take a look around and see if anything has gone missing?" Henry suggested.
Kathy gave Henry a blank stare.
"I wouldn't know if anything was missing."
Henry looked puzzled. "What do you mean?"
"This wasn't Michael's flat. He moved out of our flat when we separated. He rented this flat from a friend who is working in France at the moment. The furniture belongs to Michael's friend."
Kathy pointed to the laptop computer and the digital camera. "Those were Michael's. And of course all of the paintings and **canvases** belonged to him."
"And the bedroom?" Henry asked.
"I can look around," Kathy said.
She disappeared into the bedroom.
The paintings leaning against the wall near the large window caught Henry's attention. He began to study them. Kathy returned to the sitting room.
"It doesn't look as if anything is missing," she said.
"Did Michael paint these?" Henry asked.

Exercise 23: Hidden words. In diesem Gitternetz sind zehn Begriffe zum Thema „Wohnen“ versteckt. Welche sind es?

A	B	E	D	R	O	O	M	A	M	P	L
T	R	A	N	I	W	N	E	V	B	M	O
L	K	I	H	A	L	L	W	A	Y	M	Y
F	U	R	N	I	T	U	R	E	R	A	X
T	R	A	C	K	I	N	G	E	N	T	O
N	B	E	N	T	L	A	K	T	J	F	Y
D	O	O	R	W	E	R	E	P	S	L	Q
E	V	M	R	E	I	N	Y	R	O	A	A
S	N	S	T	L	E	P	S	L	Y	T	S
K	W	E	R	K	F	Q	Y	P	E	D	O
I	S	T	A	I	R	S	H	N	F	U	F
S	L	T	B	V	L	O	C	K	E	I	A

1. ______________________ 6. ______________________

2. ______________________ 7. ______________________

3. ______________________ 8. ______________________

4. ______________________ 9. ______________________

5. ______________________ 10. ______________________

subject	*hier*: Modell
to knock sth. over	etw. umstoßen
to file	abheften

"Yes." Kathy smiled. "He started painting Aristotle's customers for fun a few months ago. Michael worked as a barman at Aristotle's, you know. In the beginning, painting the customers was just a hobby. Then one of his **subjects** asked to see the results. Michael showed it to him and the man actually bought the painting. Other customers heard about the paintings and started to buy them, too. Some of them were even coming to him and asked him to paint them."

"Did Michael paint while he was at work?"

"Oh, no," Kathy replied. "He took pictures of the customers. When he got home, he downloaded them and later painted from the images on the laptop."

"Interesting," Henry said.

Kathy continued to look at the paintings while Henry was looking out of the window. He imagined how Michael's body must have looked in the garden below.

It would be easy to push someone out of this window, he thought. The flat is not full of furniture, so two people could have struggled without **knocking** anything **over**. The scream that Olivia heard was possibly Michael's when he fell. The thief must have picked the lock. That was why the police had not found any evidence of a break-in. The only question is, what would a thief want to steal from Michael Finn?

Kathy drove Henry back to his office.

"I have to be honest," he told her. "I don't have much evidence to work with at the moment. However, I have a feeling that you are right. I don't think your husband killed himself. I'll call you as soon as I get more information."

"Thank you, Mr Shipman."

Jennifer was **filing** papers when Henry entered the waiting room. She stopped as soon as she saw him.

Exercise 24: Plural forms. **Wie lautet die Pluralform der folgenden Substantive? Gibt es eine?**

1. information	__________	**5.** robbery	__________
2. hobby	__________	**6.** employee	__________
3. furniture	__________	**7.** advice	__________
4. thief	__________	**8.** cup	__________

"Did you find anything?" she asked.

Henry shook his head. He sat down in front of her desk.

"Not really. The neighbour heard a scream, but she didn't see anybody running from the building. Nothing appears to have been stolen. And Kathy Finn said that her husband didn't have any enemies. It's all quite mysterious."

"Do you think he killed himself after all?" Jennifer asked.

"That's the strange thing. I think someone else killed him. He seemed to have been doing very well for himself financially. And his neighbour said that he was excited about making up with Kathy. Michael Finn had everything to live for."

"He wasn't investing in the stock market, was he? A lot of people have lost quite a lot of money lately. I've just read about a seventy-year-old man who lost everything. He has to go back to work now," Jennifer told Henry.

"No," Henry said. "Michael took pictures of the customers at Aristotle's. He used the pictures to paint paintings and then sold these paintings to the subjects."

"You mean he took pictures of the customers at Aristotle's?"

"Yes. You seem surprised," Henry said.

"A lot of important and **influential** people go to Aristotle's. I can't imagine that all of them would be happy to be caught on film. Would you want someone to take a picture of you if you were where you shouldn't be?"

"Or with someone you shouldn't be with[i]," Henry added.

"I certainly wouldn't want to be caught on film in a **compromising** situation."

Henry jumped up and gave Jennifer a kiss on the cheek.

"You're a **genius**," he said. "That's the **missing link**. Michael must have taken a picture of something or someone that he shouldn't have seen. His death must be related to that picture."

influential	einflussreich
compromising	kompromittierend
genius	Genie
missing link	fehlendes Bindeglied
to dial	wählen (Telefon)
to hold a secret	ein Geheimnis bergen
to mix business with pleasure	das Angenehme mit dem Nützlichen verbinden
to keep sth.	etw. absperren

Henry picked up the phone and **dialled** Kathy's number.

"Hello, Mr Shipman. Do you have any more information about Michael's death?" Kathy's voice was hopeful.

"Not really information, just a theory. I'm interested in any pictures Michael may have taken last night."

"I don't know what pictures he took last night. I've been too sad to think about his pictures."

"I understand. But the pictures he took may **hold the secret** to his death. Would you mind looking at them?" Henry asked.

"If it will help you to find his killer, I'll do it. However, I won't be able to go back to his flat until after work."

"That's fine, I'll call you this evening."

Um die etwas umständliche Konstruktion **someone *with whom* you shouldn't be** zu umgehen, kann man **someone you shouldn't be with** sagen.

Exercise 25: Tenses. **Formulieren Sie die Sätze mit Past Continuous und Simple Past um!**

1. Jennifer files papers. Henry enters the waiting room.

   Jennifer was filing papers when Henry entered the waiting room.

2. Jennifer decides what to have for lunch. A client knocks on the door.

   ____

3. Tobias changes his tie. He hears a noise.

   ____

4. Olivia goes to the market. She sees Kathy and Henry.

   ____

5. Roberta gets out of the lift. Oscar calls her into his office.

   ____

6. Stewart pours himself a drink. Tobias arrives.

   ____

"Don't forget that you are supposed to meet Oscar Peters tonight," Jennifer said.
"Thanks for reminding me."
Henry picked up the phone again. He was greeted by Oscar's message on an answering machine.
"Oscar, meet me at Aristotle's. Ten o'clock," he said before he turned to Jennifer. "Nothing like **mixing business with pleasure**."
Henry was surprised that an expensive place like Aristotle's only

off limits

to beg so.'s jmd. um

had one functioning toilet. After Henry introduced himself, Frederic, the manager, was quick to explain.

"There was a murder here last night. The police agreed that the restaurant could open tonight, but asked us to **keep** the men's toilets **off limits**."

"The victim was killed in the toilets?"

"Yes," Frederic said. "His name was Tobias James. This morning was terrible. First I found out about Mr James's death and then about Michael Finn's."

Exercise 26: Unscramble the dialogue. Lesen Sie weiter und bringen Sie den Dialog in die richtige Reihenfolge!

1. "Of course. What was Michael like last night?"
2. "Did Michael take any other pictures last night?"
3. "Who told you about Michael Finn's death?" Henry asked.
4. "He was excited about a picture he had taken. I can't believe Michael would have gone home and killed himself."
5. "His wife, Kathy. I had been calling Michael all day. The police wanted to talk with all of last night's staff members," Frederic replied.
6. "He may have, but he only talked about that one picture."

1	2	3	4	5	6

"And you said he took it at the end of the evening?" Henry asked the manager.
"That's right. Now that I think about it, it even could have been at the same time Tobias James was killed."
"I **beg your pardon**," Henry said.

pardon	Entschuldigung bitten
to point to sth.	auf etw. zeigen
↯ socialite	Angehöriger der feinen Gesellschaft
to request	etw. erfordern
to provide	bereitstellen
proud	stolz

"Tobias James was killed near closing time. That's why we didn't find his body until this morning."
"And do you remember where the subjects of Michael's picture were sitting?"
"There," said Frederic, **pointing** to a table near the door.
"Who were they?"
"Some London **socialites**."
Henry remembered his earlier conversation with Jennifer about people being photographed in a public place.
"Were they happy to have their picture taken (i)?"
"Oh yes. They even **requested** it. Like I said, they were having so much fun, they didn't want to leave."

To have one's picture taken ist nach derselben Konstruktion gebildet wie **to have one's hair cut** oder **to have one's car fixed.** Damit drückt man aus, dass jemand etwas *machen lässt*: Carol *lässt* sich ihr Buch *signieren*. **Carol has her book *autographed*.**

"Can you give me their names?"
"Yes. I have to **provide** a list of last night's customers to the police anyway. I'll talk to Ross and Eddie to make sure I have all of the names of the people at the table that Michael photographed. They were serving the table."
"You know your customers well," Henry said.
"Yeah, I do. It's my job." Frederic **proudly** said.

Exercise 27: Adjectives and adverbs. **Setzen Sie die Adjektive in die passende Form!**

1. Oscar drove very **1.** fast ______________ to the scene of the crime.

2. Tobias worked very **2.** hard ______________.

3. Tobias and Elisabeth **3.** rare ______________ spoke to each other.

4. She rose **4.** slow ______________.

5. Your behaviour is very **5.** risky ______________.

6. He died **6.** mysterious ______________.

Oscar Peters arrived at exactly ten o'clock. He was happy to see his old friend, Henry, sitting at the bar.

"Henry, it has been too long," he said. "When did we last see each other? ... I think it was at Roberta's birthday party."

"Wow, that was six months ago. It was good to see all of you again," Henry replied.

"The feeling was **mutual**. We miss you at the station."

"You have Sam Meadows. He's a lot like me from what I hear."

mutual	gegenseitig
disillusioned	desillusioniert

"Hopefully he won't become **disillusioned** and leave the force like you did."

"Listen to his instincts and he'll stay," Henry said.

"If we had listened to your instincts, poor Joseph Myers wouldn't have been put in prison."

"At least I was able to prove that he was innocent."

to observe	beobachten
high-profile case	prominenter Fall
coincidence	Zufall
to disagree	anderer Meinung sein
to erase	löschen

"We were all glad that you found out the truth in the end."
"All of you?" Henry asked with a smile.
"Maybe not everyone was exactly glad, but you didn't have to leave the force."
"I thought it was best for everyone," Henry said.
Oscar observed the people in the restaurant.
"I could use your help now," he said to Henry.
"Are you working on a high-profile case at the moment?"
"Yes. In fact it is quite a coincidence that you asked me to meet you here."
"You're investigating Tobias James's death, aren't you?" Henry asked.
"How did you know?"
"I just guessed. I was talking to Frederic, the manager, before you came."
"You aren't working on the same case, are you?"
"No, I'm investigating the death of Michael Finn," Henry replied.
"Roberta told me about the suicide," Oscar said. "I was even wondering if I should consider him a suspect."
"Michael Finn? A suspect?" Henry asked in surprise.
"You sound like Roberta. She didn't think the two deaths were related."
"I disagree with her about that. I think the two cases are related."
"What do you mean?" Oscar asked.
"I think that Michael caught the killer on film. I've asked Kathy Finn to check Michael's camera. But if I'm right, the photos he took last night won't be there."
"That's an interesting theory. You think the killer broke in to erase the photographs?"

Exercise 28: Word spiral. Finden Sie die gesuchten Begriffe und fügen Sie sie in die Wortspirale ein!

1	2	3	4	5	6	7
22	23	24	25	26	27	8
21	36	37	38	39	28	9
20	35	42	41	40	29	10
19	34	33	32	31	30	11
18	17	16	15	14	13	12

1-8: person who killed someone
8-16: your parents, uncles, aunts, sisters and brothers
16-21: the last day of the week
21-24: day, month and...
24-28: floating water
28-33: why something is the way it is
33-42: information you periodically receive via e-mail

“That would be my guess. Michael was probably getting ready to go to bed when he heard noises in the sitting room.”
“Then we are looking for the same person.”
“It sounds like it,” Henry said.
Henry’s mobile phone rang. Oscar listened to Henry’s end of the conversation.
“You aren’t **disturbing** me, Kathy. Were you able to find any photographs from last night?” Henry paused. “I see… No, no. Don’t worry, Kathy. That’s what I suspected. I’ll call you tomorrow. Good night.”

"Let me guess," Oscar said. "There are no photographs from last night."

Henry laughed.

"It's easy to see how you **rose to the ranks of** Detective Chief Inspector."

"I guess that I should tell you what I've found out so far," Oscar replied.

to disturb	stören
to rise to the ranks of ...	zum ... aufsteigen (Position)
back alley	*hier*: Hinterhof

While Oscar and Henry were sharing information, Ross and Eddie were smoking in the restaurant's **back alley**.

"Did Frederic ask you about those customers last night?" Eddie asked Ross quietly.

"Yes," Ross replied. "Do you think he knows something?"

Eddie shook his head.

"Use your head. If he knew something, he wouldn't have asked us."

"Yeah, you're right."

Eddie smiled and put out his cigarette.

"I think we have some very valuable information."

Exercise 29: Synonyms. Welche Wörter haben eine ähnliche Bedeutung? Ordnen Sie zu!

1. ☐ very important	a) suspect
2. ☐ bother	b) valuable
3. ☐ have a strong feeling	c) rank
4. ☐ picture	d) employees
5. ☐ worth a lot	e) disturb
6. ☐ staff	f) photograph
7. ☐ position	g) high-profile

4 The Funeral

The next morning Roberta stepped out of the lift at 8:30 a.m. Sam almost fell out of his chair when he saw her.

"You arrived on time today. Finally got yourself an alarm clock?"

Roberta poured a cup of coffee. She sat down in front of Sam.

"No. I was just eager to get in early today."

She directed her attention to Oscar's office.

"Where's the boss?"

to step out	hinaustreten
to pour	einschenken
to get a lead on sth.	einen Hinweis auf etw. bekommen
to grin	grinsen
to point. sth. at sb	mit etw. auf jmd. zeigen
cause of death	Todesursache
sheet	Blatt

"He called earlier. He will be here soon. He said that he got a lead on the Tobias James case last night. He also said that I was right about Michael Finn."

Sam grinned.

"Oh, I thought you said that Michael Finn killed himself."

Sam pointed his pencil at Roberta.

"That was the official cause of death."

"So he was murdered?"

"It seems so. Henry Shipman's investigating the case." Sam's attention returned to the report on his desk.

"He is, is he?" Roberta said softly.

She wrote Henry's name on a sheet of paper on her desk. Then she drew a picture around his name. It was a picture of a heart. When Oscar arrived she covered the drawing with the palm of her hand.

palm of one's hand	Handinnenfläche

"I'm sorry I'm late," he said to Roberta.
Roberta quickly put the piece of paper in her handbag.
"That's okay. I heard that you got a lead in the investigation last night."
"You could say that. I'll tell you about it on the way to Paul Windsor's office."

Exercise 30: True or false. Welche der folgenden Aussagen sind wahr? Markieren Sie mit richtig ✔ oder falsch – !

1. Roberta is always on time. ☐
2. Roberta likes Henry Shipman. ☐
3. The police think that Michael Finn was murdered. ☐
4. Everyone knows that Roberta likes Henry Shipman. ☐
5. Roberta likes to solve crimes. ☐
6. Oscar is Roberta's supervisor. ☐

Paul Windsor's office was located near Berkeley Square. Oscar and Roberta were told that they could find him on the second floor. Paul Windsor was not happy to see the two investigators when they arrived in his office at ten o'clock.

space	Raum
canteen	Kantine
to motion for sb. to do sth.	jmd. ein Zeichen geben, etw. zu tun
to threaten	bedrohen
word of mouth	Mundpropaganda

"We can't talk here," he said. "As you can see, I share this space with two other people. They might return at any time."

"Where can we talk?" Oscar asked.

Paul Windsor sighed. "If we must speak to one another, we can talk in the canteen."

He took the investigators to the canteen on the top floor. There he led them to a table in the corner where they could not be seen by other people.

"Why do you want to talk to me?"

"We're investigating the murder of Tobias James. His secretary said that you had a fight with him on the day of his death," Oscar said.

"I have fights with many people. But I don't kill them afterwards," Paul Windsor replied.

"We didn't say that you killed Tobias James," Roberta said. "We just want to know more about what happened on the day that Mr James died."

"I'm not going to say another word without my lawyer. I know my rights."

Oscar rose. He motioned for Paul Windsor to follow him.

"If that is the way you want it, I suggest that we go to the police station. You can get your lawyer to meet us there."

Roberta touched Paul's arm.

"You can save yourself a lot of trouble if you talk to us here, Mr Windsor. We aren't accusing you of anything. We're just trying to figure out what happened during Tobias James's last days. The more we know, the easier it will be[i] for us to find the real killer."

Mit der Konstruktion **the... the** lässt sich im Englischen das deutsche **je... desto** ausdrücken. **The more we know, the easier it will be.**

Paul looked at Oscar. "You can sit down. I'll co-operate."
The smile that Oscar gave Roberta disappeared so quickly that Paul Windsor did not see it.
"So tell us. Is it true that you **threatened** Mr James? I think you said that you would have his head served on a platter," Oscar said.

Exercise 31: Fill in the blanks. **Lesen Sie weiter und fügen Sie die passenden Wörter in die Lücken ein!**

bad luck | effective | suffer | motive | dramatic | sense | figurative

"Yeah, yeah. But anyone with any 1. ______ would know that I was only using the term in a 2. ______ way. I'm in the advertising industry. I am a little 3. ______ from time to time."
"So you didn't really blame Mr James for your 4. ______ on the stock market?" Roberta asked.
"Oh, I blamed him. I was going to get even with him and I wanted to make him 5. ______. But not by killing him. That would have been too easy. I was going to make it known that he could not be trusted with people's money. **Word of mouth** is a very 6. ______ tool," Paul Windsor chuckled. "I had more to fear from Tobias James than he did from me. He is the one who had a 7. ______ to kill me.

outrage	Schande, Frevel
gaze	starrer Blick
triumphantly	triumphierend
to tick off	abhaken

Roberta and Oscar were not amused by his statement.
"To keep you from talking," Roberta said.
"That's right." Paul Windsor was no longer laughing.
"Did you see Tobias James later in the evening?" Oscar asked.
Paul moved in his chair and looked at his hands.
"No."
"It would be best for you to tell us the truth now, Mr Windsor," Roberta said.
"All right. I didn't see him, but I was in the area. I went to a bar that is located on the same street as Aristotle's."
"Were you alone?" Oscar asked.
"I was with some friends."
"We'll need their names and addresses."
"What? This is an **outrage**! I didn't kill anyone. I don't want you to involve my friends in this," Paul Windsor replied angrily.
"It is standard procedure," Roberta said. "If you were with them at the time of Mr James's death, you have nothing to worry about."
Paul Windsor's **gaze** moved from Roberta to Oscar and then back to Roberta. "Do you have a piece of paper?"
Roberta tore a sheet of paper out of her note pad.
"Here you go."
Paul Windsor wrote down several names. After he had finished, he folded the paper and gave it to Roberta.
"You're free to go, Mr Windsor, but don't make any plans to leave town until this case is solved," Oscar said.
"I just gave you my alibi. Am I still a suspect?"
"Standard procedure," Roberta said.
Paul Windsor's office was empty when he returned. Good, he thought. I have a few things to take care of. He grabbed his mobile phone and started to search for a phone number.

"Got it," he said triumphantly.
A voice answered after a few rings.
"Brown Investments. Terrance Brown speaking."
"Terrance. This is Paul. Paul Windsor."
"Paul. Good to hear from you. Does this call mean that you've changed your mind?"

Exercise 32: Tenses. Wie heißen die folgenden Verben im Simple Past und im Past Participle?

1. catch __________ __________
2. know __________ __________
3. leave __________ __________
4. fight __________ __________
5. draw __________ __________
6. find __________ __________
7. give __________ __________

"Yes. You were right. I was wasting my time and money with Tobias James. He's dead now anyway. Can we meet? I'm interested in hearing about the plans you have for the money I have left."
"Of course. What about coming by next Monday. Say nine o'clock," Terrance replied.
Paul looked up as one of his colleagues entered the room.
"Okay. I'll see you then."
Terrance hung up the phone. He ticked off Paul Windsor's name on the list by his computer. Sorry Tobias, old boy, he thought.

Exercise 33: Choose the correct alternative. **Lesen Sie weiter und unterstreichen Sie die richtige Variante!**

Superintendent Anderson couldn't believe his **1.** eyes / sight. The headlines of the morning newspaper were about the mysterious string of murders associated with Aristotle's. He had already received phone calls from **2.** too / two angry citizens this morning. One call had come from Aristotle's multi-millionaire owner. The other had come from Tobias James's influential father.

Both **3.** callers / phoners wanted the cases to be **4.** solved / found quickly. So did Superintendent Anderson.

He dialled Oscar Peter's **extension**. Sam Meadows **5.** answered / replied the phone.

"Where's Chief Inspector Peters?" Superintendent Anderson asked.

"He went to question Paul Windsor. He's one of the **6.** investigators / suspects in the Tobias James **7.** murder / death case."

"When DCI Peters returns tell him to come straight to my **8.** bureau / office."

"Yes, sir," Sam Meadows answered.

"And Meadows...," Superintendent Anderson continued.
"Yes, sir."
Superintendent Anderson recognized Sam Meadows' tone. He wants to know why I didn't hang up after leaving the message for Chief Inspector Peters, he thought.

Superintendent	Hauptkommissar
extension	*hier*: Durchwahl

"Who continued investigating Michael Finn's death?"
"No one here, sir."
Superintendent Anderson grunted.
"I had better not find out otherwise. Make sure DCI Peters gets my message."
It was midday when Oscar and Roberta returned to the police station. Sam Meadows gave Oscar Superintendent Anderson's message.
"He said that you were to go there straight away, sir."
"He did, did he? Did he also say what he wants to talk to me about?" Oscar asked.
"Not directly, sir," Sam Meadows replied. "But he did ask me about the news that Michael Finn didn't kill himself. He wanted to know who had continued the investigation. I told him that no one here had (i)."

Eine sehr häufige Art und Weise im Englischen, auf **Fragen mit who** zu antworten, ist die Wiederholung des Hilfsverbs aus der Frage, ohne das konjugierte Verb noch einmal aufzugreifen: „**Who has** called you? **Peter has.**" Oder „**Who had** continued the investigation? **No one had.**" Im Deutschen hingegen würde man lediglich das Subjekt, also „niemand" oder „Peter" nennen. Das ist im Englischen nicht üblich.

"Good job, Sam."
"Good luck, boss," Roberta said as Oscar walked to the lift. "I'm sure you'll need it."
Superintendent Anderson was talking on the phone when Oscar arrived. Oscar took the time to prepare his answers to the

questions he knew Superintendent Anderson was going to ask him. The questions started as soon as Superintendent Anderson hung up the phone.

Exercise 34: Fill in the blanks. Vervollständigen Sie die Sätze mit dem passenden Begriff!

commit suicide | inquire | replied | report | photograph | surveyed

1. Michael would never ______________________.
2. Michael took a ______________________ of Aristotle's customers.
3. I am going to ______________________ about that.
4. Have you read the ______________________ about Michael's death?
5. I ______________________ to his e-mail yesterday.
6. Oscar ______________________ the scene.

"Oscar. What the hell are you doing? My phone hasn't stopped ringing."

"Nice to see you, too," Oscar answered.

"Look, Oscar. We don't have time for formalities. Where are you going with this investigation?"

Oscar was used to the **treatment** he was getting. In fact, he was surprised he hadn't received a call earlier. These conversations always go better when we talk as **equals**, he thought. He pulled out a chair and sat down.

treatment	Behandlung
equal	Gleichgestellte/r

"We have several suspects, sir."
"And they are all members of London's high society," Anderson continued.

to lean forward	sich nach vorne lehnen
plenty of	eine Menge, viele
taxpayer	Steuerzahler

Here we go, Oscar thought. He **leaned forward**.
"What's your point, sir?"
"What a nonsense. There are **plenty of** criminals on London's streets. Have you ever thought that one of them may have murdered Tobias James?"
"It's possible, but very unlikely."
"You and I both know that. But at least make it look like it's something you've thought about," the superintendent said.
"Sir, we both know that following that route is a waste of **taxpayers'** money."
"Lots of things are a waste of taxpayers' money. That doesn't stop people from doing them."

Exercise 35: Match up. **Verbinden Sie und bilden Sie sinnvolle Sätze!**

1. ☐ Oscar was used to	a) be solved quickly.
2. ☐ He seems to	b) of London's high society.
3. ☐ The suspects are members	c) too late.
4. ☐ He wanted the cases to	d) the treatment he was getting.
5. ☐ I was supposed to	e) be nervous.
6. ☐ You sold my shares	f) meet him at Aristotle's.

some	*hier*: irgendein
tramp	Obdachloser
superior	Vorgesetzter

"So you want me to find a way to connect **some** poor **tramp** to the murders of Tobias James and Michael Finn?" Oscar asked his **superior**.

Superintendent Anderson leaned forward and looked directly into Oscar Peter's eyes. "I don't want a repeat of the situation with Joseph Myers. Just make sure you have a solid case when an arrest is made."

"I wouldn't make an arrest under any other circumstances," Oscar replied calmly as he stood up.

The next day, Oscar, Roberta and Henry attended Tobias James's funeral. Oscar had made fun of Roberta on the drive to the **graveyard**.

"You never look like that in the office."

"You look a bit more stylish than usual yourself."

"Touché," Oscar grinned.

Exercise 36: Prepositions. Lesen Sie weiter und setzen Sie die richtige Präposition ein!

for near on (2x) out up with

As Henry approached their spot **1.** ________ a hill overlooking the grave, Oscar noticed that Roberta **adjusted** her jacket and **smoothed** her hair.

"Hi Henry," she said **2.** ________ a smile.

Henry's eyes lit **3.** ________ when he saw Roberta.

"Hi Roberta. I didn't know you were going to be here, too. How have you been?"

"Fine. And you?"

"Can't complain," Henry replied.

Oscar **cleared his throat**. "This is probably a good time **4.** ________ me to point **5.** ________ some of the people I know. The blond woman standing **6.** ________ the grave is Elisabeth James. The woman **7.** ________ her right is Tina Cutter, her best friend."

"And the woman standing behind them who can't stop crying?" Henry asked.

"Tobias James's secretary, Sarah," Roberta said.

Henry pointed to three men and two women.

"Who are those other people standing close to Elisabeth James?"

"I don't know," Oscar replied.

"They must be close to the family," Roberta observed.

The funeral ended. After they had **paid their** last **respects**, the **mourners** walked towards their cars. The three investigators walked towards the three men they had noticed earlier. One was walking with Tina Cutter. The other two were also walking with women at their sides.

graveyeard	Friedhof
to adjust	in Ordnung bringen
to smooth	glätten
to clear one's throat	sich räuspern
to pay one's last respects	jmd. den letzten Dienst erweisen
mourners *pl*	Trauergemeinde

"Excuse me," Oscar said. "I know this is a sad time for all of you, but we're investigating Tobias James's death. Can we have a few words with you?"

The man next to Tina Cutter nodded to her. She gave Oscar and

shy — schüchtern

Roberta a shy glance and joined Elisabeth James. The other two women followed Tina Cutter.

The man who had been with Tina spoke first.

"Of course. We'll help in any way possible," he said. "My name is Daniel Cutter. This is Sean Campbell and Terrance Brown. We were with Tobias at university. Tina told me that she met you at Elisabeth's house."

Exercise 37: Verb forms. Welche Verbform ist korrekt? Unterstreichen Sie!

1. I was / have been shocked when I heard the news.
2. Last year we have arrested / arrested the wrong man.
3. We didn't see / haven't seen each other lately.
4. Have you seen / Have you been seen Michael Finn today?
5. I called / have called him last night, but there was no answer.
6. Everyone has liked / liked Michael Finn.
7. You want me finding / to find the murderer.
8. What is / should be your point, sir?
9. It started / will start as soon as he hung up.

"We were shocked to hear about Tobias's death," Sean Campbell said.

dreadful	schrecklich
in denial	verneinend

"We've always been very close. We've celebrated birthdays together, wedding, births, and now this," Terrance Brown added.
"Sean and Terrance are right," Daniel Cutter said. "And the way he died is dreadful. I'll never look at silk the same way again. Who would ever think that it could be so deadly?"
"When was the last time any of you saw Tobias James?" Oscar asked.
The three men looked at each other.
"We've spoken with each other, but we haven't seen each other for a long time," Terrance Brown said.
"Things have been really busy at work," Sean Campbell added.
"Daniel, didn't you and Tobias see each other recently?" Terrance Brown asked.
"No, we were going to, but he had to cancel at the last minute," Daniel said.
"Do you have any idea who would want to kill Mr James?" Henry asked.
All three men shook their heads in denial.
"Of course everybody has enemies," Terrance Brown said.
"But I can't imagine that anyone hated Tobias enough to kill him," Daniel Cutter continued.
"Thank you for your time," Oscar said. "Here's my card. Please call me if you think of anything that may be of help."

Exercise 38: Unscramble the words. Lesen Sie weiter und ordnen Sie die Buchstaben zu sinnvollen Wörtern!

Ross **1.** edrvari ____________ at the appointed meeting point, a telephone box near Archway Park, at

2. catlyex __________ two o'clock. Eddie arrived five minutes later. He **3.** delgauh __________ when he saw Ross.

"**4.** keta __________ that stupid **hood** off," he said. "You don't have to **5.** rwda __________ attention to yourself."

"I thought I would **fit in**," Ross responded.

"You watch too many films. Where's the phone **6.** bremun __________?"

Ross reached in his pocket. He pulled out a **7.** klwderni __________ sheet of paper. Eddie took the piece of paper out of Ross's hands.

"How much is our **8.** ceilsen __________ worth?" Ross asked Eddie.

"Ten thousand **quid**," Eddie **9.** deednospr __________.

"What, that much?"

"He can afford it," Eddie said.

He dialled the number on the piece of paper. A few moments later, he hung up the phone.

"No answer. We'll have to try later."

hood	Kapuze
to fit in	dazupassen
quid	Pfund

5 A Trail to Follow

to attend	beiwohnen, besuchen
attentively	aufmerksam
at a time	gleichzeitig
to gather	sich versammeln
tap	Klopfen

Oscar, Roberta and Henry **attended** their second funeral in two days. Henry **attentively** observed the people standing around him. He had already questioned many of them. Their names had been on the list that Frederic had given him. The people had been very co-operative. Michael Finn might not have been as rich as Tobias James, but he had certainly had more friends.

I've never seen people from so many different social groups in one place **at a time**. Henry thought to himself. Aristotle's regular customers must have really liked Michael. His wife Kathy Finn must be quite happy to know that both the customers and staff of Aristotle's have **gathered** together to pay their last respects.

Henry felt a **tap** on his arm.

"Aren't those Tobias James's old classmates from university?" Roberta asked, nodding towards a group of men standing under a tree.

"Yes. Aristotle's was Tobias James's favourite place to go. It's normal that his best friends would be regulars, too."

"But I guess they were not there on the night he died. Their names weren't on the customer list."

Exercise 39: Idiomatic expressions. **Wählen Sie die passende Redewendung und achten Sie auf die korrekte Zeitform!**

get rid of | get on | get wound up | get out of | get over | get off lightly

1. Tobias's classmates couldn't __________ his death.
2. Paul Windsor and Tobias didn't __________ with each other.
3. Ross __________ for not checking the toilets.
4. The killer __________ the murder weapon.
5. Ian Brown __________ whenever he thought about his finances.
6. Eddie __________ checking the toilets because he had to go home early.

Henry continued to stare at the men.
"Hey. Isn't one of them missing?"
"You're right. Daniel Cutter isn't here," Roberta replied.
Kathy Finn greeted the inspectors after the burial.
"You're going to join us for a small reception at Aristotle's, aren't you?"

Oscar and Roberta gave her a sympathetic look. Oscar spoke for both of them.
"I'm sorry, but we won't be able to join you. We have a bit of investigating to do."
"But it was a lovely **service**," Roberta said.
Kathy Finn turned to Henry. "You'll be able to come, won't you?"
"Of course," Henry responded.

burial	Begräbnis
service	*hier*: Gottesdienst
to hire	anstellen

Exercise 40: Tenses. **Setzen Sie die Verben in Klammern in die richtige Zeitform!**

When they **1.** arrive ______________ at Aristotle's, Kathy Finn led Henry to her table. From there he watched the customers. Frederic had **hired** additional staff for the afternoon. Aristotle's regular staff members and customers **2.** sit ______________ at tables together. Everyone seemed **3.** be ______________ at ease. Two tables away, Sean Campbell **4.** get ______________ up and went to the bar. Henry **5.** rise ______________ and sat in the empty seat next to Terrance Brown. Terrance **6.** recognize ______________ him. The two men **7.** shake ______________ hands.

in spite of	trotz
to assume	annehmen, vermuten
as well	ebenfalls
saddened	traurig
bond	Verbindung
involved	verwickelt
hunting accident	Jagdunfall

"I would say good to see you again, but I'm not sure it's really appropriate under these circumstances," Terrance said.

"I must say that I was surprised to see you and Sean Campbell at the cemetery today. I didn't know that you knew Michael Finn," Henry responded.

"We all came here frequently. I hope people still come in spite of the recent events."

"Will you continue to come here?"

"Oh yes. I like it here, the place has just had a run of bad luck. It happens to everyone – look at the financial industry. A few banks make some bad decisions and everyone is suffering. It's not fair."

"You said that all of you came to Aristotle's often. I assume that includes Daniel Cutter as well."

"Yes, indeed. Poor Daniel. I think it's a bit too soon for him to come back here. Tobias's death has really hit him hard."

"Harder than the rest of you?"

"Of course both Sean and I are upset and saddened by Tobias's death. We'll miss him. But Tobias and Daniel seemed to have a secret bond. Sean and I were never able to find out what it was. All I know is that Tobias helped Daniel's brother, Cedric, when he was in trouble with the law. That could have had something to do with it."

"Does Daniel's brother have a criminal record?" Henry asked, surprised.

"No. Not that I know of anyway," Terrance Brown replied. "He was involved in a hunting accident a few years ago. Shot a neighbour walking in the woods."

"I guess hunting accidents happen from time to time," Henry replied.

"That would be the normal conclusion. The police were a bit suspicious though because Daniel's brother and his neighbour were having a property dispute."

property dispute	Grundstücks-streitigkeit
seperately	getrennt, einzeln

"Oh, I see. What happened?"
"Nothing really. A friend of Tobias's, a lawyer, got involved. The neighbour finally moved."
"Has Daniel's brother been in any trouble since then?" Henry asked.
"If he has, then the family has managed to keep it a secret."
Henry saw Sean Campbell coming back, holding two drinks.
When he arrived, Henry stood up.
"I was keeping your seat warm for you."
"There's no need for you to leave," Sean Campbell said. "We can get another chair for you."
Henry considered the offer. He wondered if Sean Campbell had any additional information. I won't ask any more questions now. I can always talk to him later if necessary. It's probably better to talk to them separately anyway.

Exercise 41: True or false? Welche der folgenden Aussagen sind wahr? Markieren Sie mit richtig ✔ oder falsch – !

1. Daniel's brother has spent time in jail. ❑
2. Tobias and Daniel seemed to be close to each other. ❑
3. Aristotle's has had a lot of luck lately. ❑
4. Cedric had a good relationship with his neighbour. ❑
5. The lawyer was able to help Cedric. ❑
6. Cedric has been in trouble since the shooting. ❑

to have a temper	leicht reizbar sein
to be about to do sth.	gerade etw. tun wollen
to make progress	vorankommen
there is no use	es bringt nichts

"That's okay. I should be getting back to my table."

Henry returned to his table. He could not stop thinking about his conversation with Terrance Brown. Is this the break we've been looking for? Daniel Cutter's brother seems to have a temper. Is he connected to the deaths of Tobias James and Michael Finn? Does Daniel Cutter know? Is that the real reason he decided not to come to Michael Finn's funeral? He was about to phone Oscar when Frederic came to the table and sat down next to him.

"How's the case going?" he asked.

"We're making progress," Henry responded.

"Aristotle's owner will be happy to hear that. You and that other inspector who's investigating the death of Tobias James were here together the other[i] night. Do you think that Michael's death is related to the death of Tobias James?"

> Die englische Wendung **the other night** oder auch **the other day** bedeutet so viel wie „neulich/neulich Abend/neulich Nacht" oder „vor einigen Tagen/vor Kurzem."

"We're looking at every aspect."

Henry noticed that Ross was standing close to the table. Their eyes met. Is he listening to our conversation? Or am I just too suspicious? Ross was about to walk away when Frederic called him to the table.

"Ross," Frederic said. "This is Henry Shipman. He's the private investigator I told you about. Can you think of anything else that might help him solve the mystery of Michael's death?"

"No," Ross said.

"Are you sure?" Frederic asked.

"Yeah."

There's no use getting him to speak now, Henry thought. He

pulled one of his cards out of his wallet and gave it to Ross. "Ross, if you think of anything that might help me find Michael Finn's killer, please call me."
"Of course."
Ross took Henry's card and walked away.

Exercise 42: Short answers. Beantworten Sie die folgenden Fragen mit einer Kurzantwort!

1. Did you say something? No, ____________________.
2. Did Cedric get off lightly? Yes, ____________________.
3. Aren't you going to join Tobias later tonight? No, ____________________.
4. Is Cedric Daniel's brother? Yes, ____________________.
5. Will you be able to meet me later? No, ____________________.
6. Daniel, have you seen Cedric lately? No, ____________________.

A man opened Arabella Hornsby's front door. He studied Oscar and Roberta for a moment.
"Arabella, the interior decorators are here," he shouted into the flat. Roberta sniggered. Oscar showed the man his badge.
"Oh," the man said, surprised. "Arabella, they aren't the interior decorators. They're the police."
"Let them in anyway," a voice called from inside the flat.

wallet	Brieftasche
interior decorator	Innenausstatter
badge	*hier*: (Polizei-) Marke

"Come in," the man said.

Oscar and Roberta followed his orders. The room was full of boxes. If she's leaving, why is she expecting interior decorators, Oscar wondered.

Oscar was about to **peer** into one of the boxes when a tall, thin woman walked into the room.

She looks like a ballerina, Oscar thought. It's no wonder Tobias James hadn't been able to resist her. Any man would be happy to have her by his side.

Exercise 43: Translation. Lesen Sie weiter und unterstreichen die richtige Übersetzung der folgenden Wörter!

Unordnung | Mord | argwöhnisch | Beziehung | ansonsten | überrascht

"Hello. I'm Arabella Hornsby. Please excuse the mess," she said.

Oscar felt Roberta **nudging** his arm. He cleared his throat.

"How do you do. I'm Detective Chief Inspector Oscar Peters and this is Detective Inspector Roberta Nettles. We're investigating the murder of Tobias James. May we ask you a few questions?"

"Of course."

Arabella turned to the man who was still standing near the door. She gave him a kiss and **flashed** a smile.

"Why don't you come back later, love?"

The man gave Oscar and Roberta a suspicious look before leaving the flat.

"So, what would you like to know?" Arabella asked after everyone had been seated.

"What was your relationship with Tobias James?" Oscar inquired.

Arabella laughed.

"I'm sure you know the answer. You wouldn't be here **otherwise**. In fact, I'm surprised that it took you so long to come and question me."

"Why do you think you should have been higher on the list of suspects?" Roberta asked.

"My relationship with Tobias wasn't a secret. And neither was our break-up. I was angry enough to kill him when he told me that our relationship was over. But everything is okay now. I have a new boyfriend."

"What caused the break-up?" Oscar asked.

"Tobias claimed that I was too expensive for him. He said that he could no longer afford to pay for my flat and support my lifestyle because of the financial crisis."

Rather than ask another question, Oscar thought about the women in Tobias James's life. All of them seemed to be very cold. Neither Elisabeth James nor Arabella Hornsby had shown any

to peer	spähen
to nudge	stupsen, schubsen
to flash	*hier*: blitzen lassen
otherwise	andernfalls

source of income	Einnahmequelle

emotion when they talked about Tobias James. Oscar was glad to hear Roberta's voice. Now I have more time to observe Arabella Hornsby, he thought.

"How did you feel about that?" Roberta asked.

"How would you feel? I was very angry. I took it personally. I knew that money wasn't the problem."

Arabella's answer made Oscar curious.

"What do you mean? Wasn't he losing clients and a lot of money because of the financial crisis?"

"Yes, he was. But Tobias had another source of income. That income source, in addition to what he was earning, was enough to cover his financial obligations and more."

"Another source of income?" Roberta asked.

"Yes, that's what he told me," Arabella replied.

Exercise 44: Phrasal verbs. Lesen Sie weiter und schreiben Sie die folgenden Phrasal Verbs in der richtigen Zeitform in die Lücken!

call off | come from | wait for | move in | come in | get rid of

Oscar and Roberta **1.** ______ Arabella Hornsby to say more. When she didn't, Oscar continued to question her.

"Where did the other source of income **2.** ______?"

"I don't know. I just know that it **3.** ______

on a monthly basis. But I think that it was late this month because Tobias was more careful than usual with his money. And he was constantly checking his bank account."

"Did you see Tobias James on the day of his death?" Roberta asked.

"No. He **4.** ______________ our relationship the day before he died. I called him several times on the day of his death, but he didn't return any of my calls. I even went to his house and talked to his wife, but I never saw him."

"By the way, are you **5.** ______________ or moving out?" Oscar asked.

"**Due to my** change of fortune, I'm staying here. In fact I'm redecorating the place. It's time to **6.** ______________ old memories. I'm going to put my personal touch on the place."

Oscar and Roberta exchanged a glance.

"That's all for now, Ms Hornsby," Oscar **stated**.

"Do you think that she killed Tobias James to **get rid** of more old memories?" Roberta asked as she and Oscar **exited** the block of flats.

"Tobias James was a strong man. I don't think she could have strangled him."

"Maybe she got someone to do it for her. She seems to like to **give orders**. Did you

due to	aufgrund
to state	erklären, angeben
to get rid of sth.	etw. loswerden
to exit	verlassen
to give orders	Befehle erteilen

recognize how she ordered her new boyfriend around? She said that she had been angry enough to kill Tobias James, didn't she."

"That's just it. She had been angry enough to kill him herself. She wouldn't have hired someone else to kill him for her," Oscar replied.

to recognize	bemerken
beggar	Bettler
to rub	reiben
on sb.'s part	von jds. Seite
lead	Spur
to chuckle	kichern

Roberta sighed.

"So what do we do now? We have suspects. We have motives. But we don't have any proof that our suspects were at Aristotle's on the night of Tobias James's death. Maybe Superintendent Anderson was right."

"Roberta. Do you really think that a **beggar** could walk into a place like Aristotle's without anyone seeing him?"

"No, not really," Roberta paused. "But someone who was a regular at Aristotle's could."

"That's what I think, too. Tobias James knew his killer."

"But how did his killer know when to find him in the toilets?" Oscar **rubbed** his chin.

"Maybe his killer came in, saw Tobias James going to the toilets and followed him."

"Good timing **on the killer's part**."

"You could say that."

"So, back to my question," Roberta said. "What do we do now?"

"We follow the **lead** that Arabella Hornsby just gave us."

"You're talking about Tobias James's extra source of income."

"That's right," Roberta replied. "Where did it come from and why didn't it arrive on time this month?"

"Sounds like a lot of research," Oscar said.

"Sounds like a job for Henry, don't you think?" Roberta **chuckled**.

Exercise 45: Prepositions. Welche Präposition gehört zu welchem Verb?

1. ☐ invest		a) with
2. ☐ confess		b) down
3. ☐ sympathize		c) for
4. ☐ worry		d) in
5. ☐ calm		e) from
6. ☐ come		f) to
7. ☐ pay		g) about

Henry was still at Aristotle's talking to Frederic when his mobile phone vibrated. He looked at the name on the display.
"Excuse me," he said to Frederic.
Frederic waved goodbye and moved to another table.
"I was just going to call you," Henry said to Roberta.
He listened as Roberta told him about Tobias James's mysterious extra income.
"Do you mind checking it out?" Roberta asked.
"Not at all. In fact, what you just told me helps me to make sense of what I've found out here."
"You've uncovered something?"
"You could say that," Henry said.
"What do you mean?"
"This isn't a good place to talk. I'm still at Aristotle's. Why don't you and Oscar meet me at my office in an hour?"
"Will do," Roberta replied.

to uncover	etw. aufdecken
Will do.	Mach ich! Wird gemacht!

Exercise 46: Choose the correct alternative. Welche Antwort ist korrekt? Kreuzen Sie an!

1. What's her name?
   a) ❏ She is named Sarah.
   b) ❏ Her name is Sarah.

2. How did Tobias die?
   a) ❏ He had strangled.
   b) ❏ He was strangled.

3. Thank you for talking to me, Ross.
   a) ❏ I welcome you.
   b) ❏ You're welcome.

4. Where did the money come from?
   a) ❏ He got the money from the bank.
   b) ❏ He became the money from the bank.

5. Where were you last night?
   a) ❏ I have been visiting a friend.
   b) ❏ I had seen a friend.

Tina Cutter lifted the cushions of the couch as she hoovered it. Many of her friends had maids. But she had always cleaned her own home. As she reached under the cushion at the end of the couch,

cushion	Kissen
to hoover	staubsaugen

her hand touched something soft. She removed the cushion. "What's this doing here?" she said, staring at a wrinkled tie. This doesn't look like one of Daniel's. He would never wear one this bright. As Tina picked it up, her gaze fell upon two monogrammed letters.
"How did one of Tobias's ties end up here?" she mumbled.
"What are you doing with that?"
Tina Cutter jumped. She was surprised to hear her husband, Daniel, behind her. She detected fear in his voice.

monogrammed	mit Monogramm versehen
to detect	aufspüren
cheerful	heiter
harshly	schroff
boldly	mutig
forehead	Stirn

"Oh Daniel, I didn't know you were here." She tried to sound cheerful.
"You shouldn't have that..."
He took the tie from her.
Tina stared at her husband. His eyes were red from lack of sleep and he had bags under his eyes. She watched as he nervously slid the tie through his fingers. Do I dare ask more questions about Tobias's tie? Daniel has been so troubled since Tobias's death. I have to find out what is worrying him so much. She took a deep breath.

Kennen Sie sich aus mit **since** und **for**?
He has been troubled *since* Tobias's death. Es ging ihm nicht gut seit Tobias' Tod.
Tobias has been dead *for* over a week now. Tobias ist jetzt seit über einer Woche tot.

"How did one of Tobias's ties get here?"
"It's none of your business," Daniel answered harshly.
"I think it's my business when the tie of a dead man is found in my house," Tina said boldly.
Daniel rubbed his forehead.
"Will you shut up, Tina. You're being dramatic. Tobias probably left it here one night."

Exercise 47: Personal pronouns. Lesen Sie weiter und unterstreichen Sie im folgenden Abschnitt alle zehn Personalpronomen!

"When? He didn't come here at all last month. I clean the cushions monthly. If he had left it here I would have found it before now."
"Tina. It's not important. The poor man is dead now."
Tina Cutter gazed at her husband. Am I being dramatic? Daniel must be right. Tobias must have left his tie here. How else could it have got here? Tobias used to come to the house a lot after work. He and Daniel used to go into the library and talk for hours.
Tina hugged her husband.
"I'm sorry. I'm worried about you. You've been doing strange things lately."

"Like what, for example?" Daniel asked tensely.
Tina bit her lip. Do I dare mention the money missing in the bank account?

lately	in letzter Zeit

"You've been talking a lot in your sleep, Daniel."
"What do I say?"
"Something about it being over. Daniel, what's going on? Money is missing from our bank account. And all of those mysterious phone calls. If you're seeing another woman let me know now. The truth is better than not knowing."
Daniel held Tina tightly in his arms.

"Is that what you think? That I have a mistress?"
"Elisabeth said that I was silly to think that. She said you love me and that you would never have a mistress."
Daniel held Tina at arm's length.
"Elisabeth is right. I don't have a mistress. The money is for Cedric."
"Is that why you've been talking to him so much lately? Is your brother in trouble again?"
"I'm afraid so. In fact I am going to see him now," Daniel replied.
"You're going to see Cedric?" Tina noticed a black sports bag on the floor.
"Are you going to give him more money?"
"This is the last time. It will all be over after today."
Tina looked into her husband's eyes. She hoped he was telling the truth.

Exercise 48: Match up. **Welche Begriffe gehören zusammen? Ordnen Sie zu!**

1. ☐ wave	**a)** account
2. ☐ phone	**b)** tie
3. ☐ arm's	**c)** goodbye
4. ☐ sports	**d)** call
5. ☐ bank	**e)** length
6. ☐ wrinkled	**f)** bag

incident	Zwischenfall
to exaggerate	übertreiben
↯ slut	Schlampe

Henry decided to pay Elisabeth James a visit on his way to the office. A maid answered his knock. "My name is Henry Shipman," he introduced himself. "I would like to speak to Elisabeth James."
"You and all the rest," Mary, Elisabeth James's maid, said.
Henry showed her his ID.
"You aren't the police," Mary said.
"No, I'm a private investigator. I'm working closely with Chief Inspector Oscar Peters. He has already spoken to Mrs James, but we have some new evidence. He asked me to talk to her."
Mary stepped out of the doorway.
"You can wait for Mrs James in the library."
Henry sat down. He took his mobile phone from his pocket and dialled his office number.
"Shipman Investigations," Jennifer's cheerful voice answered.
"Jennifer. Henry here. Can you do me a favour?"
"Of course. What do you need?"
"Can you see what you can find out about Daniel Cutter and his brother, Cedric? I'm especially interested in an incident that occurred a couple of years ago. Apparently Cedric shot his neighbour."
"Oh dear. He doesn't sound like a nice person."
"No, he doesn't. See if he's been able to stay out of trouble since then."
"Okay," Jennifer replied.
Henry hung up. Elisabeth James entered the library a few minutes later.
"Good afternoon, Mr Shipman. Mary tells me that you're investigating my husband's death together with Inspector Peters. I hope all of this work isn't costing the taxpayers a lot of money. Tobias wasn't worth it."
Oscar hadn't exaggerated when he had described Elisabeth

James, Henry thought. He tried to speak without showing any emotion.
"It's our job to protect our citizens. That means doing whatever is necessary to keep criminals off the street."

Exercise 49: Fill in the blanks. Lesen Sie weiter und fügen Sie die passenden Wörter in die Lücken ein!

account | income | information | wonder | lighter | provide | puff | wealthy

Elisabeth clapped. "Bravo. Now what can I do for you? Or have
you come to give me more 1. ______ than I can find out by reading the newspaper?"
"Actually, I hope you can 2. ______ me with some information. Do you know the source of the extra 3. ______ your husband had been receiving?"
Elisabeth pulled out a cigarette. Henry noticed a 4. ______ on the table. He picked it up and lit her cigarette. Elisabeth took a long puff.
"Any information about my late husband's bank 5. ______ must have come from that slut, Arabella Hornsby."
"What do you know about it?" Henry asked again.
Arabella took another 6. ______ of her cigarette. "I don't know where it came from, if that's your

question. I've never needed Tobias's money. I'm independently **7.** ________ . When the financial crisis started I made sure my interests were protected. My husband had a **gredy streak**. I didn't want to support it with my **inheritance**. I did **8.** ________ how he was **staying afloat**."

"Why was that?" Henry inquired.

"He was losing clients. His father refused to lend him any money. Yet he was able to **maintain** his lifestyle. He still went out, and he still supported his mistress. The situation was a bit strange. I even wondered if Daniel Cutter was lending him money."

"What made you think that?"

"Tina Cutter came over on the night of Tobias's death. It seems as if Daniel had been **withdrawing** large **sums** of money. She thought that he had a mistress. I told her that it must have been for some other reason. Daniel loves her, he would never have a mistress."

Henry couldn't believe what he was hearing.

"You said that Tina Cutter was here the night of your husband's death. Where was Daniel?"

"I don't know. I assumed that he was working late. I know that he got home after she did."

"How do you know that?"

"She told me the next day. That was the day Chief Inspector Peters told me about Tobias's death. She was very upset."

greedy streak	gierige Ader, raffgieriger Charakter
inheritance	Erbschaft
to stay afloat	sich über Wasser halten
to maintain	aufrechterhalten
to withdraw	abheben
sum	Summe

Exercise 50: Crossword puzzle. Finden Sie die Übersetzungen der folgenden Begriffe im obigen Abschnitt und lösen Sie das Kreuzworträtsel!

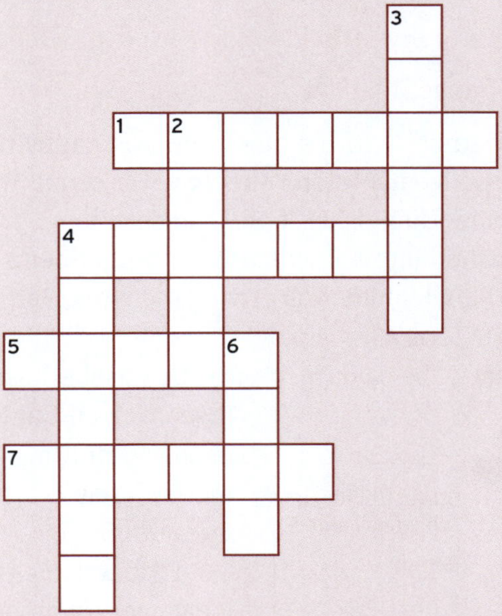

Across:

1. Kunden
4. seltsam
5. aufgebracht
7. verlieren (Simple Progressive)

Down:

2. riesig
3. Vater
4. unterstützen
6. Daniels Ehefrau

6 Exposed

Henry drove quickly to his office. He was happy that he didn't run into a policeman along the way. He certainly would have received a speeding ticket if one had seen him.

When he rushed into his office, Oscar and Roberta were already waiting for him. Jennifer was serving them tea. She poured a cup for Henry. He took a few sips.

"Sorry I'm late," he said. "I stopped by Elisabeth James's house. It seems as if Daniel Cutter has been withdrawing large sums of money lately."

speeding ticket	Strafzettel für zu schnelles Fahren
amount	Betrag
blackmail	Erpressung

Oscar grinned.

"And Tobias James was receiving large sums of money."

"The question is, was the money going out of Daniel Cutter's account the same amount as the money going into Tobias James's account?" Roberta added quickly.

"We can easily check that."

Oscar looked at Jennifer. She wrote a note to herself on the pad in front of her.

"I think we all know the answer to that." Henry took a deep breath. "The real question is, why was Daniel Cutter giving money to Tobias James?"

"And why did he stop?" Roberta added.

"Blackmail," Jennifer said.

Suddenly, all eyes were on her. She blushed.
"That's the obvious reason. Tobias James was blackmailing Daniel Cutter. Daniel Cutter decided that he wasn't going to pay anymore. He confronted Tobias James. They had a fight and Daniel Cutter killed Tobias James."

to blush	rot werden
rifle	Gewehr
to stroke	streicheln

Exercise 51: Verbs. Unterstreichen Sie die richtige Variante der Verbformen!

After leaving his house, Daniel Cutter **1.** drove / had been driving to the country to pick up his brother, Cedric. Cedric smiled as he **2.** took / takes his hunting rifle out of the glass cabinet.
"We're **3.** went / going hunting," he said.
Watching Cedric, Daniel Cutter wondered if he had **4.** did / done the right thing by involving his brother.
"What do you mean?"
"You asked me to **5.** helping / help you. I'm glad you've finally recognized my talents."
Daniel **6.** is looking / looked away as Cedric stroked his rifle.
"I don't want any violence. You said you would just scare whoever is blackmailing me."
"Don't worry, dear brother. It'll only take one shot **7.** to scare / scaring them off. No harm done." Cedric grinned.

to yawn	gähnen
drop-off point	Übergabestelle
to give the bird call	*hier*: rufen, um jmd. zu warnen

Jennifer shrugged her shoulders as if to say that it was an obvious conclusion.
Henry slapped his leg.
"Jennifer's right. I knew I was missing something. Do you remember what Daniel Cutter said at Tobias James's funeral?"
Oscar shook his head.
"Help me out here."
Roberta jumped up and down as if she were on a game show.
"He said something about not knowing how deadly silk could be."
"Right," Henry said.
Oscar finally understood.
"We never released the cause of death."
Ross **yawned**. It had been a long day. First he had attended Michael Finn's funeral. After that he had gone to the reception at Aristotle's. Now he and Eddie were on their way to Hampstead Heath.
"Keep your eyes on the road," Eddie warned.
"I am, I am."
"You know what you're supposed to do?"
"Yeah. How many times do we have to go over it? We're going to park the car. When we get to the **drop-off point**, I'm going to hide and keep watch," Ross said.
"What are you going to watch for?"
"Any funny business. Like policemen who show up with Daniel Cutter."
"Right. And what are you going to do if you see some?"
"**Give the bird call**," Ross replied.
"Good." Eddie nodded.
"What are you going to do with your half of the money, Eddie?"
"Go on holiday. Get the hell out of this depressing city. What are you going to do with yours?"

"Don't know yet. Maybe use it to **further** my education," Ross replied.

to further	fördern
disguise	Verkleidung

"You and your education. This is close enough, park here."
Ross followed Eddie's orders. The two of them got out of the car. Eddie reached into his pocket and pulled out a baseball cap and dark sunglasses.
"What's that for?" Ross asked.
"It's my **disguise**. I don't want him to recognize me."
"Now who watches too many films," Ross laughed.
Eddie pushed Ross.
"Go over there and keep watch. He's supposed to meet me here."

Exercise 52: Direct speech. Verwandeln Sie die folgenden Sätze in die direkte Rede!

1. He asked her when she had last seen him.

2. She told him to talk to Arabella Hornsby.

3. He said that he would call me later.

4. He said that he never drank alone.

5. He said that he had been talking to Tobias's father.

Ross jogged over to a big tree with low branches. He climbed high enough to have a good view of the area. It wasn't long before he saw Daniel Cutter, who was carrying a black sports bag. Ross rubbed his hands together. Here comes the money.

Ross saw Eddie jump down from another tree, wearing the cap and sunglasses. He walked up to Daniel Cutter and reached for the bag. Ross looked away as a group of birds flew by overhead. A loud bang brought his attention back to Eddie.

"Eddie," he yelled.

He jumped out of the tree and ran to Eddie. Eddie was lying on the ground, blood was **streaming** out of his **chest**. Ross shook him, but Eddie didn't move. Then Ross remembered the bag. Both it and Daniel Cutter were gone.

In panic, Ross stood up and ran faster than he had ever run before. He didn't look back. If he had, he would have seen two men following him.

Roberta **convinced** Oscar that he should inform Superintendent Anderson of their plan to pick up Daniel Cutter for questioning. Oscar went directly to the Superintendent's office when they arrived at the police station.

"Oscar. I didn't expect to see you this evening."

"I thought I should tell you that we have a **breakthrough** in the Tobias James murder case."

"You do, do you?" the superintendent asked.

"Yes, we plan to pick up Daniel Cutter for questioning."

"Daniel Cutter. You're determined to arrest one of London's leading citizens, aren't you?"

Oscar tried to remain calm.

"I was doing you a favour by letting you know of our plans before bringing him in for questioning."

"What evidence do you have against him?"

to stream	fließen
chest	Brust
to convince	überzeugen
breakthrough	Durchbruch
among	unter, inmitten

"He knows how Tobias James died, among other things."
"And I take it that we never released that piece of information."
"No, we didn't," Oscar replied calmly.
"Do what you have to do."
"Thank you, sir."

to double-lock	doppelt verschließen
to pace	rennen

Exercise 53: Passive voice. **Formulieren Sie die folgenden Sätze im Passiv!**

1. Henry picked up the phone.

   ____

2. They didn't answer my questions.

   ____

3. Superintendent Anderson gave permission to arrest Daniel Cutter.

   ____

4. Somebody killed Eddie.

   ____

5. Ross didn't let them in.

   ____

6. Ross closed the door.

   ____

7. We never released that piece of information.

   ____

Ross closed his front door behind him and double-locked it. He paced back and forth like a scared rabbit. What do I do now?

Phew!	Puh!
to whine	heulen, jammern

Daniel Cutter killed Eddie. Had he seen me? I was so stupid. I should have run away as soon as I saw Eddie fall. Or even better, just stayed where I was. Oh, man! What do I do now? What would Eddie do? Run. No, I don't want to do that. Call the police. That's it. Where's that private detective's phone number? Think, think. What did you do with it? Ross ran into the bedroom. The trousers he had worn to the funeral were on the bed. He picked them up and reached into the front pocket. Phew, here it is. He grabbed his mobile phone and dialled the number.

"Henry Shipman."

"You've got to help me, Mr Shipman. He's out to kill me," Ross yelled.

"Slow down. Who is this?"

"It's Ross. Ross from Aristotle's. Eddie's dead."

"Eddie. Your friend Eddie?" Henry asked, confused.

"Yeah. He killed him and now he's probably going to try to kill me."

"Ross. Where are you? Who's trying to kill you?"

"I'm at home. Daniel Cutter had Eddie killed. Now they'll come after me. I know they will."

"Okay. I have your address, I'll be right over. Don't let anyone in. Do you understand, Ross?"

"Yes, Mr Shipman. Please hurry."

Daniel Cutter's car was parked outside Ross's flat. Daniel Cutter and Cedric had a clear view of Ross as he paced back and forth in front of his upstairs window.

"You didn't tell me there were two of them," Cedric said.

"I didn't know. I only spoke to one of them." Daniel Cutter put his face in his hands. "This is such a mess."

"Now's not the time to start whining." Cedric opened the car door.

"Where are you going?" Daniel asked.

Exercise 54: Fill in the blanks. **Lesen Sie weiter und fügen Sie die passenden Wörter in die Lücken ein!**

life | jail | barman | business | accident | murder | control | sitting room | blackmail

"To take care of **1.** ______."
For the first time in his **2.** ______, Daniel was scared of his brother. "You aren't going to kill him, are you?"
"Look, little brother. You didn't seem to have any problems killing your best friend and that **3.** ______.
And who's idea was it to do something about the other one who tried to **4.** ______ you?"
"Tobias's death was an accident. He just made me so angry talking to me like that. I couldn't **5.** ______ myself."
"And the barman?"
"Another **6.** ______. I just wanted to delete the picture he took that had me in it. I thought he had gone to bed, but he must have heard me and came into the **7.** ______. We struggled and he fell out of the window."
"Maybe you could have convinced people that the first two deaths were accidents. But the one I just killed wasn't. It was cold-blooded **8.** ______ and unless we want to spend the rest of our lives in **9.** ______, we have another one to take care of."

peephole	Guckloch, Spion
to go off	losgehen (Gewehr)
to mean harm	Böses wollen

Oscar had just come back to his office when his mobile phone rang.
"Yes?" he answered.
"Oscar, it's Henry. Ross, the waiter from Aristotle's, has just called. He thinks Daniel Cutter is trying to kill him."
"What?"
"You heard right. I'm going over there now." Henry gave Oscar Ross's address and hung up.
"Roberta," Oscar called. "Come on. We've got an emergency."

Ross hesitated. I wish I had a peephole. If I live through this, the next flat I get will have a peephole. He put his ear to the door, but didn't hear anything.
"Who is it?"
"Police."
Ross opened the door.
"You got here fast."
Cedric pushed his way into the flat.
"Sorry, old boy. They didn't get here fast enough."
Daniel Cutter followed his brother and closed the door behind him. "Cedric. Stop pointing that rifle. It might go off."
"Wouldn't it be sad if it did?"
Daniel Cutter stood between his brother and Ross.
"Ross don't be afraid. All of this has got out of control. I don't want to kill you. I didn't want to kill your friend, I just wanted to scare him. Was it Eddie?"
Ross merely nodded.
"I thought so. I should have known that you two had seen me. You were waiting on the table at the entrance when I walked in that night."
"Sorry, Mr Cutter. We just thought we could get some extra spending money. We didn't mean any harm."

confession	Geständnis
content	zufrieden
to play for time	auf Zeit spielen
to plead with so.	jmd. anflehen
to pay up	vollständig bezahlen
to stop by	kurz vorbeischauen

"Isn't this a sad story. The **confessions** of a murderer and a blackmailer."
"Cedric will you shut up."
Ross didn't know how much longer Cedric would be **content** holding the rifle without shooting him. He needed to **play for time**.
"Mr Cutter, why did you kill Tobias James? I thought that the two of you were friends."
"Now that's a good question," Cedric said. "You haven't even told me that."
"He was blackmailing me."
"What did he have on you, Mr Cutter?" Ross asked.
"I never graduated from university."
"What?" Cedric shouted in disbelief. "The big man around town never graduated from university?"
"No. No, I didn't. Tobias helped me obtain a fake diploma. I've always lied on my CV. He was going to tell the bank. If that came out, I would be ruined. Tobias knew that, but he didn't care. He just wanted money to cover his losses. Losses created by his own bad investments."
"So you paid him to keep quiet," Cedric said.
"I did for a long time. But then he increased the amount. I couldn't afford it. I didn't know what to do. I **pleaded with** him, but he wouldn't listen. He just told me to **pay up**, or else."
Daniel sighed.
Ross tried to think of something else to say. Talking seemed to be working.
"Did you plan to kill him in Aristotle's?"
"No. I just **stopped by** to talk to him. Then I saw him going into the toilets and I followed him. If only I hadn't. If I had talked to

him at the bar, he might still be alive."
"Along with Michael Finn and Eddie," Ross mumbled.
Cedric quickly stepped around his brother and pointed the rifle at Ross.
"We'll be able to add you to that list soon."

Exercise 55: Choose the correct alternative.
Welche Mengenangaben sind korrekt? Unterstreichen Sie!

1. Michael Finn didn't have many / much money last year.
2. He had a lot of / plenty debts.
3. Henry only had few / a few minutes to get to Ross.
4. Daniel was a little / little annoyed with his brother.
5. Kathy Finn didn't have plenty of / much confidence in the police.
6. There weren't many / much things Sarah didn't know about Tobias.

Henry was the first to arrive at Ross's flat. He was standing on the doorstep when Oscar and Roberta arrived. He waved to them.
"Do we know what's going on up there?" Oscar asked.
"I have no idea. We should be prepared for the worst," Henry replied.
Oscar, Roberta and Henry took the lift to Ross's flat. They prepared their guns as they got out. Henry reached Ross's door first. He heard voices.

"They're in there," he informed the others.
"What do you think? Should we break down the door or pick the lock?" Oscar asked.
Henry studied the lock.
"I could pick it."
Oscar nodded for him to proceed. Henry gave Roberta his gun and quickly unlocked the door. Roberta handed him his gun and slowly turned the knob.

to lunge at so.	sich auf jmd. stürzen
to ring out	sich lösen (Schuss)
capable	fähig
to back out	rückwärts hinausgehen

"Police," the three inspectors yelled.
Cedric pointed the rifle at Ross.
"I'll shoot."
Daniel Cutter **lunged** at him.
"No, you won't, Cedric."
He was trying to take the rifle away from his brother when suddenly a shot **rang out**. Daniel Cutter fell to the floor, while Cedric grabbed Ross.
"Come near me and I'll shoot."
The three investigators stood still. They knew that anyone who would kill their own brother was **capable** of doing anything.
"Good," Cedric said. "Now slowly put your guns down on the floor."
Oscar, Roberta and Henry carefully placed their guns on the floor.
"You," Cedric said to Roberta, "kick them over here. Good. Now Ross and I are going to leave. And you aren't going to follow us. If you do, Ross is dead."
Slowly, Cedric **backed out** of the flat with Ross. He closed the door. As soon as they were gone, Oscar, Roberta and Henry picked up their guns. They ran out of the flat, but Cedric and Ross were gone.
"Damn," Henry said.

They rushed downstairs and were about to exit the block of flats when they heard two shots. Carefully, Henry opened the door. Cedric was bleeding heavily on the steps. Sam Meadows was standing over him, holding a gun.
An hour later, Henry accompanied Oscar, Roberta and Sam to the police station. Ross, who was suffering from shock, had been taken to the hospital until he could be questioned.
Oscar walked into his office. He wasn't there long when his phone rang.
"Okay, we'll be right up," he said.
Roberta, Sam and Henry were discussing the case.
"Let me guess. Superintendent Anderson wants to see you," Roberta said when she saw Oscar.
"Actually, he wants to see all of us."
"All of us?" Henry asked.
"Yes, all of us."

That couldn't be helped.	Das war nicht zu verhindern.
to frown	die Stirn runzeln
villain	Schurke

Superintendent Anderson stood up when he saw the investigative team at his door.
"Come in, come in," he said. He shook their hands.
"Great work. A bit bloody in the end, but I guess that couldn't be helped."
"No. We didn't have much control over that," Oscar said.
"That Cedric Cutter was always a wild one. That young waiter, Ross, said that Daniel Cutter saved his life."
Oscar frowned.
"I beg your pardon."
"You know if we co-ordinate our stories, Daniel Cutter can come out as the hero and his crazy brother as the villain. They are both dead. Dead men can't talk."
"You mean to say that Cedric Cutter killed Tobias James and Michael Finn?" Oscar asked.

"I didn't say that. It's just something to think about."
Superintendent Anderson turned his attention to Henry.
"Henry, it's good to see you again. Do you ever think about coming back to the force?"
"To tell you the truth, sir, no."
Henry turned around and walked out of Superintendent Anderson's office followed by Oscar, Roberta and Sam Meadows.

Final Test

Answers

Glossary

Final Test

Death at Land's End

Exercise 1: Verb forms. Wie lautet das Present Simple und Past Simple der folgenden Verben in der dritten Person?

1. to find	*finds*	*found*
2. to see		
3. to sell		
4. to give		
5. to take		

Exercise 2: Spot the mistake. Welcher Satz ist fehlerfrei? Kreuzen Sie an!

1. a) ❐ Old George is working when Hartley arrives.
   b) ❐ Old George works when Hartley arrives.
2. a) ❐ I am thinking you should call the police!
   b) ❐ I think you should call the police!
3. a) ❐ Bad news travels fast.
   b) ❐ Bad news travel fast.
4. a) ❐ Say me the whole story.
   b) ❐ Tell me the whole story.
5. a) ❐ The police is looking for the murderer.
   b) ❐ The police are looking for the murderer.

Learning by Killing

Exercise 3: True or false? Welche der folgenden Aussagen zur Geschichte „Learning by Killing" sind wahr? Markieren Sie mit richtig ✔ oder falsch – !

1. Eastcastle is a small town in the North of England. ❐
2. Colonel Lessons wants to retire to Brighton. ❐
3. Tracy Dean was born in Ireland. ❐
4. Jim Ryan is a Catholic from Dublin. ❐
5. Mrs Bradley is a cleaner at the school. ❐
6. Elke comes from Switzerland. ❐

Exercise 4: If or when? Setzen Sie in die Lücken das passende Wort ein!

1. Tracy enters the classroom to find out __________ everything is going smoothly.
2. Karl wants to check the words in his dictionary __________ he goes back in his hotel.
3. __________ all pupils learn their text by heart, the play will be a success.
4. There will be a future for Tracy and Jim __________ he loves her as much as she does.
5. __________ she realizes that he doesn't love her, she is very sad.

The Butterworth Mystery

Exercise 5: Verb forms. **Setzen Sie die richtige Verbfom ein!**

1. After the phone call was finished, Michael open ________ ________ the car window.

2. He saw her rush ________ into the room, looking very frightened.

3. Two people hide ________ in some bushes underneath a tree.

4. Tomorrow, someone come ________ round and check for fingerprints.

Exercise 6: Word search. **Finden Sie im Suchrätsel sieben Begriffe aus "The Butterworth Mystery"!**

C	H	O	K	I	N	G	T	U	Z
Y	G	V	U	G	T	R	A	J	E
I	O	B	S	H	H	E	B	O	D
S	R	I	C	A	I	K	B	X	W
E	G	R	A	V	E	Y	A	R	D
M	E	X	R	I	F	L	Z	Q	B
I	O	H	Y	C	I	S	S	A	J
Z	U	P	A	I	N	T	I	N	G
O	S	F	L	T	W	A	F	M	E
P	Q	A	G	H	O	S	T	U	C

Exercise 7: Contracted forms. Bilden Sie die verneinte Kurzform!

1. I can ________________
2. I will ________________
3. I do ________________
4. you are ________________
5. we could ________________
6. it is ________________
7. he should ________________

Long Time No Kill

Exercise 8: Who did what? Verbinden Sie Täter und Aktion!

1. ☐ crashed the car	a) no one
2. ☐ made aggressive phone calls	b) the chambermaid
3. ☐ found Penny's phone	c) some teenagers
4. ☐ killed Rebecca Bracknell	d) Mr Wiley

Exercise 9: Translation. Übersetzen Sie!

1. Margaret gab ihnen ihre Visitenkarte.

____

2. Die Schülerinnen hatten Angst vor der Schulleiterin.

____

3. Was zum Teufel macht er hinter dem Zaun?

____

4. Miss Musty und Miss Foster waren eng befreundet.

____

5. Sie sind damit beschäftigt, den Schubkarren zu untersuchen.

____

Exercise 10: Boarding School. Finden Sie neun Begriffe!

B	A	F	E	H	E	T	C	O	S	E	L	Y	L
O	S	T	U	E	M	U	L	E	P	R	E	T	O
T	C	I	D	A	O	N	A	L	O	T	S	S	Y
S	H	E	A	D	M	I	S	T	R	E	S	S	X
Y	O	R	M	G	P	F	S	A	T	A	O	R	O
D	O	R	M	I	T	O	R	Y	S	C	N	E	Y
O	L	M	E	R	T	R	O	U	S	H	B	A	Q
R	T	A	A	L	E	M	O	M	A	E	R	Y	A
L	E	D	A	R	E	T	M	E	N	R	P	E	S

Exercise 11: Multiple choice. Welcher Satz ist korrekt? Kreuzen Sie an!

1. a) ☐ Miss Paddington is interesting in Hudson's work.
   b) ☐ Miss Paddington is interested in Hudson's work.

2. a) ☐ Penny turned up at the school.
   b) ☐ Penny turned off at the school.

3. a) ☐ The police is looking for the murder.

b) ☐ The police are looking for the murderer.

4. a) ☐ Penny is dead, I'm afraid.

b) ☐ Penny is dead, I'm frightened.

Exercise 12: Where is Shepton Mallet? Lösen Sie das Kreuzworträtsel!

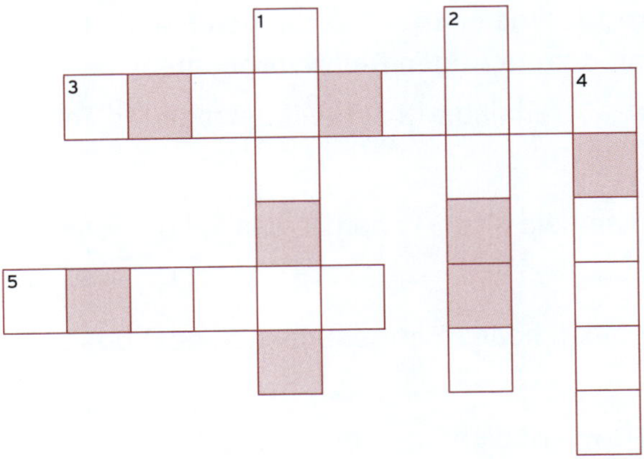

Lösung: _ _ _ _ _ _ _ _

Across:

3. DI Bradley would like to have an ...
5. If you do something illegal, you ... a crime.

Down:

1. Penny was the ... of a violent crime.
2. Miss Musty was only interested in her ...
4. Mrs Motherwell killed Miss Foster with the sports ...

Exercise 13: Definitions. **Schreiben Sie das beschriebene Wort auf!**

1. This helps you to see something far away. ______
2. A step up in your career. ______
3. A very small town. ______
4. The political leader of the UK. ______

Death Wasn't the Deal

Exercise 14: Who or that? **Verbinden Sie die folgenden Sätze mit dem richtigen Relativpronomen!**

1. He was strangled with a tie. It belonged to Tobias James.

______

2. The man held a sports bag. It was full of money.

______

3. The woman heard a noise. She lives next door.

______

4. Tina is worried about her husband. She is Elisabeth's best friend.

______

5. The man was trapped. He let the hostage go.

______

6. Ross works in a restaurant. It is very expensive.

______

Exercise 15: Unscramble the words. Ordnen Sie die Buchstaben zu sinnvollen Wörtern!

1. ltneic __ __ ☐ __ __ __
2. mnabra __ __ __ __ __ ☐
3. ysruev __ __ __ ☐ __ __
4. htsce __ __ ☐ __ __
5. cusspsuioi __ __ ☐ __ __ __ __ __ __ __
6. wrteia __ __ __ ☐ __ __
7. vtesni ☐ __ __ __ __ __
8. ugn ☐ __ __
9. reghta __ ☐ __ __ __ __
10. ite ☐ __ __
11. uolabit __ __ ☐ __ __ __ __
12. toh hsufl __ ☐ __ __ __ __ __ __
13. situnerivy __ ☐ __ __ __ __ __ __ __ __

Lösung: ☐☐☐☐☐☐☐☐☐☐☐☐☐

Exercise 16: Opposites. Finden Sie die Gegenteile der folgenden Begriffe!

1. repeat ____________
2. close ____________
3. remember ____________
4. truth ____________

Exercise 17: Tenses. **Setzen Sie die Verben in der richtigen Zeitform ein!**

1. I read ______________________ a book when I heard a noise.
2. If I know ______________________ he was in trouble, I would have called the police.
3. I work ______________________ here for ten years.
4. I think we find ______________________ the killer.
5. We separate ______________________ three months ago.
6. Daniel not act ______________________ like himself lately.
7. Daniel wonder ______________________ if he had done the right thing by involving his brother.

Exercise 18: Word forms. **Bilden Sie zu den Substantiven das jeweilige Adjektiv!**

1. success ______________________
2. accident ______________________
3. sympathy ______________________
4. drink ______________________
5. brother ______________________
6. blood ______________________
7. emotion ______________________
8. mess ______________________
9. suspect ______________________

Exercise 19: Who is who? **Ordnen Sie die Beschreibungen der richtigen Person zu!**

1. ☐ This person is Tobias's wife.
2. ☐ This person is Tobias's mistress.
3. ☐ This person is Tobias's best friend.
4. ☐ This person is a waiter.
5. ☐ This person is a barman.
6. ☐ This person is Henry's secretary.

a) Daniel
b) Ross
c) Stewart
d) Elisabeth
e) Jennifer
f) Arabella

Exercise 20: Fill in the blanks. **Ergänzen Sie die Sätze mit den angegebenen Begriffen!**

blackmailed | buy | gathered | shrieks | knack | fortune

1. Tobias had a ________________ for making money.
2. Hysterical ________________ came from the dining room.
3. A few bystanders had ________________ behind the police tape.
4. Ross tried to ________________ some time by talking to Daniel.
5. I'm staying here due to my change in ________________.
6. Tobias James had ________________ Daniel Cutter.

Exercise 21: Idiomatic expressions. **Welche Bedeutung haben die folgenden Ausdrücke? Kreuzen Sie an!**

1. Don't hold your breath!
   a) ❐ Don't expect it.
   b) ❐ Don't turn blue.

2. Roberta gulped down her coffee.
   a) ❐ Roberta drank her coffee slowly.
   b) ❐ Roberta drank her coffee quickly.

3. It's human nature to look for a scapegoat.
   a) ❐ It's human nature to want to raise goats.
   b) ❐ It's human nature to look for someone to blame.

4. She pumped Sam for information.
   a) ❐ She kept asking Sam for information.
   a) ❐ She beat Sam to make him talk.

5. Tobias blackmailed Daniel.
   a) ❐ Tobias sent Daniel letters without paying for them.
   b) ❐ Tobias forced Daniel to give him money.

Exercise 22: Questions to the text. **Kreuzen Sie die richtige Antwort an!**

1. Detective Chief Inspector ... is Roberta's boss.
   a) ❐ Sam Meadows
   b) ❐ Peter Oscar
   c) ❐ Oscar Peters

2. Elisabeth told Tina that ...
   a) ❐ Daniel had a mistress.

b) ❒ Daniel would never betray Tina.
c) ❒ she had a love affair with Daniel.

3. Daniel Cutter was giving money to
   a) ❒ Elisabeth James.
   b) ❒ Cedric Cutter.
   c) ❒ Tobias James.
4. Arabella Hornsby is
   a) ❒ Tobias James's ex-mistress.
   b) ❒ Tobias James's secretary.
   c) ❒ Daniel Cutter's ex-wife.

Answers

Death at Land's End

Exercise 1: **1.** large **2.** noisy **3.** unfriendly **4.** expensive

Exercise 2: **1.** true **2.** true **3.** false (He calls the coastguard.) **4.** false (McGregor works with his partner, Sam Nolan.) **5.** false (He smokes a cigarette and watches the sun set.)

Exercise 3: **1.** repeats **2.** tells **3.** tell **4.** is **5.** get

Exercise 4: **1.** you're (your) **2.** tell (say) **3.** it (him) **4.** easily (easy) **5.** thinks (things) **6.** German (german)

Exercise 5: **1.** d **2.** c **3.** b **4.** a

Exercise 6:
1. O'Reilly doesn't think she is a liar.
2. Did you see him?
3. They identify his body.
4. Walker keeps it at Sennen Cove.
5. Do you believe her?

Exercise 7: **1.** onto **2.** to **3.** to **4.** for **5.** on **6.** at

Exercise 8: **1.** nosy **2.** nasty **3.** dirty **4.** empty **5.** angry

Exercise 9: **1.** When **2.** What **3.** Where **4.** who

Exercise 10: **1.** sit down **2.** husband **3.** lost **4.** love **5.** strong

Exercise 11: **1.** name's **2.** I'm **3.** She's **4.** isn't **5.** We'll

Exercise 12: **1.** false (Walker went to Cornwall to sail his yacht one last time.) **2.** true **3.** true **4.** false (Giles often goes sailing. He lied to O'Reilly.)

Exercise 13: **1.** Where **2.** What is **3.** her **4.** men **5.** thinks

Exercise 14: **1.** are you going **2.** be **3.** Are **4.** has **5.** goes

Exercise 15:

M	A	L	W	E	M	W	O	T	S
O	V	E	R	B	O	A	R	D	A
G	K	I	S	R	T	V	D	E	I
D	E	S	U	A	O	E	A	C	B
P	E	W	R	T	R	I	C	K	O
I	L	I	F	E	B	U	O	Y	T
L	E	M	I	N	O	T	U	Z	N
L	Y	T	S	E	A	S	I	C	K
O	R	E	T	S	T	M	A	B	E
D	E	A	K	Y	A	C	H	T	E

Learning by Killing

Exercise 1: **1.** laugh/cry **2.** plump/slim **3.** whisper/shout **4.** cheap/expensive **5.** late/early **6.** short/tall **7.** superb/terrible **8.** heavy/light **9.** fast/slow

Exercise 2: **1.** ugly **2.** car **3.** garden **4.** stay **5.** clever **6.** secretary **7.** huge **8.** seagull **9.** sailor

Exercise 3: **1.** smile **2.** laugh **3.** looks **4.** come **5.** means **6.** know **7.** think **8.** can **9.** produce **10.** depends **11.** have

Exercise 4: **1.** magazine **2.** desk **3.** biro **4.** briefcase **5.** folder **6.** chips **7.** redhead **8.** class

Exercise 5: **1.** is **2.** am talking **3.** am trying **4.** means **5.** nods **6.** says

Exercise 6: **1.** You can put logs on a fire. **2.** Karl picks up his biro. **3.** Pierre speaks with a French accent. **4.** People meet their friends in a pub. **5.** She decides that Karl must die. **6.** You are an innocent witness. **7.** Jim is happy that the ice is broken.

Exercise 7: **1.** false **2.** false **3.** false **4.** true **5.** false **6.** false **7.** true

Exercise 8: **1.** by **2.** about **3.** for **4.** at **5.** out **6.** off **7.** off

Exercise 9: **1.** cocky/impertinent **2.** cut/commission **3.** hip flask/bottle **4.** under false pretences/ illegally **5.** calm/relaxed **6.** grand/thousand **7.** vigorously/energetically

Exercise 10: **1.** think **2.** leaves **3.** runs **4.** hurries **5.** follows **6.** is lying **7.** is dying

Exercise 11: **1.** Sie sind bereit, ihre Aufgaben zu präsentieren. **2.** Die Studenten lachen und unterhalten sich. **3.** Sie freuen sich auf die Aufführung. **4.** Mahdi verschwindet hinter den/dem Vorhang. **5.** Ich fahre weg und dann schießt du. **6.** Karl putzt seine Brille. **7.** Einige Studenten fangen an zu weinen.

Exercise 12: **1.** was **2.** were **3.** understood **4.** left **5.** knew **6.** heard **7.** thought

Exercise 13: **1.** Ryan's class can give no useful information because they are upset. **2.** The toy gun cost £5.50. **3.** Olsen's seat was in the second row. **4.** Olsen heard three sounds. **5.** Tracy was at home on Friday. **6.** The cleaner's name is Mrs Bradley. **7.** Olsen lives in Denmark.

Exercise 14: **1.** Is Watson doing his interviews? **2.** Do they order another gin? **3.** Does he turn to the gun collection? **4.** Does his school pay local taxes? **5.** Is she cleaning the floor? **6.** Is the sun setting on Eastcastle?

The Butterworth Mystery

Exercise 1: **1.** Felder **2.** Dorf **3.** mitfühlend **4.** alt **5.** Häuschen **6.** geschehen **7.** Tor **8.** Gemälde

Exercise 2: **1.** b **2.** c **3.** b

Exercise 3: **1.** brought **2.** had **3.** walked **4.** were **5.** was **6.** told **7.** stood

Exercise 4: **1.** e **2.** g **3.** f **4.** c **5.** b **6.** d **7.** a

Exercise 5: **1.** Where **2.** What **3.** When **4.** Which **5.** Why **6.** Who

Exercise 6: **1.** After **2.** about **3.** at **4.** to **5.** in **6.** with **7.** for

Exercise 7: **1.** e **2.** c **3.** f **4.** h **5.** a **6.** g **7.** i **8.** d **9.** b

Exercise 8: **1.** quickly **2.** close **3.** serious **4.** full **5.** clear **6.** alive

Exercise 9: **1.** cook **2.** torchlight **3.** murderer **4.** sell **5.** box **6.** museum **7.** soldier **8.** clue

Exercise 10: **1.** mansion **2.** torch **3.** sculptor **4.** mobile **5.** cemetery **6.** confident
Lösung: stolen

Exercise 11: **1.** went **2.** wrote **3.** heard **4.** were living **5.** to find **6.** of **7.** bring

Exercise 12: **1.** false (He's 85.) **2.** true **3.** true **4.** false (No, not without a search warrant.) **5.** false (They lost contact much later.) **6.** true

Exercise 13: **1.** She **2.** They **3.** We **4.** He **5.** them **6.** us **7.** her **8.** him **9.** her **10.** you

Exercise 14: **1.** thieves **2.** women **3.** galleries **4.** information **5.** memories **6.** noises **7.** systems **8.** witches

Exercise 15: **1.** Sylvia Butterworth stole the paintings because she thinks they belong to her.
2. Agnes Cott was burned as a witch at Lancaster Castle in the 17th century.
3. They are bored and are partying at the cemetery. They are lighting candles and listening to music.
4. They think the house is haunted because sometimes strange noises can be heard and lights can be seen at the house.
5. It is named after John Oswald, who built the house the gallery is in.

Long Time No Kill

Exercise 1: lovely, blue, young, ugly, grey, yellow, terrible, bossy, arrogant

Exercise 2: **1.** at **2.** through **3.** on **4.** behind **5.** above

Exercise 3: **1.** true **2.** false (Miss Foster was very popular.) **3.** true **4.** false (Penny is a lawyer.)

Exercise 4: **1.** get **2.** leads **3.** is standing **4.** pours

Exercise 5: **1.** them **2.** it **3.** her **4.** They

Exercise 6: **1.** morning **2.** watch **3.** thinks **4.** Perhaps **5.** reception

Exercise 7: **1.** She is the headmistress of Shepton Mallet Boarding School for Girls.
2. She meets Fiona at the Queen's Arms pub.
3. Fiona thinks Penny was a teacher's pet.
4. She finds it in room 14 when she is cleaning.

Exercise 8: **1.** is **2.** knocks **3.** were **4.** found **5.** thought

Exercise 9: **1.** c **2.** d **3.** a **4.** b

Exercise 10: **1.** is standing (standing) **2.** give (gives) **3.** 14-year-old boy (14-years-old boy) **4.** a lot of (lot of) **5.** through (threw) **6.** mobile (handy)

Exercise 11: **1.** emergency **2.** pile **3.** proud **4.** message
Lösung: clue

Exercise 12: **1.** b **2.** a **3.** d **4.** c

Exercise 13: **1.** I've **2.** he's **3.** You're **4.** It's **5.** you'll

Exercise 14: **1.** colleague **2.** husband **3.** assistant **4.** boss

Exercise 15: **1.** Was ist los? **2.** Sie macht ihre Sache gut.
3. Macht nichts! **4.** Ich komme einfach nicht voran!

Exercise 16: **1.** turns off **2.** walks **3.** replies **4.** is **5.** go

Exercise 17: **1.** d **2.** c **3.** b **4.** a

Exercise 18: **1.** what **2.** Why **3.** What **4.** Who **5.** What

Exercise 19: **1.** rings **2.** calling **3.** loved **4.** than

Exercise 20: **1.** surprise **2.** number **3.** text **4.** message

Exercise 21:

1 N	2 E	3 T	4 B	5 A	6 L
20 Y	21 E	22 L	23 L	24 O	7 L
19 C	32 B	33 E	34 C	25 W	8 I
18 N	31 E	36 A	35 C	26 O	9 T
17 E	30 R	29 E	28 D	27 N	10 T
16 G	15 R	14 E	13 M	12 E	11 L

Exercise 22: **1.** hard **2.** heavy **3.** terrible **4.** closer **5.** deep **6.** dark

Exercise 23: **1.** bottom **2.** late **3.** serious **4.** dangerous **5.** death **6.** find

Exercise 24: **1.** d **2.** b **3.** a **4.** c

Exercise 25: **1.** Next Hudson drives back to Scotland Yard.
2. He meets Jarvis outside an interview room.
3. "Morning, sir!" she says brightly.
4. "Morning, Jarvis. How is Mr Wiley this morning?"

Exercise 26: **1.** d **2.** c **3.** a **4.** b

Exercise 27: **1.** seat **2.** office **3.** shakes **4.** breath **5.** crime

Exercise 28: **1.** I spent the weekend sitting at my computer.
2. She tries to escape.
3. He keeps complaining.
4. I am renting a small flat.

Exercise 29: **1.** b **2.** d **3.** a **4.** c

Exercise 30: **1.** new (knew) **2.** to (too) **3.** of (off) **4.** right (write) **5.** her (she) **6.** know (no)

Exercise 31: **1.** true **2.** false. (He has no idea who she was.) **3.** false. (She doesn't find one.) **4.** true

Exercise 32: **1.** arrives **2.** thick **3.** round **4.** hard **5.** sits down

Exercise 33: **1.** arrival **2.** choice **3.** thought **4.** reply **5.** death **6.** connection

Exercise 34: **1.** window **2.** receptionist **3.** windowsill **4.** afternoon

Exercise 35: **1.** scared **2.** important **3.** unusual **4.** continue

Exercise 36: **1.** quiet **2.** here **3.** some **4.** me **5.** sadly

Exercise 37: **1.** d **2.** a **3.** b **4.** c

Exercise 38: **1.** edge **2.** behind **3.** get out **4.** busy **5.** want to wait

Exercise 39: **1.** firm **2.** nervous **3.** strong **4.** tight

Exercise 40: **1.** leaving **2.** rings **3.** is **4.** have **5.** missing **6.** thought

Exercise 41: **1.** b **2.** d **3.** a **4.** c

Exercise 42: **1.** tray **2.** truth **3.** persuade **4.** accident **5.** reputation **6.** harmless **7.** liar
Lösung: Australia

Exercise 43: **1.** told **2.** argument **3.** about **4.** died **5.** upset

Exercise 44: **1.** Übrigens, ich heiße Nancy.
2. Reiß dich zusammen!
3. Jetzt kommen wir endlich voran.
4. Ich hole die Schlüssel.

Exercise 45: **1.** past **2.** towards **3.** Next to **4.** in **5.** in **6.** at

Exercise 46: **1.** hysterically **2.** stupid **3.** gentle **4.** broken **5.** tightly

Exercise 47: **1.** think (thing) **2.** carefully (careful) **3.** knew (new) **4.** how (who) **5.** an (a) **6.** die (died)

Exercise 48: **1.** false (Mrs Motherwell killed her before she could talk to Miss Sharp.) **2.** false (They were friends.) **3.** false (It was an accident.) **4.** true

Exercise 49: **1.** car boot **2.** handcuffs **3.** key ring **4.** hockey stick

Death Wasn't the Deal

Exercise 1: **1.** wait **2.** toe **3.** kind **4.** owner **5.** destruction

Exercise 2: **1.** crooked **2.** wrinkled **3.** lingered **4.** repu-tation **5.** temper **6.** scapegoat

Exercise 3: **1.** by **2.** into **3.** near **4.** at **5.** of **6.** at

Exercise 4: **1.** false (Tobias hasn't lost Ethan Smith as a client.) **2.** false (Sarah doesn't plan to meet Tobias at Aristotle's.) **3.** true **4.** false (The Canary Wharf cafés have turned into recruitment centres.) **5.** false (Tobias is not very happy to see Wallace.) **6.** true **7.** true **8.** false (Sarah is Tobias's secretary.) **9.** true **10.** false (Tobias smoked a cigar after Paul left.)

Exercise 5: **1.** d **2.** h **3.** a **4.** e **5.** g **6.** c **7.** b **8.** f

Exercise 6: **1.** The British government is recruiting. **2.** You seem to be in a good mood. **3.** You have been smoking a cigar. **4.** It is human nature to look for a scapegoat. **5.** I have just had a very successful meeting. **6.** I am meeting Ethan Smith for dinner.

Exercise 7: **1.** e **2.** d **3.** a **4.** b **5.** g **6.** f **7.** c

Exercise 8: **1.** pushed **2.** making **3.** round up **4.** know **5.** placed **6.** scribbled **7.** saw

Exercise 9: **1.** When was Tobias James killed? **2.** Where was his body found? **3.** Who found his body? **4.** How did the inspector get to Aristotle's? **5.** Why are we going to Aristotle's? **6.** Why did it take them so long to find the body?

Exercise 10: **1.** lead **2.** medical examiner **3.** might **4.** unless

Exercise 11: **1.** b **2.** a **3.** b **4.** a **5.** b

Exercise 12: **1.** will **2.** had **3.** hadn't **4.** remember **5.** wouldn't **6.** won

Exercise 13: **1.** Roberta's pad **2.** Mr James's financial problems **3.** Stewart's words **4.** her husband's death **5.** his customers' visits **6.** Wallace's friend

Exercise 14: **1.** for **2.** at **3.** to **4.** of **5.** with **6.** in **7.** about

Exercise 15: **1.** d **2.** f **3.** a **4.** c **5.** b **6.** e

Exercise 16: **1.** made **2.** cloth **3.** hold **4.** top **5.** sealed **6.** gulped **7.** knack **8.** puff

Exercise 17: **1.** personal items **2.** entered **3.** phoned **4.** inspected **5.** commented **6.** hated **7.** mad

Exercise 18: **1.** won't you **2.** did you **3.** didn't you **4.** hasn't he **5.** didn't she **6.** will we **7.** do you

Exercise 19: **1.** line (ryhmes with fine) **2.** take (rhymes with shake) **3.** show (rhymes with know) **4.** to pick (rhymes with kick) **5.** try (rhymes with sigh) **6.** phone (rhymes with bone)

Exercise 20: **1.** was reading **2.** knocked **3.** to talk **4.** sitting **5.** wants **6.** returned **7.** tell

Exercise 21: **1.** false (Kathy Finn was Michael Finn's wife.) **2.** false (Roberta and Oscar do not think so.) **3.** true **4.** true **5.** true **6.** true **7.** true

Exercise 22: **1.** She said she was sorry to hear about Michael's death. **2.** She said she had heard a scream. **3.** She said she would let me know if she thought of anything else. **4.** She asked me what I meant. **5.** She said she didn't think anything was missing. **6.** She asked me where I had gone yesterday.

Exercise 23:

A	B	E	D	R	O	O	M	A	M	P	L
T	R	A	N	I	W	N	E	V	B	M	O
L	K	I	H	A	L	L	W	A	Y	M	Y
F	U	R	N	I	T	U	R	E	R	A	X
T	R	A	C	K	I	N	G	E	N	T	O
N	B	E	N	T	L	A	K	T	J	F	Y
D	O	O	R	W	E	R	E	P	S	L	Q
E	V	M	R	E	I	N	Y	R	O	A	A
S	N	S	T	L	E	P	S	L	Y	T	S
K	W	E	R	K	F	Q	Y	P	E	D	O
I	S	T	A	I	R	S	H	N	F	U	F
S	L	T	B	V	L	O	C	K	E	I	A

Exercise 24: **1.** information **2.** hobbies **3.** furniture

4. thieves 5. robberies 6. employees 7. advice 8. cups

Exercise 25: 1. Jennifer was filing papers when Henry entered the waiting room. 2. Jennifer was deciding what to have for lunch when a client knocked on the door. 3. Tobias was changing his tie when he heard a noise. 4. Olivia was going to the market when she saw Kathy and Henry. 5. Roberta was getting out of the lift when Oscar called her into his office. 6. Stewart was pouring himself a drink when Tobias arrived.

Exercise 26: 1. c 2. e 3. a 4. d 5. b 6. f

Exercise 27: 1. fast 2. hard 3. rarely 4. slowly 5. risky 6. mysteriously

Exercise 28:

1 M	2 U	3 R	4 D	5 E	6 R	7 E
22 E	23 A	24 R	25 I	26 V	27 E	8 R
21 Y	36 S	37 L	38 E	39 T	28 R	9 E
20 A	35 W	42 R	41 E	40 T	29 E	10 L
19 D	34 E	33 N	32 O	31 S	30 A	11 A
18 N	17 U	16 S	15 E	14 V	13 I	12 T

Exercise 29: 1. g 2. e 3. a 4. f 5. b 6. d 7. c

Exercise 30: 1. false (Roberta is not always on time.) 2. true 3. true 4. false (Not everyone knows that Roberta likes Henry Shipman.) 5. true 6. true

Exercise 31: 1. sense 2. figurative 3. dramatic 4. bad luck 5. suffer 6. effective 7. motive

Exercise 32: 1. caught, caught 2. knew, known 3. left, left 4. fought, fought 5. drew, drawn 6. found, found 7. gave, given

Exercise 33: 1. eyes 2. two 3. callers 4. solved 5. answered 6. suspects 7. murder 8. office

Exercise 34: **1.** commit suicide **2.** photograph **3.** inquire **4.** report **5.** replied **6.** surveyed

Exercise 35: **1.** d **2.** e **3.** b **4.** a **5.** f **6.** c

Exercise 36: **1.** on **2.** with **3.** up **4.** for **5.** out **6.** near **7.** on

Exercise 37: **1.** was **2.** arrested **3.** haven't seen **4.** Have you seen **5.** called **6.** liked **7.** to find **8.** is **9.** started

Exercise 38: **1.** arrived **2.** exactly **3.** laughed **4.** Take **5.** draw **6.** number **7.** wrinkled **8.** silence **9.** responded

Exercise 39: **1.** get over **2.** get on **3.** got off lightly **4.** got rid of **5.** got wound up **6.** got out of

Exercise 40: **1.** arrived **2.** sat **3.** to be **4.** got **5.** rose **6.** recognized **7.** shook

Exercise 41: **1.** false (Daniel's brother never was in jail.) **2.** true **3.** false (Aristotle's had a lot of bad luck lately.) **4.** false (Cedric didn't have a good relationship with his neighbour.) **5.** true **6.** false (Cedric apparently hasn't been in any trouble since the shooting.)

Exercise 42: **1.** No, I didn't. **2.** Yes, he did. **3.** No, I'm not. **4.** Yes, he is. **5.** No, I won't. **6.** No, I haven't.

Exercise 43: **1.** mess **2.** nudging **3.** murder **4.** suspicious **5.** relationship **6.** otherwise **7.** surprised

Exercise 44: **1.** waited for **2.** come from **3.** came in **4.** called off **5.** moving in **6.** get rid of

Exercise 45: **1.** d **2.** f **3.** a **4.** g **5.** b **6.** e **7.** c

Exercise 46: **1.** b **2.** b **3.** b **4.** a **5.** a

Exercise 47: **1.** He **2.** I **3.** he **4.** I **5.** I **6.** He **7.** I **8.** I **9.** you **10.** You

Exercise 48: **1.** c **2.** d **3.** e **4.** f **5.** a **6.** b

Exercise 49: **1.** information **2.** provide **3.** income **4.** lighter **5.** account **6.** puff **7.** wealthy **8.** wonder

Exercise 50:

							3 F	
							A	
		1 C	2 L	I	E	N	T	S
			A				H	
	4 S	T	R	A	N	G	E	
	U		G				R	
5 U	P	S	E	6 T				
	P			I				
7 L	O	S	I	N	G			
	R			A				
	T							

Exercise 51: **1.** drove **2.** took **3.** going **4.** done **5.** help **6.** looked **7.** to scare

Exercise 52: **1.** When did you last see him? **2.** Talk to Arabella Hornsby. **3.** I'll call you later. **4.** I never drink alone. **5.** I have been talking to Tobias's father.

Exercise 53: **1.** The phone was picked up by Henry. **2.** My questions weren't answered by them. **3.** Permission to arrest Daniel Cutter was given by Superintendent Anderson. **4.** Eddie was killed by somebody. **5.** They weren't let in by Ross. **6.** The door was closed by Ross. **7.** That piece of information was never released by us.

Exercise 54: **1.** business **2.** life **3.** barman **4.** blackmail **5.** control **6.** accident **7.** sitting room **8.** murder **9.** jail

Exercise 55: **1.** much **2.** a lot of **3.** a few **4.** a little **5.** much **6.** many

Final Test

Exercise 1: **1.** finds, found **2.** sees, saw **3.** sells, sold **4.** gives, gave **5.** takes, took

Exercise 2: **1.** a **2.** b **3.** a **4.** b **5.** b

Exercise 3: **1.** false **2.** false **3.** false **4.** false **5.** true **6.** true

Exercise 4: **1.** if **2.** when **3.** If **4.** if **5.** When

Exercise 5: **1.** opened **2.** rush **3.** were hiding **4.** will come

Exercise 6: **Across: 1.** CHOKING **2.** GRAVEYARD **3.** PAINTING **4.** GHOST
Down: 1. GORGEOUS **2.** SCARY **3.**THIEF

Exercise 7: **1.** I can't **2.** I won't **3.** I don't **4.** you aren't **5.** we couldn't **6.** it isn't **7.** he shouldn't

Exercise 8: **1.** c **2.** d **3.** b **4.** a

Exercise 9: **1.** Margaret gave them her business card. **2.** The schoolgirls were afraid of the headmistress.
3. What on earth is he doing behind the fence?
4. Miss Musty and Miss Foster were close friends.
5. They are busy examining the wheelbarrow.

Exercise 10:

B	A	F	E	H	E	T	C	O	S	E	L	Y
O	S	T	U	E	M	U	L	E	P	R	E	T
T	C	I	D	A	O	N	A	L	O	T	S	S
S	H	E	A	D	M	I	S	T	R	E	S	S
Y	O	R	M	G	P	F	S	A	T	A	O	R
D	O	R	M	I	T	O	R	Y	S	C	N	E
O	L	M	E	R	T	R	O	U	S	H	B	A
R	T	A	A	L	E	M	O	M	A	E	R	Y
L	E	D	A	R	E	T	M	E	N	R	P	E

Exercise 11: **1.** b **2.** a **3.** b **4.** a

Exercise 12:

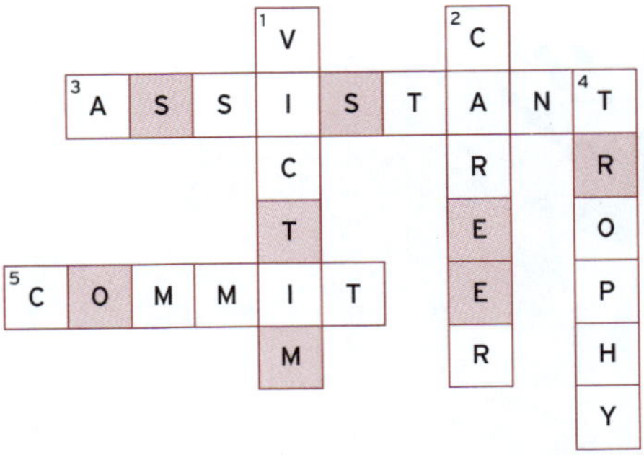

Lösung: Somerset

Exercise 13: **1.** binoculars **2.** promotion **3.** village **4.** prime minister

Exercise 14: **1.** He was strangled by a tie that belonged to Tobias James. **2.** The man held a sports bag that was full of money. **3.** The woman who lives next door heard a noise. **4.** Tina, who is Elisabeth's best friend, is worried about her husband. **5.** The man who was trapped let the hostage go. **6.** Ross works in a restaurant that is very expensive.

Exercise 15: **1.** client **2.** barman **3.** survey **4.** chest **5.** suspicious **6.** waiter **7.** invest **8.** gun **9.** gather **10.** tie **11.** bailout **12.** hot flush **13.** university **Lösung:** investigation

Exercise 16: **1.** stop **2.** open **3.** forget **4.** lie

Exercise 17: **1.** was reading **2.** had known **3.** have worked/have been working **4.** have found **5.** separated **6.** hasn't been acting **7.** wondered

Exercise 18: **1.** successful **2.** accidental **3.** sympathetic **4.** drunk **5.** brotherly **6.** bloody **7.** emotional **8.** messy **9.** suspicious

Exercise 19: **1.** d **2.** f **3.** a **4.** b **5.** c **6.** e

Exercise 20: **1.** knack **2.** shrieks **3.** gathered **4.** buy **5.** fortune **6.** blackmailed

Exercise 21: **1.** a **2.** b **3.** b **4.** a **5.** b

Exercise 22: **1.** c **2.** b **3.** c **4.** a

Glossary

↯ = umgangssprachlich
pl = Plural

accelerator	Gaspedal
accident	Unfall, Unglück
accommodation	Unterkunft
accounts *pl*	Geschäftsbücher
actor/actress *m/f*	Schauspieler(in)
to add	hinzufügen
to adjust sth.	etw. zurechtrücken, in Ordnung bringen
to admire	bewundern
to afford	sich leisten
afloat	über Wasser
against	gegen
ajar	angelehnt, halboffen
to alert sb.	jmd. alarmieren, warnen
allotment	Schrebergarten
allowance	*hier*: Beihilfe, Zulage
among	unter, inmitten, zwischen
amount	Betrag
angry	ärgerlich, verärgert
anxious	besorgt, ängstlich
anything else	sonst noch etwas
apart from	außer
APB (all points bulletin)	Fahndungsaufruf
to apologize	(sich) entschuldigen
apparently	anscheinend
to appear	auftauchen, erscheinen
appointment	Termin
appreciation	Anerkennung

to approach	sich nähern
archive	Archiv
armed	bewaffnet
to arrest	festnehmen, verhaften
art restoration	Gemälderestaurierung
as well	ebenfalls
asap	schnellstmöglich
assembly hall	Aula
to assume	annehmen, vermuten
at a time	gleichzeitig
at first hand	*hier*: mit eigenen Augen
at once	sofort; gleichzeitig
at the seaside	an der Küste
at the top of one's game	in Bestform
at top speed	mit voller Geschwindigkeit
attached	befestigt
to attend	beiwohnen, besuchen
attentive(ly)	aufmerksam
audience	Publikum
awful	furchtbar
awkwardly	ungeschickt
ϟ Aye, aye!	Jawohl! Zu Befehl!
back alley	*hier*: Hinterhof
to back out	rückwärts hinausgehen
back-up plan	Plan B
bad news travels fast	schlechte Nachrichten verbreiten sich schnell
badge	*hier*: (Polizei-)Marke
badly	heftig, schwer
bailout	Notverkauf
bald	kahlköpfig
bangers and mash	Würstchen mit Kartoffelbrei
bankrupt	bankrott
bargain	günstiges Angebot, Schnäppchen
to be in charge	zuständig sein
to be related to	in Verbindung stehen mit
to be about to do sth.	im Begriff sein, etw. zu tun
to be blindfolded	die Augen verbunden haben
to be cut from a different cloth	aus einem anderen Holz geschnitzt sein
to be deep in conversation	ins Gespräch vertieft sein

to be echoed	widerhallen
to be in a terrible hurry	es schrecklich eilig haben
to be in charge	die Verantwortung tragen
to be involved in	beteiligt sein an
to be just about to	gerade dabei sein, etw. zu tun
to be on fire	brennen, in Flammen stehen
to be performed	aufgeführt werden
to be sb.'s pride and joy	jmds. ganzer Stolz sein
to be under arrest	verhaftet sein
bead of sweat	Schweißperle
bedsit	möbliertes Zimmer, Einzimmer- wohnung
to beg sb.'s pardon	jmd. um Entschuldigung bitten
to beg sb. for sth.	jmd. anflehen um
to beg	(an)flehen
beggar	Bettler
to bend	biegen
to bet (bet, bet)	wetten
betrayal	Verrat
betrayed	betrogen; verraten
binoculars *pl*	Fernglas
biro	Kugelschreiber
blackmail	Erpressung
blank	verständnislos, leer
bloodstain	Blutfleck
blow	Schlag
to blush	rot werden, erröten
Board of Directors	Aufsichtsrat
boarding school	Internat
body	*hier*: Leiche; Körper
boldly	mutig
bond	Verbindung
bossy	bestimmend, herrisch
bottom	Boden
bow tie	Fliege
to bow	(sich) verbeugen
brave	mutig
to break the ice	das Eis brechen
to break the law	das Gesetz brechen
breakthrough	Durchbruch
breathlessly	atemlos

briefcase	Aktentasche
bright	intelligent; hell; strahlend
bruise	blauer Fleck
to bully	mobben, schikanieren
to bump (into)	zusammenstoβen mit, anrempeln
bureaucracy	Bürokratie
burglary	Einbruch(-diebstahl)
to burgle sth.	einbrechen in
burial	Begräbnis
burning	brennend
to bury	begraben
business associate	Geschäftspartner(in)
business card	Visitenkarte
by force	mit Gewalt
by heart	auswendig
by the way	übrigens
can	Dose
to cancel a contract	einen Vertrag kündigen
to cancel	absagen
canteen	Kantine
canvas	Leinwand, Gemälde
capable	fähig
to capsize	kentern
car boot	Kofferraum
car jack	Wagenheber
care	Pflege, Betreuung
caretaker	Hausmeister
to carve	meiβeln
case	Fall
to cast	*hier*: werfen
to catch (caught, caught)	*hier*: einholen
to catch one's foot	mit dem Fuβ hängenbleiben
cause of death	Todesursache
CCTV (closed-circuit television)	Überwachungskamera
ceiling	(Zimmer-)Decke
cemetery	Friedhof
chambermaid	Zimmermädchen
to change one's mind	sich anders entschlieβen
to change the subject	das Thema wechseln

Channel	Ärmelkanal
Charming!	Wie charmant!
to chat	sich unterhalten, plaudern
to check sth. out	etw. untersuchen
cheek	Wange
cheeky	frech
cheerful(ly)	heiter, fröhlich
chest	Brust
choir	Chor
to choke	ersticken; würgen
to chuckle	kichern, in sich hineinlachen
church hall	Gemeindesaal
churchyard	Friedhof
to claim	behaupten
to clap	klatschen
to clear one's throat	sich räuspern
to cling onto	sich festklammern an
closely	genau
clue	Hinweis, Spur
coastal	Küsten...
coastguard	Küstenwache
⚡ cocky	großspurig, frech
coincidence	Zufall
to collapse	zusammenbrechen
to come to no good	böse enden
to commit (a crime)	(ein Verbrechen) begehen
community	Gemeinschaft
to compare	vergleichen
to complain	sich beschweren
complexion	Teint
comprehensive school	Gesamtschule
compromising	kompromittierend
concrete paving slab	Betonplatte
to confess	gestehen
confession	Geständnis
confidence	(Selbst-)Vertrauen, Zuversicht
confident	selbstsicher; zuversichtlich
confidential	vertraulich
to confirm	bestätigen
confused	verwirrt

confusing	verwirrend
ϟ conman	Schwindler
connection	Verbindung
to consider sth. be sth.	etw. für etwas halten
constable	Wachtmeister, Polizist(in)
Constabulary	Polizeirevier
content	zufrieden
contract	Vertrag
to convince	überzeugen
convincing	überzeugend
to cordon off	absperren
corpse	Leiche
cottage	Häuschen, kleines Landhaus
council	Gemeinderat
court	*hier*: Gericht
cover	Abdeckung
to creep up to	sich anschleichen an
crime scene	Tatort
crime	Verbrechen
Crimestoppers number	Telefonnummer für sachdienliche
crooked	*hier*: zerknittert
cruel	grausam
CU (see you)	Wir sehen uns.
cubicle	Kabine
curious	neugierig
curly	lockig
curtain	Vorhang
cushion	Kissen
cut	*hier*: Anteil, Provision; Schnitt
to damage	beschädigen
dare	Mutprobe
database	Datenbank
to deal (dealt, dealt)	sich beschäftigen mit, zu tun haben
deal	Handel
debriefing session	Abschlussbesprechung
decision	Entscheidung
deckchair	Liegestuhl
dedicated	engagiert
denim jacket	Jeansjacke
to depend on	abhängen von

deputy	Stellvertreter(in)
desperately	verzweifelt
to detect	aufspüren
detective work	Ermittlungsarbeit
to dial	wählen
to dig	graben
direction	Richtung
dirty work	Drecksarbeit
to disagree	anderer Meinung sein
to disappear	verschwinden
to disappoint sb.	jmd. enttäuschen
disease	Krankheit
disguise	Verkleidung
disillusioned	desillusioniert
to disturb	stören
diving squad	Polizeitaucher
divorce	Scheidung
divorced	geschieden
Don't hold your breath.	Da kannst du lange warten.
doorway	Türöffnung
dormitory	Schlafsaal
Dorset	Grafschaft in Südengland
to double-lock	doppelt verschließen
doubt	Zweifel
down	*hier*: offen, lose
to drag	schleppen
dreadful	schrecklich
dress rehearsal	Generalprobe
drive(way)	Auffahrt zu einem Haus
to drop	fallen lassen
drop-off point	Übergabestelle
to drown	ertrinken
drunk	betrunken
drunkenly	betrunken
due to	aufgrund
dumb	dumm
to dump sb.	jmd. den Laufpass geben
↯ dump	Drecksloch
to dust for fingerprints	Fingerabdrücke sichern
to earn	verdienen

eavesdropper	Lauscher(in)
edge	Rand, Kante
to educate	(aus)bilden
elderly	ältere(r/s)
embarrassed	verlegen
emergency	Notfall
to emphasize	betonen, hervorheben
encouraging(ly)	ermutigend
enemy	Feind(in)
engine	Motor
entrance	Eingang
to envelop	einhüllen
envelope	Briefumschlag
equal	Gleichgestellte/r
equipment	Ausrüstung
to erase	löschen
to escape	fliehen, flüchten
to estimate	schätzen
estranged wife	Noch-Ehefrau
even	sogar
evidence	Beweis(mittel)
to exaggerate	übertreiben
to examine	untersuchen
except (for)	bis auf, außer
to exchange	wechseln, austauschen
excited(ly)	aufgeregt, begeistert
to exclaim	ausrufen
exhibition	Ausstellung
to exist	bestehen, existieren
to exit	verlassen
to expect	erwarten
to explore	erkunden
expression	(Gesichts-)Ausdruck
extension	*hier*: Durchwahl
factory	Fabrik
factual	sachlich
fairly	ziemlich
familiar (with)	vertraut (mit), sich auskennen (mit)
fault	Fehler
fee	*hier*: Schulgeld; Gebühr

to feel at ease	sich wohl fühlen
to feel sorry for sb.	mit jdm. Mitleid haben
fellow	Kerl, Bursche
fence	Zaun
to fetch	herbeiholen
figure	Gestalt; Figur
to file	abheften
file	Akte
filing cabinet	Aktenschrank
fingerprint	Fingerabdruck
fire precautions *pl*	Brandschutzmaßnahmen
fireplace	(offener) Kamin
fireproof	brandsicher, feuerfest
firmly	fest
fist	Faust
to fit in	dazupassen
fit	Anfall
to flash	*hier*: blitzen lassen
to flow	fließen
for practice	zum Üben
forehead	Stirn
Foreign Office UK	Außenministerium
forensic officer	Gerichtsmediziner(in)
forensic	gerichtsmedizinisch
forensics	Kriminaltechnik
former	ehemalig
frame by frame	Bild für Bild
frantic	völlig verzweifelt
freak	*hier*: außergewöhnlich
fright	Schreck
to frighten sb.	jdn. erschrecken
to frown	die Stirn runzeln
funeral	Beerdigung
further	fördern
gagged	geknebelt
gate	Tor
to gather	(ein)sammeln; (sich) versammeln
gaze	starrer Blick
gelled	gegelt (Haar)
genius	Genie

gently	sanft
to get a lead on sth.	einen Hinweis auf etw. bekommen
to get on with sth.	mit etw. weitermachen
to get drunk	sich betrinken
to get in touch	Kontakt aufnehmen
to get on with sb.	mit jmd. auskommen
to get one's hands on sb.	jmd. in die Finger kriegen
to get rid of sb./sth.	jmd./etw. loswerden
to get somewhere	vorankommen (mit etw.)
to get sth. off one's chest	sich etw. von der Seele reden
ghost	Gespenst
ghostly	unheimlich
to giggle	kichern
to give orders	Befehle erteilen
to give the bird call	*hier*: rufen, um jmd. zu warnen
glad	froh
glance	Blick
glasses *pl*	Brille; Gläser
glow	Leuchten
to glow	leuchten
to go (went, gone) off	*hier*: losgehen
to go for a run	joggen gehen
to go into business	ein Geschäft gründen
ϟ good-for-nothing	Taugenichts
gorgeous	herrlich, wunderschön
gossip	Klatsch
to grab	greifen, fassen
grades *pl*	*hier*: Noten
ϟ grand	tausend Pfund
to grasp	ergreifen, begreifen
grave	Grab
gravestone	Grabstein
graveyard	Friedhof
greedy streak	gierige Ader, raffgieriger Charakter
to greet sb.	jmd. grüßen
grimly	grimmig, streng
to grin	grinsen
to groan	ächzen
guardian	Wächter(in)
gulp	(großer) Schluck

habit	Gewohnheit
halfway human	halbwegs menschlich
hall	Flur; Saal
hallway	Diele, Hausflur
to hand in one's notice	kündigen
to handcuff sb.	jmd. Handschellen anlegen
handcuffs *pl*	Handschellen
handicapped	behindert
handicrafts *pl*	Handarbeiten
handle	Griff
handsome	gutaussehend
to hang (hung, hung) up	*hier*: auflegen
to hang sb.	jmd. erhängen
harbour	Hafen
harshly	schroff
to hate	hassen
to haunt	spuken (in)
to have a knack for sth.	eine Vorliebe für etw. haben
to have (had, had) a fight	streiten
to have a bad temper	schlecht gelaunt sein
to have a temper	leicht reizbar sein
He wouldn't hurt a fly.	Er kann keiner Fliege etwas zu-
head girl	Schulsprecherin
headache	Kopfweh
headline	Schlagzeile
headmistress	Schulleiterin
headstone	Grabstein
height	Größe, Höhe
to hesitate	zögern
to hide (hid, hidden)	(sich) verstecken
high-profile case	prominenter Fall
hip flask	Flachmann
to hire	einstellen, anheuern
to hit (hit, hit) sb.	jmd. schlagen
to hold (held, held)	den Atem anhalten
to hold a secret	ein Geheimnis bergen
to hold on tight	fest halten
honeymoon	Flitterwochen
hood	Kapuze
hooded	mit Kapuze

hoover	staubsaugen
hosepipe	Wasserschlauch
hot flush	Hitzewallung
housekeeper	Haushälterin
How dare you!	Was erlauben Sie sich!
to hug	umarmen
to hum	summen
to hunt	jagen
hunting accident	Jagdunfall
to hurt (hurt, hurt)	verletzen; schmerzen
identity parade	polizeiliche Gegenüberstellung
I'm afraid	Es tut mir leid, aber ...; leider
imagination	Fantasie; Vorstellung
to imagine	sich vorstellen
immortalized	verewigt
impatiently	ungeduldig
impertinence	Frechheit, Dreistigkeit
impostor	Betrüger(in)
to impress sb.	jmd. beeindrucken
impressed	beeindruckt
in charge (of)	verantwortlich, zuständig (für); leiten
in denial	verneinend
in despair	verzweifelt
in his mid-40s	Mitte vierzig
in person	persönlich
in silence	schweigend
in spite of	trotz
in tears	in Tränen aufgelöst
in the distance	in der Ferne
incident	Zwischenfall, Ereignis
influential	einflussreich
inheritance	Erbschaft
innocent	unschuldig; ahnungslos
to inquire	nachfragen
to insist	auf etw. bestehen
instead	stattdessen
insulting	beleidigend
insurance	Versicherung
intercom	Gegensprechanlage
interior decorator	Innenausstatter

to interview	befragen, verhören
investigation	Ermittlung, Untersuchung
involved	verwickelt, involviert
It's on me.	Das geht auf mich.
It's none of your business!	Das geht dich nichts an!
it's not like her.	Es ist nicht ihre Art.
jealous	neidisch; eifersüchtig
to join in	mitmachen
to joyride	eine Spritztour machen
jumble sale	Flohmarkt, Basar
to jump up	aufspringen
keel	Kiel
keen	leidenschaftlich, eifrig
to keep sth. off limits	etw. absperren
to keep an eye on sb.	jmd. im Auge behalten
key ring	Schlüsselbund
to kick sb. out	jmd. rausschmeißen
kind	Art, Sorte
to knock over	umwerfen, umstoßen
knot	Knoten
to know the drill	wissen, wie etw. läuft
lab	Labor
laboured	mühsam, schwerfällig
lad	Junge, Bursche
Lancashire	engl. Grafschaft, benannt nach der Stadt Lancaster
landlady/landlord	Wirtin/Wirt
landscape	Landschaft
lately	in letzter Zeit
law firm	Anwaltskanzlei
lawn	Rasen
lawyer	Anwalt/Anwältin
lazy	faul
lead	Spur
to lean forward	sich nach vorne lehnen
leather	Leder
to let (let, let) sb. down	jmd. im Stich lassen
↯ Let's call it a day.	Machen wir Schluss (für heute).
Let's take her for a spin.	Lass uns eine Spritztour machen.
letter of resignation	Kündigungsbrief

liar	Lügner(in)
life buoy	Rettungsboje
lifeboat	Rettungsboot
to light (lit, lit)	*hier*: anzünden
to linger	verweilen
link	Verbindung
local man	Einheimische(r)
to lock up	abschließen
lock	Schloss
loner	Einzelgänger(in)
to look ashamed	beschämt aussehen
to look blank	verständnislos schauen
to look forward to sth.	sich auf etw. freuen
to loosen one's collar	den Kragen lockern
to lower	senken
to lunge at so.	sich auf jmd. stürzen
mad	verrückt
magic spell	Zauberspruch
to magnify	vergrößern
magpie	Elster
maid	Dienstmädchen
maiden name	Geburtsname
mainland England	das englische Festland
to maintain	aufrechterhalten
to make a mental	sich etw. merken
to make fun of sb.	sich über jmd. lustig machen
to make progress	vorankommen
to make sth. up	eine Geschichte erfinden
to make up	Frieden schließen
male	männlich
to manage to do sth.	es schaffen, etw. zu tun
manners *pl*	Benehmen
mansion	Villa, Herrenhaus
marble	Marmor
married	verheiratet
marvellous	wunderbar, fantastisch
to match (with)	(zusammen)passen; vergleichen (mit)
match	*hier*: Treffer
ϟ mate	Kumpel
to mean harm	Böses wollen

meanwhile	währenddessen
mellowed brickwork	alter Ziegelsteinbau
memory	Erinnerung
merely	lediglich
mess	Durcheinander, Unordnung
middle-aged	mittleren Alters
to mind one's own business	sich um seine eigenen Angele-
to mind sth.	etw. dagegen haben
miserable	elend
missing link	fehlendes Bindeglied
mist	Nebel
mistress	Geliebte
to mix business with pleasure	das Angenehme mit dem Nützlichen verbinden
mobile	Handy
mock	*hier*: gespielt; falsch
modest(ly)	bescheiden
ϟ money for old rope	leicht verdientes Geld
monogrammed	mit einem Monogramm versehen
mood	Stimmung, Laune
ϟ moonlighting	Schwarzarbeit
to mop	wischen
to motion sb. to do sth.	jmd. ein Zeichen geben, etw. zu tun
mourners *pl*	Trauergemeinde
moustache	Oberlippenbart
to move out	ausziehen
to move	*hier*: umziehen
to mow the lawn	Rasen mähen
to mumble	murmeln
murder	Mord
murderer	Mörder(in)
mutual	gegenseitig
My goodness!	Meine Güte!
narrow	sich verschmälern
nasty	böse, gemein
nearby	in der Nähe
neat and tidy	ordentlich, picobello
necessary	notwendig
neither ... nor	weder ... noch

Never mind.	Macht nichts.
next-of-kin	nächster Angehörige
nightmare	Albtraum
night-watchman	Nachtwächter
to nod	nicken
noisy	laut
nosy	neugierig
note	Notiz, Zettel
to notice	(be)merken
to nudge	stupsen, schubsen
oak	Eiche
to observe	beobachten
obsessed (with)	besessen (von)
obvious(ly)	offensichtlich
to offend	kränken, beleidigen
to offer	(an)bieten
old people's home	Seniorenheim
old-fashioned	altmodisch
on sb.'s part	von jmds. Seiten
on duty	im Dienst
only child	Einzelkind
open day	Tag der offenen Tür
opportunity	Gelegenheit, Möglichkeit
to order	befehlen
ordinary	normal, gewöhnlich
otherwise	andernfalls
out of breath	atemlos
out of the blue	unerwartet, aus heiterem Himmel
outcome	Ausgang, Ergebnis
outgoing calls *pl*	ausgehende Anrufe
outrage	Schande, Frevel
to oversleep (-slept, -slept)	verschlafen
to overtake (-took, -taken)	überholen
to pace	rennen
package	Paket
pale	blass
palm of one's hand	Handinnenfläche
paper clip	Büroklammer
passionate(ly)	leidenschaftlich
to pat	tätscheln

path	Pfad, Weg
patroness	Mäzenin
pay one's last respects	jmd. den letzten Dienst erweisen
to pay sb. a visit	jdm. einen Besuch abstatten
to pay up	vollständig bezahlen
PC (Police Constable)	Polizist(in)
PDA	Organizer (Personal Digital Assistant)
pebble	Kieselstein
peephole	Guckloch, Spion
peeping Tom	Spanner
to peer	spähen
people in authority	Autoritätspersonen
ϟ pep talk	aufmunternde Worte
perpetrator	Eindringling
to persuade sb.	jmd. überreden, überzeugen
ϟ Phew!	Puh!
physically	körperlich
to pick	*hier*: knacken (Schloss)
piercing	durchdringend
ϟ pig	*hier*: Bulle
pile	Haufen
pipe	Tabakspfeife
platter	Servierplatte
to play for time	auf Zeit spielen
to plead with sb.	jmd. anflehen
plenty of	eine Menge, viele
plump	pummelig, mollig
to point (to)	zeigen (auf)
to point sth. at sb.	mit etw. auf jmd. zeigen
polite	höflich
possession	Besitztum
potential	möglich
to pour	einschenken
praise	Lob
to prepare	vorbereiten
prime minister	Premierminister(in)
prime suspect	Hauptverdächtige(r)
prison	Gefängnis
probably	wahrscheinlich
progress	Fortschritt

to promise	versprechen
promotion	Beförderung
property dispute	Grundstücksstreitigkeit
property	*hier*: Immobilien
props *pl*	Requisiten
to protect	schützen
protective clothing	Schutzbekleidung
proud(ly)	stolz
to provide	bereitstellen
to pull oneself together	sich zusammenreißen
to pump sb. for information	etw. aus jmd. herausquetschen
Punch and Judy show	Kasperletheater
to purr	schnurren
to put sb. behind bars	jmd. hinter Gitter bringen
puzzled	verblüfft, verwirrt
to question sb.	jmd. befragen
quid	Pfund
Rather you than me!	Lieber Sie als ich!
rather	eher, ziemlich
to reach for sth.	nach etw. greifen
reason	Grund
receipt	Quittung
recent	aktuell
recently	kürzlich, in letzter Zeit
reception	Empfang
recipe	Kochrezept
to recognize	bemerken, erkennen
record	*hier*: Akte
recruitment centre	Jobbörse
red herring	falsche Fährte
registration number	Autokennzeichen
regular	*hier*: Stammgast
relationship	Beziehung
relative	Verwandte(r)
to release	hinausgeben, freigeben
relieved	erleichtert
reluctantly	widerwillig
to remember sth.	sich erinnern an
to remind sb. (of sth.)	jmd. (an etw.) erinnern

to rent	mieten
to report	melden, berichten; anzeigen
reputation	Ruf
to request	etw. erfordern
rescue officer	Rettungshelfer(in)
resident	Bewohner(in)
responsible	verantwortlich
to rest in peace	in Frieden ruhen
to retire	in Rente gehen
Retirement Home	Altersheim
to retrieve	herausholen
rifle	Gewehr
right away	sofort
to ring out	sich lösen (Schuss)
to rise the ranks of …	zum … aufsteigen (Position)
robbery	Raubüberfall
rocking chair	Schaukelstuhl
row	Reihe
to rub	reiben
rude	unhöflich
Rumour has it…	Es geht das Gerücht herum …
rumour	Gerücht
rumpled	zerknittert
to run (ran, run) past	vorbeirennen
to run (ran, run)	*hier*: leiten
to rush	eilen, sich beeilen
sack race	Sackhüpfen
saddened	traurig
safety	Sicherheit
sailor	Matrose
sample	Probe
scapegoat	Sündenbock
to scare sb. to death	jmd. zu Tode erschrecken
scared	verängstigt
school fees *pl*	Schulgebühren
scoop	Knüller
to scramble	stürzen, hasten
scrapyard	Schrottplatz
to scratch	kratzen
scratch	Kratzer

to scream	schreien, kreischen
scuff mark	Abnutzungsspur
sculptor	Bildhauer(in)
scum	Abschaum
sea shanty	Seemannslied
sealed	versiegelt
search warrant	Durchsuchungsbefehl
seasick	seekrank
security camera	Überwachungskamera
security guard	Sicherheitsbedienstete(r)
security	Sicherheit
selfish	egoistisch
to send daggers	tödliche Blicke zuwerfen
separated	getrennt
seperately	getrennt, einzeln
serious(ly)	ernst
service	*hier*: Gottesdienst
to set (set, set) a date	einen Termin festlegen
to set (set, set)	*hier*: untergehen
setting	Schauplatz
to settle back	sich zurücklehnen
several times	mehrmals
shadow	Schatten
shaky	zitternd
shame	Schande; Scham
shape	Form
She didn't want me to know.	Sie wollte nicht, dass ich es erfahre.
shed	Schuppen
sheet	Blatt
shelf	Regal
shepherd's pie	Auflauf aus Hackfleisch und Kartoffelbrei
shift	Schicht(dienst)
to shiver	frösteln, schaudern
shoulder-length	schulterlang
shriek	Schrei
to shrug	mit den Schultern zucken
to shudder	schaudern
to shuffle	*hier*: schlurfen
shy	schüchtern

to sigh	seufzen
sight	Anblick
to sign	unterschreiben
sign	Zeichen, Hinweis
to silence	zum Schweigen bringen
silk	Seide
sink	Waschbecken
sip	kleiner Schluck
to sip	nippen
siren	Sirene
sitting room	Wohnzimmer
skull	Schädel
to slam	zuschlagen, zuknallen
to slap	einen Klaps geben
to sleepwalk	schlafwandeln
sleeve	Ärmel
slightly	etwas, ein bisschen
slim	schlank
ϟ slut	Schlampe
smart	*hier*: schick
to smash	zerschlagen, zerschmettern
to smirk	süffisant lächeln
to smooth	glätten
smoothly	problemlos, reibungslos
to snatch	schnappen
to sniffle	die Nase hochziehen
ϟ So what?!	Ja und?!
sober	nüchtern
ϟ socialite	Angehöriger der feinen Gesellschaft
soldier	Soldat(in)
solution	Lösung
to solve	lösen
some	*hier*: irgendein
to sort sth. out	etw. regeln
source of income	Einnahmequelle
space	Raum
to sparkle	funkeln
speck	Körnchen; Pünktchen
to speed (sped, sped)	rasen
speeding ticket	Strafzettel für zu schnelles Fahren

spider's web	Spinnennetz
to spit (spat, spat)	spuken
to splash	schwappen
splinter	Splitter
to splutter	hervorstoßen, stammeln
sprawled	ausgestreckt
spray paint	Sprühfarbe
squad car	Streifenwagen
squeeze	drücken
staff	Kollegium; Personal
to stagger	wanken, torkeln
stall	Verkaufsstand
to stand out from	sich abheben von
to stare	starren
startled	erschrocken
to state	erklären, angeben
state	Zustand
to stay afloat	sich über Wasser halten
to stay in touch	in Kontakt bleiben
stay	Aufenthalt
to steal (stole, stolen)	stehlen
steering wheel	Lenkrad
to step out	hinaustreten
stern	streng
still-life	Stillleben
stock market	Aktienbörse
to stop by	kurz vorbeischauen
straight away	sofort
straight	direkt, geradewegs
strange	merkwürdig, seltsam
stranger	Fremde(r)
streak	Ader, Charakter
to stream	fließen
strict	streng
to stroke	streicheln
to stub out	ausdrücken
to stuff	stopfen
stunned	benommen; fassungslos
subject	*hier*: Modell
success	Erfolg

successful(ly)	erfolgreich
sum	Summe
to summon back	zurückrufen
Superintendent	Hauptkommissar
superior	Vorgesetzter
supplier	Lieferant
surprised	überrascht
surrounded by	umgeben von
to survey	überwachen
suspect	Verdächtige(r)
to suspect	verdächtigen
suspicious of	misstrauisch gegenüber
suspicious(ly)	argwöhnisch, verdächtig
to swallow	schlucken
sweat	Schweiß
to sweat	schwitzen
swiftly	flink, schnell
to switch on	anschalten (Motor) anlassen
swollen	angeschwollen
tabby	getigerte Katze
to take a puff	einen Zug nehmen, paffen
to tap	klopfen, tippen
tap	Klopfen; Wasserhahn
tape	Klebeband
tax-free	steuerfrei
taxpayer	Steuerzahler
ϟ teacher's pet	Lehrers Liebling, Streberin
temptation	Versuchung
tension	Spannung
terraced house	Reihenhaus
terrible	furchtbar, schrecklich
terror alert	Terroralarm
Thank goodness!	Gott sei Dank!
That couldn't be helped.	Das war nicht zu verhindern.
That's a shame!	Wie schade!
The Jolly Roger	Totenkopfflagge, wörtl.: der fröhliche Roger
The time is up.	Die Zeit ist abgelaufen.
there is no use	es bringt nichts
thief, thieves *pl*	Dieb(in)
to think long and hard	es sich reiflich überlegen

thoughtfully	nachdenklich
to threaten	bedrohen
thrilled	begeistert, hingerissen
throat	Hals, Kehle
thud	dumpfes Geräusch
to tick off	abhaken
to tickle sb.'s fancy	jmd. reizen
tied	gefesselt
ties *pl*	Bindungen
ϟ tiff	Geplänkel, kleiner Streit
to tighten	sich zusammenziehen, enger werden
tiled	gefliest
to tip	*hier*: Trinkgeld geben
to strike	*hier*: ergreifen; schlagen (Uhrzeit)
to to gasp	nach Luft schnappen, kurz einatmen
to occure	passieren, vonstattengehen
to rewind (rewound, rewound)	zurückspulen ridiculous lächerlich
ϟ to roar off	davondonnern
toad-in-the-hole	in Teig gebackene Würstchen
tongue	Zunge
torch	Taschenlampe
tousled	verwuschelt (Haar)
to trace	aufspüren
track	Spur
to trail off	verstummen
trail	Spur
tramp	Obdachlose(r)
tranquillity	Stille
trapped	gefangen
tray	Tablett
to treat	behandeln
treatment	Behandlung
trial period	Probezeit
trial	Gerichtsverfahren
triumphantly	triumphierend
to trust	vertrauen
truth	Wahrheit
unconscious	bewusstlos
to uncover	aufdecken

under false pretences	unter Vorspiegelung falscher Tatsachen
underage	minderjährig
unemployed	arbeitslos
unison	Einklang
unlikely	unwahrscheinlich
to unlock	aufschließen
to unpack	auspacken
unsolved	ungelöst
to untie	losbinden
up one's sleeve	im Ärmel
to upset sb.	jmd. ärgern
upset	aufgeregt, verärgert
urgently	dringend
versus	gegen
victim	Opfer
vigorously	energisch, kräftig
villager	Dorfbewohner(in)
villain	Schurke
violent crime	Gewaltverbrechen
violent	gewalttätig, brutal
volume	*hier*: Band, Buch
wallet	Geldbeutel
wave	Welle
wavy	gewellt
wedding	Hochzeit
weeds	Unkraut
well	Brunnen
What on earth...!	Was zum Teufel...?!
⚡ What's up?	Was ist los?
wheelbarrow	Schubkarre
to whine	heulen, jammern
to whisper	flüstern
to whistle	pfeifen
white as a sheet	kreidebleich
wicked	böse
widow	Witwe
wig	Perücke
Will do.	Mach ich! Wird gemacht!
windowsill	Fensterbank
witch	Hexe

with ease	mit Leichtigkeit
to withdraw	abheben
witness	Zeuge/Zeugin
witty	geistreich, witzig
to wonder	sich fragen
wood	kleiner Wald
wooden	aus Holz
word of mouth	Mundpropaganda
to worry about	sich Sorgen machen um
to wrap	wickeln
wrinkle	(Gesichts-)Falte
wrinkled	faltig, runzelig
to yawn	gähnen
to yell	schreien, brüllen
yet	schon, bis jetzt
You don't say!	Allerdings! Sie sagen es!
You can say that again.	Das kannst du laut sagen.
zip-locked	mit Reißverschluss